"Richard Hughes Gibson and James E. Beitler III offer a refreshing alternative to agonistic argumentation, inviting us—readers and writers, teachers and students—to reimagine writing with humility as its cornerstone. Assembling a polyptych of saints as m~~~~ what such charitable writing might look like. ~~~~ ~~~~ lded themselves to this great cloud of ~~~~ us book led me to rethink the habits ~~~~ , and teaching; may it do the same fo ~~~~

Peter Wayne Moe, assista ~~~~ ...npus writing at Seattle Pacific University, a ~~~~ Leviathan

"Who we are is absolutely foundational for anything we write. Gibson and Beitler take us to the heart of this largely unexamined principle. Without being grounded as people, our writing will run into a ditch, or we will, or both. As just one instance of this, the authors unmask the menacing metaphor of argument as a form of war, generously offering alternatives to reshape us. Throughout they gently yet firmly guide us to embrace loving others not only in what we write but in how we write."

Andrew T. Le Peau, author of *Write Better*

"I have lived my life attempting to follow Christ and have devoted my academic career to understanding rhetoric and religion. Yet *Charitable Writing* challenged me to think about writing as spiritual practice in ways I never had. Listening humbly, arguing lovingly, keeping time hopefully: take these concepts even remotely seriously, and they will transform your idea of what writing ought to be. Kudos to Gibson and Beitler. This is important work."

Jeff Ringer, associate professor of English at the University of Tennessee, Knoxville, author of *Vernacular Christian Faith and Civil Discourse*

"In *Charitable Writing*, Richard Gibson and James Beitler achieve the worthy goal they set for themselves: they draw on rhetorical theory as well as art and writers in the Christian tradition to explore the all-encompassing effects of Christian love (charity) on the practice of academic writing. When Christians compose with the aim of enacting charity, they listen with humility, they respond to others as fellow children of God, and they demonstrate the discipline required by the metanoic process of writing. Gibson and Beitler offer fresh and worthy models for writers as they seek to embody the law of love."

Elizabeth Vander Lei, professor of English and academic dean at Calvin University

"Gibson and Beitler draw upon a broad, deep understanding of the Christian tradition as it is represented in both word and image. *Charitable Writing* will inspire students and their teachers to approach the task of composing argumentative prose in a new way: as a spiritual discipline animated by love of God and love of neighbor. For as long as I continue to teach and to write, I will keep their wise book close at hand."
Paul J. Contino, professor of great books at Pepperdine University

"In this delightful book, Richard Hughes Gibson and James E. Beitler III take an approach unusual in writing studies—something I can best call ekphrastic criticism—to offer us a lovely new way to consider the art and craft of writing and the vital ways it is linked to our very discipleship. For Gibson and Beitler, to 'listen humbly, argue lovingly, and keep the time of writing hopefully' is to understand our own faith incarnated in our words, the high calling of writing as spiritual practice."
Jennifer L. Holberg, professor of English at Calvin University, founding coeditor of *Pedagogy*

"*Charitable Writing* offers a transformative vision of writing as a Christian spiritual practice. It is a compelling book that invites readers to reimagine the generative ways Christian tradition can animate writing practices, rhetorical education, and rhetoric itself."
Michael-John DePalma, associate professor of English and coordinator of professional writing and rhetoric at Baylor University, author of *Sacred Rhetorical Education in 19th Century America*

"At this time of cultural polarization that is undermining the basis of democracy and threatening the unity of Christians, *Charitable Writing* offers lessons of the highest importance, not just to Christians but to all who care for the future of our civilization."
Timothy Radcliffe, OP, author of *Alive in God: A Christian Imagination*

Richard Hughes Gibson
and James Edward Beitler III

Foreword by Anne Ruggles Gere
Afterword by Alan Jacobs

Cultivating Virtue
Through Our
Words

Charitable
Writing

Academic
An imprint of InterVarsity Press
Downers Grove, Illinois

InterVarsity Press
P.O. Box 1400, Downers Grove, IL 60515-1426
ivpress.com
email@ivpress.com

InterVarsity Press® is the book-publishing division of InterVarsity Christian Fellowship/USA®, a movement of students and faculty active on campus at hundreds of universities, colleges, and schools of nursing in the United States of America, and a member movement of the International Fellowship of Evangelical Students. For information about local and regional activities, visit intervarsity.org.

Scripture quotations, unless otherwise noted, are from the New Revised Standard Version Bible, copyright © 1989 National Council of the Churches of Christ in the United States of America. Used by permission. All rights reserved worldwide.

Cover design and image composite: David Fassett
Interior design: Daniel van Loon

ISBN 978-0-8308-5483-7 (print)
ISBN 978-0-8308-5484-4 (digital)

Printed in the United States of America ♾

InterVarsity Press is committed to ecological stewardship and to the conservation of natural resources in all our operations. This book was printed using sustainably sourced paper.

Library of Congress Cataloging-in-Publication Data
A catalog record for this book is available from the Library of Congress.

P	25	24	23	22	21	20	19	18	17	16	15	14	13	12	11	10	9	8	7	6	5	4	3	2	1
Y	41	40	39	38	37	36	35	34	33	32	31	30	29	28	27	26	25	24	23	22	21	20			

For Our Students

Charity is a good dish, set in the middle of Solomon's banquet. With the sweet scent of its many virtues, like a medley of fragrant spices, it refreshes those who hunger and delights them as they are refreshed. It is seasoned with peace, patience, kindness, long-suffering, and joy in the Holy Spirit; and if there are any other fruit of truth or wisdom, they are mixed in, too. Humility's course is part of the spread, the bread of suffering and the wine of remorse. Truth offers these first to beginners, to whom it is said: Rise up after you have eaten, you who eat the bread of sorrow. *Contemplation brings the solid food of wisdom, made of the finest flour. Served with wine, it makes the human heart glad. To this food Truth invites the mature, saying:* Eat, my friends, and drink and take your delight, my best-beloved.

BERNARD OF CLAIRVAUX

To write in such a way as to invite both thought and love is to write on behalf of others. It is to practice writing as a spiritual discipline that has the good of others at its heart. It is to write in a way that exposes one's hopes and motivations, that betrays one's love. It is to write in language that invites rather than excludes, in forms that are full of doors through which a reader might walk. To write this way requires time and a certain measure of solitude. But it also requires that each writing project begin and end with others, both those near at hand, and those we may never know, but to whom and for whom we write.

STEPHANIE PAULSELL

Contents

List of Illustrations

Figure 1. Andrea Mantegna, *San Luca Altarpiece*, Pinacoteca di Brera Collection, Milan / Wikimedia Commons

Figure 2. Andrea Mantegna, *San Luca Altarpiece*, detail of Luke the Evangelist, Pinacoteca di Brera Collection, Milan / Wikimedia Commons

Figure 3. David Holgate, *Julian of Norwich*, photo: Matt Brown / Flickr. Used under Creative Commons license 2.0.

Figure 4. Albrecht Dürer, *St. Jerome in His Study*, Cleveland Museum of Art Collection, Cleveland, Bequest of Mrs. Severance A. Millikin / Wikimedia Commons

Figure 5. Nicolás Francés (fl. 1425–1468), *Saint Jerome Translating the Gospels*, c. 1450, tempera on panel, 98 x 59 cm, NGI.1013, National Gallery of Ireland Collection. Photo © National Gallery of Ireland. Used with permission.

Figure 6. John Collier, *Annunciation*, © John Collier, www.hillstream.com. Used with permission.

Figure 7. Sandro Botticelli, *Madonna of the Magnificat*, Uffizi Gallery Collection, Florence / Wikimedia Commons

Figure 8. Attributed to Benedetto di Bindo, *Virgin of Humility and Saint Jerome Translating the Gospel of John*, Philadelphia Museum of Art Collection, Philadelphia / Wikimedia Commons

Figure 9. *The Luminous One*, 2015–2017. 7.5' x 15' glass, ceramic, stone mosaic for the Wheaton College President's Art Commission. Designed by Jeremy Botts, facilitated by Leah Samuelson, constructed with the help of John Mark Daniel, Hannah Frankl, Diane Greenberg,

Foreword

Anne Ruggles Gere

After I had invited students in my composition class to come by if they had questions about their drafts, a young woman entered my office hesitantly, clutching her paper. When she sat down, she knitted her fingers together and asked, "What if I write about being a Christian?" As I reassured her that the only requirement was to write an evidence-based argument, my mind raced back to my own uncertainty about revealing to colleagues my commitment to and activities in a Christian church. I was a tenured full professor before I could utter phrases like "singing in my church choir" or "the homeless shelter sponsored by my church" at the university. Like many of my Christian colleagues who teach writing in secular institutions, I actively contributed to what George Marsden calls the "near exclusion of religious perspectives from dominant academic life." *Charitable Writing* demonstrates that we have an alternative.

By creating this wise, eloquent, and innovative book, Richard Gibson and James Beitler set forth new perspectives on the long-standing discussion about the relationship between rhetoric and religion. They show how writing instruction and spiritual formation connect with one another. They demonstrate that the rich Christian tradition can shape approaches to and processes of writing. They offer a grammar of faith that can guide writers and teachers of writing. The "charitable writing" they espouse "embodies the distinctive Christian understanding of love, which used to go by the name 'charity' in English." This is not a book that merely advocates; the authors provide clear lessons—or, as they put it, "spiritual threshold concepts"—that can be enacted by writers and their teachers.

Threshold concepts are a topic of current conversation in the field of writing studies, so it seems fitting for *Charitable Writing* to call on them. However, the authors give them new meaning by translating them into spiritual terms that emphasize specific activities writers can employ and instructors can encourage. Their key terms, *imitation* and *practice*, are both familiar to writing instructors, but these words take on new meanings in the hands of Gibson and Beitler. Imitation reaches beyond following models and into the pursuit of virtue through a combination of looking back on the Christian tradition and into the present moment in order to engage in the "creative remembering" that invents "something new by remaking the old." Practice, as represented here, also takes virtue as its goal, and while it encompasses the traditional meaning of repeating actions over and over again, it focuses on spiritual formation.

Transfer, another contemporary term in writing studies, does not appear as a key concept in this book, but its sense of taking up knowledge from one space and employing it in another is present everywhere. Lessons for writers draw on passages from Scripture, texts written by Christian leaders throughout history, and the works of contemporary spiritual leaders as well as an impressive array of artists. The authors encourage writers to become what Rebecca Nowacek calls "agents of integration": people who take up spiritual resources, adjust them to various projects of writing, and become themselves transformed in the process.[1]

One of the most powerful aids for this transformation is the authors' use of art. Amplifying key points with images that illustrate the concepts under discussion, the authors add another dimension to the lessons they offer. While some of the images are clearly religious, like altarpieces and paintings of figures from the Scriptures, other images of people like Maya Angelou and objects like pottery do not immediately conjure a spiritual dimension. With images of statues, engravings, and photographs, along with a wide variety of paintings, the authors add an aesthetic dimension to their argument. But it is an aesthetic that is tightly bound to the textual message, and the authors ensure that readers will understand the images as well as the words. Gently but firmly they guide the reader to look here, notice that, and see how the image conveys a meaning linked to the central messages of the book.

---

[1]Rebecca Nowacek, *Agents of Integration: Understanding Transfer as a Rhetorical Act* (Carbondale: Southern Illinois University Press, 2011).

In his book *The Gift*, Lewis Hyde distinguishes between commodities and gifts. While the recipient of a commodity returns to the seller a specified amount of money, the recipient of a gift responds to its transformative powers, and passing the gift along is an act of gratitude.[2] *Charitable Writing* is a gift. It is a gift to writers in all circumstances and stages of life, to teachers of writing, and to students—especially those with questions, like the young woman who walked into my office. It is a gift that has transformed my thinking about what it means to write and teach writing, and I am confident that you, dear reader, will let it work its powers on you. Then you can pass it along.

ANNE RUGGLES GERE

Arthur F. Thurnau Professor of English, Gertrude Buck Collegiate
Professor of Education, University of Michigan

---

[2]Lewis Hyde, *The Gift: Creativity and the Artist in the Modern World*, 25th anniv. ed. (New York: Vintage, 2007).

Opening Meditation

At the Gallery

T his book is a writing guide, yet unlike most manuals it offers no advice about comma placement, the passive voice, or how to compose the perfect conclusion. This book is concerned, instead, with how we *conceive* of and, in turn, *practice* writing. To put it another way, this book examines how we think about writing as well as how we go about it. In both respects, the conceptual and the practical, this book argues that our spiritual commitments can and should provide bearings for our academic and professional work. Unthinkingly, many of us—the authors included—often check those commitments at the door when we sit down to write. We say now: let them in.

Charitable Writing began as the authors' attempt to reconceive the labor of writing as an aspect of the Christian life, the life of discipleship. Yet our striving to do a new thing—to reimagine writing—has repeatedly shown us that nothing new was needed. The resources were already there, waiting patiently for us, on the walls of churches and art galleries; in the lives of saints ancient and modern; in theologies and spiritual devotions; and, above all, in the words of Scripture. We set out to craft a new image; instead, we rediscovered the old. *Charitable Writing* is thus no mere manual of style. It is better understood as a work of creative remembrance. This book invites you, reader, to take up your inheritance: the inexhaustible wealth of the Christian tradition.[1]

---

[1]We are not claiming that the Christian tradition is static. The tradition grows and changes with the contributions of the generations. We must recognize, too, that our tradition has privileged some voices over others, and efforts to uncover the neglected voices of our tradition are far from complete. (Perhaps you'll engage in this work through your writing!) In this book, we attempt to draw on a diverse collection of voices, and we hope that readers will add examples

One example of this wealth awaits in Milan's Pinacoteca di Brera, one of the finest public galleries in Italy. Found here are masterpieces by Caravaggio and Raphael, paintings of saints in brilliant costumes, and vividly rendered scenes from our Lord Jesus' life and breathtaking depictions of his death. The walls furnish a feast for the eye. Our particular interest is hard to miss given its bright gold-painted frame. The Saint Luke Altarpiece (figure 1) was created by the artist Andrea Mantegna in 1453–1454 for the monastery of Saint Giustina in the Italian city of Padua. It is a "polyptych," meaning that it contains multiple panels, and in each of its honeycomb-like cells we meet a

Figure 1. Andrea Mantegna, *San Luca Altarpiece*

from their own denominational and cultural backgrounds. If you are interested in the field of writing studies' efforts to explore the riches and complexities of Christian tradition, a good starting place is Elizabeth Vander Lei et al., eds., *Renovating Rhetoric in Christian Tradition* (Pittsburgh: University of Pittsburgh Press, 2014). For a wonderful annotated bibliography on the intersections of religion and writing studies, see Paul Lynch and Matthew Miller, "Twenty-Five Years of Faith and Writing: Religion and Composition, 1992–2017," *Present Tense: A Journal of Rhetoric in Society* 6, no. 2 (2017), www.presenttensejournal.org/volume-6/twenty-five-years-of-faith-in-writing-religion-and-composition-1992-2017. And for another take on a writing guide written from a Christian perspective, see John H. Timmerman and Donald R. Hettinga, *In the World: Reading and Writing as a Christian* (Grand Rapids, MI: Baker Academic, 2004).

Figure 2. Andrea Mantegna, *San Luca Altarpiece*, detail of Luke the Evangelist

saint. Some are well-known now, including Augustine, Jerome, and Mary (all of whom will reappear later in this book); some, such as Scholastica and Justina, are not. All were meaningful to the community for which the piece was made: the seeming hodgepodge of men and women is, in fact, a kind of spiritual genealogy. Rightly, the highest figure in the group is Jesus, bearing the wounds of the cross.

We begin this meditation on writing in this gallery, gazing at this picture, because of the figure who sits immediately beneath Jesus in the piece's largest panel. He is Saint Luke, author of the Gospel that bears his name (figure 2). Mantegna's Luke is equipped with all the tools of the writer's trade: writing desk, quill, inkpot, and several books, including the one in which we witness him busily scribbling. The historical Luke didn't compose like this, of course. The saint didn't work at a throne-like desk chiseled out of Italian marble. The kind of book in use here, the codex, hadn't been invented yet—the original Gospel of Luke was a scroll. Luke himself may not have even been holding the pen: that work may have fallen to a scribe, a common practice in antiquity. We may be tempted to fault the artist for a lack of historical realism. But to do so is to miss the *spiritual* meaning of the portrait. Mantegna depicts Luke's deskwork as a scene of high drama, of beauty, of glory—even though it consists of nothing more than writing in a book.

In this way, this oversized panel testifies to a deep truth about the Christian faith, one that though patently obvious is often forgotten or overlooked. For Christians, the seemingly ordinary labor of writing can rival—if not exceed in significance—the undertakings of generals, captains of industry, and heads of state. Within the Christian tradition, the acts of reading and writing can assume the weight of epic feats.

Remarkably, Luke portrays his writing not as the fruit of a state of ecstatic rapture but as the down-to-earth chore of sifting through the sources:

> Since many have undertaken to set down an orderly account of the events that have been fulfilled among us, just as they were handed on to us by those who from the beginning were eyewitnesses and servants of the word, I too decided, after investigating everything carefully from the very first, to write an orderly account for you, most excellent Theophilus, so that you may know the truth concerning the things about which you have been instructed. (Lk 1:1-4)

Regarding these words, our college's writing center director, Alison Gibson, astutely observes, "Luke is a meticulous researcher: he has gathered eyewitness accounts that were handed down and has investigated everything carefully. Others have undertaken this project, but Luke seems committed to a more expansive and thorough research process than has preceded him. His purpose in this accumulation of evidence is not to hoard his knowledge but to share it."[2] Luke presents his writing as a gift—one designed to help his reader to "know the truth concerning the things about which you have been instructed." That reader's name is suggestive. Theophilus means "God-loving," or "loved by God," or even "God's friend." It may refer to a specific person, but it may also serve as an invitation to any of God's beloveds to take up the book and read. Either way, whether Luke addresses his particular friend or all of God's friends, Luke presents his book as an act of love.

Once we recognize the centrality of writing to the central panel, its neighboring panels take on new meaning. Many of the figures here are

---

[2]Alison Gibson, "Welcoming the Student Writer: Hospitable Christian Pedagogy for First-Year Writing" (faculty paper, Faith and Learning Program, Wheaton College, January 4, 2018).

famous for their writings—including the aforementioned Jerome and Augustine. To Luke's immediate left, Mantegna depicts Saint Benedict busily reading a book. To his left, Saint Justina holds one. On the other side of the polyptych, Saint Scholastica (according to tradition, Benedict's sister) is equipped with one, too. In so many ways, the Saint Luke Altarpiece celebrates the Christian faith's ancient love affair with writing. All of these figures are, to borrow Luke's expression, "servants of the word."

Mantegna restricted himself to figures from the early church, but the sprawling form of the polyptych also permits gestures to subsequent ages, even the artist's own day. As we bring this opening meditation to a close, we invite you to join us in imaginatively extending the Saint Luke Altarpiece, for the Christian history of writing doesn't end in the fifteenth century. To the polyptych we might add the images of Christian mystics such as Marguerite d'Oingt and Julian of Norwich; celebrated theologians such as Thomas Aquinas, John Calvin, and John Wesley; later writers such as C. S. Lewis, Pandita Ramabai, and Dorothy L. Sayers; and contemporary guides such as Maya Angelou and Rowan Williams. The open form of polyptych allows us to add figures from every age and continent. Here we may behold the All Saints' Day of the written word.

We encourage you, reader, to add figures to this polyptych as you see fit. Attach panels for famous Christian authors whose books line your shelves. Provide space for the local "servants of the word"—the teachers, pastors, mentors, and friends—whose writing (or counsel on writing) you revere. And leave room for one more. It should be decorated with all of the tools of the modern writer's trade—laptop, pad, pens and pencils, stacks of paper, books, and other source materials. This panel is reserved for you. Step in when you are ready.

Introduction

At the Threshold

+ C + M + B +

Traditional Christian Door-Marking

This book began with a professional crisis. After a few years of teaching at a Christian liberal arts college, the authors had an unsettling realization: we had been teaching the craft of writing in almost the same way that we had previously done at state universities. In fact, we were still using the same textbooks, dispensing the same handouts, and assigning the same exercises. Our writing classrooms were largely indistinguishable from those in the academy at large. All of this, we recognized, was a problem. But as we pondered these issues, we had a second difficult realization. We had never given much thought to *our own* writing practices. Did they reflect our Christian commitments? We had the worrying sense that we were, to use an unflattering biblical reference, "blind guides" (Mt 15:14). Our classrooms didn't just need work; we did, too.

Centuries ago, one of the saints mentioned in our opening meditation faced a related crisis, and his solution offered a model for handling ours.[1] Shortly after his conversion, the North African bishop Saint Augustine decided that he had to give up his teaching post in Milan because his subject matter (aptly summed up by one scholar as a "passport to success") seemed to jar with that of his newfound Christian

---

[1] We adapt this example, with some variation, from James E. Beitler III, *Seasoned Speech: Rhetoric in the Life of the Church* (Downers Grove, IL: IVP Academic, 2019), 1-3.

faith.[2] This moment was significant for us because Augustine was a teacher of rhetoric, the art of persuasion. He thus had the ancient version of our job as teachers of writing. In his autobiography, *The Confessions*, the saint writes that he sought to honor God by discontinuing "the service of my tongue from the market of speechifying, so that young boys who were devoting their thoughts not to your law, not to your peace, but to lying follies and legal battles, should no longer buy from my mouth the weapons for their frenzy."[3]

Now, this example would appear to be a rather despairing one. Augustine would seem to be showing rhetoric the door—and teaching us that we ought to go and do likewise with our own rhetorical educations. However, Augustine never really abandoned rhetoric. He spent the remainder of his life making arguments, and his religious writings have been treasured for centuries for the force and eloquence of those arguments. Most important of all, Augustine would himself argue that rhetoric could serve Christian ends. His most important statements on this subject appear in *On Christian Teaching*, a book that he initially published ten years after his conversion. The topic remained a vital one to him in the decades to come, and he would even add a final section to *On Christian Teaching* a few years before his death.

In that book, Augustine defends the use of rhetoric as long as it is practiced within the bounds of Christian belief.[4] He argues in the book's final section that since rhetoric can be used "to give conviction to both truth and falsehood," those who would stand on the side of truth must learn its techniques in order to resist error.[5] In that same section, moreover, Augustine observes that rhetoric isn't simply some foreign art: the Christian tradition itself provides manifold examples of eloquent persuasion. He claims that for the student with a lot of free time for this kind of reading, "time will run out" before one runs out of texts.[6] Ultimately, then, Augustine did not disavow rhetoric. Rather, he sought

---

[2]Augustine, *The Confessions*, trans. Maria Boulding, OSB (New York: Vintage, 1998), 170-71; Catherine Conybeare, "Augustine's Rhetoric in Theory and Practice," in *The Oxford Handbook of Rhetorical Studies*, ed. Michael J. MacDonald (Oxford: Oxford University Press, 2017), 301.
[3]Augustine, *Confessions*, 171.
[4]Augustine, *On Christian Teaching*, trans. R. P. H. Green (Oxford: Oxford University Press, 1997), 64-65, 101-2.
[5]Augustine, *On Christian Teaching*, 101.
[6]Augustine, *On Christian Teaching*, 105.

out models for communication within the Christian tradition and directed the practices of the rhetorician toward a new set of goals. In short, Augustine *repurposed* rhetoric.[7]

From Augustine's example, we took the lesson that we need not throw out our old textbooks, handouts, and assignments. Our syllabi didn't need to be rewritten from scratch or our classroom exercises rebuilt from the ground up. We could (and, in fact, *should*) continue to teach the parts of an argument, the basic structure of an introduction, how to use discipline-specific terminology—all of "the moves that matter in academic writing."[8] In one respect, then, our job remained the same as it had been before our crisis: to train students to become savvy academic and professional writers. Yet our engagement with Augustine revealed that we could no longer go about this business in the same way. Education in writing, we saw, needed to be interwoven with education in Christian Scripture and tradition. Students' progress, as well as our own, needed to be measured not only by the mastery of skills but also by growth in virtue. Our responsibility wasn't simply to teach up-to-date information about effective writing. As Augustine knew, writing is inescapably bound up with spiritual formation. That, too, is part of the Christian educator's charge. *Charitable Writing* represents our attempt to answer it.

This book does not enumerate a list of "dos and don'ts" or "writing rules." Such matters are handled in the many excellent writing manuals, style guides, and research primers already available. We address the big picture. To recall the phrasing of the opening meditation, we examine how Christians might *conceive* of and, in turn, *practice* writing in light of our religious commitments. How do we imagine our work as writers? How do we relate to our fellow writers and our readers? How do we handle the writing of others? How do we respond to those with whom we disagree? Can we argue with them lovingly? How do we connect the time we spend writing to our spiritual lives? As this list of questions suggests, we take a step back from the traditional subjects of writing textbooks, like organization and voice, in order to reflect on how our

---

[7]Nello Cipriani, "Rhetoric," in *Augustine Through the Ages: An Encyclopedia*, ed. Allan D. Fitzgerald et al. (Grand Rapids, MI: Eerdmans, 1999), 724.
[8]Gerald Graff and Cathy Birkenstein, *They Say/I Say: The Moves That Matter in Academic Writing*, 4th ed. (New York: W. W. Norton, 2018).

Christian commitments can enter into and grow out of our writing lives. The grammar of the schoolbook—though important!—is not our direct concern; we inquire, instead, into how we might write according to the grammar of faith.

We will be highlighting a variety of examples of Christian writing in the chapters that follow. But we have also tapped into other channels, other media, through which the Christian tradition has meditated on the craft of writing. Our opening meditation has already made plain our interest in painting. At the close of this introduction, we will consider a sculpture. We have multiple reasons for gathering these materials, as we will explain below. For now, though, we want to emphasize the most important lesson about our use of these artifacts: this book does not strive to be original. Our tradition is deep and wide. Our tradition is wise. *Charitable Writing* is our attempt to let the tradition speak.

What Is "Charitable Writing"?

We concluded the opening meditation by inviting you to join the tradition of Christian writing—to step into your own panel in the polyptych of Christian writers. That might now seem like a tall order. "What do *I*," you may be thinking to yourself, "have to contribute to the tradition?" Our book aims to address this question. We aren't simply trying to show you that the Christian tradition is pertinent to writing; we also hope to persuade you, reader, that *your writing* can be an expression of and contribution to the tradition. That last statement, moreover, applies to *any* kind of writing. A legal brief, a scientific article, an op-ed piece on local affairs, a short story, correspondence with a patient, a libretto: all of these genres can—and, in fact, *should*—be occasions for the practice of what we call "charitable writing."

The definition of the term *charitable writing* might be said to constitute the entirety of this book, and we are quite confident that our chapters have not exhausted the topic. Yet we recognize that it will be helpful to attempt a preliminary definition now, which the ensuing pages will thicken and complicate. In brief, "charitable writing" is writing that embodies the distinctive Christian understanding of love, which used to go by the name "charity" in English. In the King James Bible, for example, Paul's famous hymn to love concludes, "And now abideth faith, hope, charity, these three; but the greatest of these is charity" (1 Cor 13:13).

More specifically, "charitable writing" is writing that seeks to fulfill our Lord's great "double commandment" to love God and our neighbors. Here is how the Gospel of Matthew records this commandment:

> "You shall love the Lord your God with all your heart, and with all your soul, and with all your mind." This is the greatest and first commandment. And the second is like it: "You shall love your neighbor as yourself." On these two commandments hang all the law and the prophets. (Mt 22:37-40)

As we will see, Jesus frames the commandment so that it admits no exceptions: there is no activity, however mundane, to which the "law of love" does not apply. So here already is evidence that the present book isn't at all original. We are simply telling you to do what Scripture itself commends—or, better said, *demands*! We aren't trying to convince you that you ought to be a more loving writer. (You may debate that point with your Lord.) We strive, instead, to offer guidance on how to reach that goal.[9]

Spiritual Threshold Concepts

In recent years, educators have adopted the image of the threshold to explain how we learn, and you can easily see why: to be a student in many ways resembles standing at a threshold of a new experience. On the first day of class, we do just that: breathe deeply and walk through the door. Educational theorists Jan H. F. Meyer and Ray Land coined the term *threshold concepts* to describe the ideas one must learn to take part in academic disciplines, such as mathematics, biology, or philosophy.[10] For example, a threshold concept from the discipline of mathematics is the notion of complex numbers—that is, numbers that include imaginary elements.[11] About this example Meyer and Land write,

---

[9]To be clear, we are not saying that all Christians are called to write. Rather, we are contending that the law of love ought to be followed in everything we do, including writing. If and whenever we write, we are called to obey Christ's twofold commandment.

[10]Jan H. F. Meyer and Ray Land, "Threshold Concepts and Troublesome Knowledge: An Introduction," in *Overcoming Barriers to Student Understanding: Threshold Concepts and Troublesome Knowledge*, ed. Jan H. F. Meyer and Ray Land (New York: Routledge, 2006), 3. We first encountered Meyer and Land's work in *Naming What We Know: Threshold Concepts of Writing Studies*, ed. Linda Adler-Kassner and Elizabeth Wardle (Logan: Utah State University Press, 2016), ix-x.

[11]Meyer and Land, "Threshold Concepts," 4.

"The idea of the imaginary part . . . is, in fact, absurd to many people and beyond their intellectual grasp as an abstract entity. But although complex numbers are apparently absurd intellectual artifacts they are the gateway to the conceptualization and solution of problems in the pure and applied sciences that could not otherwise be considered."[12] According to Meyer and Land, learning a threshold concept of this sort is like passing through "a portal, opening up a new and previously inaccessible way of thinking about something."[13] Since this learning often challenges our ways of being, knowing, and acting, it can be risky, difficult, and even painful—but it is also "transformative."[14] Crossing thresholds changes us.

Like mathematics, biology, and philosophy, writing is a field of study. Many of our students are surprised to learn that writing is not only an activity we engage in; it is also an academic discipline.[15] Though that discipline goes by different names, we will refer to it as "writing studies" throughout the remainder of this book. Scholars working in the field of writing studies explore the history of writing, its processes, how it is taught, and much more. As a field, writing studies has its own threshold concepts, and scholars Linda Adler-Kassner and Elizabeth Wardle gather thirty-seven of them in their edited book *Naming What We Know: Threshold Concepts of Writing Studies*.[16] Here are several examples:

- Writing is a social and rhetorical activity.
- Writing involves making ethical choices.
- Writing speaks to situations through recognizable forms.
- Disciplinary and professional identities are constructed through writing.
- Writing enacts and creates identities and ideologies.
- All writers have more to learn.

Charitable Writing reinforces many of these threshold concepts, directly or indirectly, throughout its pages.[17] But that is not the book's primary

---

[12]Meyer and Land, "Threshold Concepts," 4.

[13]Meyer and Land, "Threshold Concepts," 3.

[14]Meyer and Land, "Threshold Concepts," 7; Adler-Kassner and Wardle, *Naming What We Know*, ix.

[15]Elizabeth Wardle and Doug Downs, *Writing About Writing: A College Reader*, 3rd ed. (Boston: Bedford/St. Martin's, 2017), 2.

[16]Adler-Kassner and Wardle, *Naming What We Know*, v-viii.

[17]To give one significant example, our project extends the notion that "writing involves making ethical choices." The underlying argument of *Charitable Writing* is that writing not only in-

purpose. Rather, we aim to introduce you to *spiritual* threshold concepts. Spiritual threshold concepts, as we define them, are ideas that one can learn to help integrate academic disciplines (such as writing studies) with spiritual disciplines and practices. Over the course of our three sections, we will introduce you to three such concepts: humble listening, loving argument, and hopeful timekeeping. The central claim of this book is that charitable writers listen humbly, argue lovingly, and keep the time of writing hopefully.

This list is not exhaustive. It is a starting point, a set of preliminary suggestions that we hope will catalyze conversations that will yield new insights about writing as a spiritual practice. (If writing studies can come up with thirty-seven threshold concepts, then surely we have a lot of work to do!) Yet our trio is not a scattershot attempt. Taken together, these concepts are designed to address multiple aspects of the writing life, including one's initial entrance into writing communities, both local and disciplinary; one's ways of conceiving of and practicing argument; and the rhythms of the writing process.

Writing studies' thirty-seven threshold concepts are portable. They don't just apply to the writing done by scholars working in the field of writing studies but to *any* writing situation; you can take them with you on the journey across the disciplines and along a future professional track.[18] We see the same promise in ours. In fact, we hold out a bolder hope: that our threshold concepts will not only improve your writing but also enrich your spiritual life. Though learning these spiritual threshold concepts may be challenging at times, it can be transformative. Our prayer for you is that you would be transformed, to an ever-greater degree, into the likeness of our Lord (2 Cor 3:18).

Writing into Virtue

Writing studies' threshold concepts have a decidedly practical bent. Notice the emphasis on *action* in several of the concepts we've listed

---

volves making *ethical* choices but also (always) *theological* and *spiritual* choices. For excellent reflections on the connections between writing, ethics, and virtue, see John Duffy, *Provocations of Virtue: Rhetoric, Ethics, and the Teaching of Writing* (Logan: Utah State University Press, 2019); "The Good Writer: Virtue Ethics and the Teaching of Writing," *College English* 79, no. 3 (2017): 229-50; and "Writing Involves Making Ethical Choices," in *Naming What We Know*, ed. Adler-Kassner and Wardle, 31-32. Whereas Duffy tends to focus on Aristotelian virtues, our focus is on Christian virtues.

[18] Adler-Kassner and Wardle, *Naming What We Know*, xi-xii

above; they involve making, speaking, constructing, enacting, and creating. Our book adopts this emphasis. Grasping spiritual threshold concepts does not, we want to suggest, simply involve mastering the definitions of abstract theological terms or memorizing general ethical principles. Learning to listen humbly, argue lovingly, and keep time hopefully involves a deeper, embodied kind of understanding—these are activities not only of the head but also of the heart and hands.

Christians have long talked about this aspect of faith using the language of *virtue*. As the philosopher James K. A. Smith explains, virtues are "good moral habits . . . character traits that become woven into *who you are* so that you are the *kind* of person who is inclined to be compassionate, forgiving, and so forth."[19] In describing virtue, Smith calls our attention to the apostle Paul's letter to the Colossians, which offers us several examples:

> As God's chosen ones, holy and beloved, clothe yourselves with compassion, kindness, humility, meekness, and patience. Bear with one another and, if anyone has a complaint against another, forgive each other; just as the Lord has forgiven you, so you also must forgive. Above all, clothe yourselves with love, which binds everything together in perfect harmony. (Col 3:12-14)

This passage is packed with virtues! A single sentence gives us five: compassion, kindness, humility, meekness, and patience. Paul then adds the disposition to forgive, which moral philosophers call "forgivingness."[20] And last comes love, "the big belt that pulls together the rest of the ensemble," as Smith well puts it.[21]

The question that Paul's and Smith's words raise, of course, is "*how do* [we] acquire such virtues?"[22] To use Paul's image, where can we get some of that cloth of many virtues and a nice belt to match? Smith reminds us that the Christian tradition has long set before us two strategies for growth in virtue, and they are both pertinent to our approach in this book.

[19]James K. A. Smith, *You Are What You Love: The Spiritual Power of Habit* (Grand Rapids, MI: Brazos Press, 2016), 16.

[20]See, for example, Robert C. Roberts, "Forgivingness," *American Philosophical Quarterly* 32, no. 4 (1995): 289-306.

[21]Smith, *You Are What You Love*, 16.

[22]Smith, *You Are What You Love*, 17, emphasis added.

The first is imitation. "We learn to be virtuous," Smith writes, "by imitating exemplars of justice, compassion, kindness, and love."[23] Our *ultimate* model is, of course, the Lord Jesus. Yet, as Christian ministers and theologians have long recognized, our growth in virtues is also aided by reflecting on how fellow Christians have sought to live their lives in imitation of Christ. Again, Smith invites us to consider Paul's words, this time in 1 Corinthians 11:1: "Be imitators of me, as I am of Christ." And Paul is not the only saint who has provided an example of virtue. As Smith notes, churches have long surrounded themselves with "the stained-glass 'wallpaper'" of saintly model lives.[24] Even churches with simple taste in design do this, such as through the practice of reading missionaries' journals and autobiographies.

The importance of imitation to the present book is likely already apparent to you, but let us take a moment to acknowledge one particularly significant influence on our approach: the theologian Stephanie Paulsell. In a 2001 essay, "Writing as a Spiritual Discipline," which is reprinted at the end of our book, Paulsell relates how the subject of her dissertation— the medieval mystic writer Marguerite d'Oingt—became "a challenge to me as a writer":

> Marguerite worked hard to forge an authorial identity in the midst of a culture that often mistrusted women's writing, and she pushed me to embrace the identity of writer as well. Writing matters, she seemed to say. On days when cleaning my apartment seemed preferable to writing my dissertation, she goaded me. Do your work, she said. Writing is your work. Finishing a degree or getting a grade is the least of it. Write to learn, to understand, to communicate with another, to seek what is real and true.[25]

Paulsell provided us with many insights—about humility, about attention, about revision, about community—and thus you will see her name at several key junctures in this book.[26] But the contribution that matters now is her modeling of imitation itself. Paulsell is herself a

---

[23]Smith, *You Are What You Love*, 18.
[24]Smith, *You Are What You Love*, 18.
[25]Stephanie Paulsell, "Writing as a Spiritual Discipline," in *The Scope of Our Art: The Vocation of the Theological Teacher*, ed. L. Gregory Jones and Stephanie Paulsell (Grand Rapids, MI: Eerdmans, 2002), 20.
[26]Paulsell, "Writing as a Spiritual Discipline," 22, 23, 25, 26-29.

Protestant, but in Marguerite, a medieval nun and one of the first French women writers, she recognized a spiritual precursor that cut across our contemporary denominational lines. Notice how she describes the effect of reading Marguerite's devotional works and epistles. These writings didn't just give her ideas about the spiritual life of the past. They become goads to her to get to work this very moment, and to get to work for the right reasons (learning, understanding, communicating —rather than amassing academic trophies). From Marguerite, Paulsell gained a powerful idea: that writing can be a *spiritual discipline*, "a discipline within which we might meet God."[27] We have gratefully received that lesson from Paulsell, in turn. Equally importantly, Marguerite offered Paulsell a model writing life—an example of discipline to follow. Paulsell thus exemplifies the process of "creative remembrance" that we mentioned in the opening meditation of the book. In the tradition of Christian women's writing, she found a catalyst for her own vocation as a writer.

In Marguerite and Paulsell, we add two more figures to our expanded polyptych. Our selections across this book have been chosen with two ends in view. First, they provide patterns for reflecting on and reshaping one's writing practices. Second, they show something of the diversity of contributors to the Christian tradition, mixing saints ancient and modern, male and female, and from a variety of cultural contexts. Our teachers include the aforementioned African bishop, Augustine; an ancient scholar from the fringes of the Roman Empire (modern Croatia or Slovenia), Jerome; a modern Indian social reformer, Pandita Ramabai; and many others. As you come up with your own examples, we encourage you to look for models closer to home, perhaps even in the seat next to you.

Imitation, let us also recognize, has a historic place in the teaching of writing.[28] Ancient rhetoricians introduced the art of rhetoric through exercises in which students imitated model texts. Some modern instructors continue to use these practices. Even teachers of writing who don't directly incorporate the ancient exercises in their classes often employ practices of imitation, such as training students to use templates (for argument, for introductions, even for sentence construction). A

---

[27]Paulsell, "Writing as a Spiritual Discipline," 21.
[28]In this paragraph, we adapt material from Beitler, *Seasoned Speech*, 22-23.

common exercise in introductory courses, moreover, asks students to examine the structure of a sample document—say, an article by a prominent scholar—for the purpose of imitation in the students' own writing. The goal of these exercises, ancient and modern, is not simply to copy others' work. Imitation, instead, has long been understood as a catalyst for what rhetoricians call *invention*, "the making of something new by remaking the old."[29] The ancient rhetor and the modern writer, on this understanding, use existing forms dynamically, to meet the needs of their particular moments. We encourage you to think about virtues in the same way: as ancient patterns for the Christian life, indeed of Christ's own life, which by his grace may find fresh expression in our lives now. Across this book, we will discuss how these two modes of imitation may be joined. We argue that virtues like humility, love, faith, and hope can be cultivated through the writing process, not simply alongside it.

We have in fact already begun to address Smith's second strategy for virtue acquisition: *practice*.[30] Smith's point—which is an ancient one—is that you don't develop a virtue simply by reading about it or by imitating it once. You grow in it by doing it over and over.

This emphasis on practice runs counter to prevalent cultural views about virtue. Consider the case of love. In our culture, we tend to characterize love as a spontaneous feeling—something that just happens to us. We are, as the saying goes, "swept off our feet." But this isn't the way that the New Testament describes its ideal of love. Charity, which comes from the Latin *caritas* and also goes by the Greek name *agapē*, is not an uncontrollable feeling that arises from time to time (or once in a lifetime). It is a disposition, a character trait, a "baseline inclination" that ought to permeate our everyday affairs.[31] Such a deep-rooted loving orientation toward the world doesn't come easy. Nobody "gets it" on the first try. Celebrated writer Maya Angelou captures this point well in an interview that appeared in *The Paris Review*'s famous "Art of Fiction" series. When asked if she reads the Bible for inspiration as a writer, she responded,

---

[29]Beitler, *Seasoned Speech*, 23; Michael C. Leff, "Hermeneutical Rhetoric," in *Rethinking Rhetorical Theory, Criticism, and Pedagogy: The Living Art of Michael C. Leff*, ed. Antonio de Velasco, John Angus Campbell, and David Henry (East Lansing: Michigan State University Press, 2016), 313-15.

[30]Smith, *You Are What You Love*, 18.

[31]Smith, *You Are What You Love*, 16.

For melody. For content also. I'm working at trying to be a Christian and that's serious business. It's like trying to be a good Jew, a good Muslim, a good Buddhist, a good Shintoist, a good Zoroastrian, a good friend, a good lover, a good mother, a good buddy—it's serious business. It's not something where you think, Oh, I've got it done. I did it all day, hotdiggety. The truth is, all day long you try to do it, try to be it, and then in the evening if you're honest and have a little courage you look at yourself and say, Hmm. I only blew it eighty-six times. Not bad. I'm trying to be a Christian and the Bible helps me to remind myself what I'm about.[32]

Angelou's words are so arresting because she grasps how hard it is to live out the virtues that we claim to value. And no virtue is harder to practice than love. Like our bodies, love requires nourishment (through prayer, for example) and regular exercise. Like any form of serious training, we will likely fail at it often. To return to Paul's metaphor, the virtues must be our daily attire. We add: like our workaday clothing, our virtues will often be in need of cleaning, pressing, and mending. Seeking to grow in virtue provides regular reminders of one's terrific need for God's grace.

Virtues, once again, are learned through imitation and practice, and this dual understanding of virtue acquisition dictates the structure of the book. Our three main sections are organized around our three threshold concepts: humble listening, loving argument, and hopeful timekeeping. To illuminate what these concepts look like in practice, we look at the writing and images of charitable writers of the past—saintly individuals who, we believe, are worth modeling our own writing lives after. Each section then moves from these reflections to practical recommendations. While our recommendations directly address students in writing classes, they are translatable to other contexts in which writing is shared, such as writing groups, church staffs, and workplaces. Most of our suggestions involve infusing your writing community with spiritual practices such as prayer, acts of hospitality, and rest. This last point highlights one of our great hopes for this book. The goal of charitable writing isn't simply to use Christian practices to smooth out

---

[32]Maya Angelou, "The Art of Fiction No. 119," interview by George Plimpton, *The Paris Review*, no. 116 (Fall 1990): www.theparisreview.org/interviews/2279/maya-angelou-the-art-of-fiction-no-119-maya-angelou.

wrinkles in the writing process. It's to turn the writing process into an occasion for spiritual growth.

How to Use This Book

In his treatise *On the Trinity,* Saint Augustine pauses at one point to address how the reader should approach his book:

> Reader, where you are equally certain, press on with me; where you are equally hesitant, seek with me; where you detect your own misstep, come back to me; where you detect mine, call me back. In this way, let us set off together on the Way of Charity, striving toward Him of whom it is said, "Seek His face always."[33]

Augustine is drawing on the Christian vision of life itself as a pilgrimage through the world, its ultimate destination being the New Jerusalem. Here he uses that metaphor as a framework in which to understand his labor of writing and his audience's of reading: fellow traveler, he is saying, let's make this effort of learning into a stage along the Way of Charity. We are peers, he suggests. At one place you go astray, at another I do. We encourage you to read our book in the spirit suggested by this passage: when you share our certainties, stride along with us, reader; when matters give you pause, explore with us; when you find an error in your thinking, circle back to us; when we err, call us back. But let us ever remember Whose Way it is that we walk.

Receive this book from us as a conversation starter rather than a series of edicts on what counts as good writing or proper Christian spirituality. As we suggested above, *Charitable Writing* represents our preliminary findings; we are well aware that there are further resources to mine and insights to glean from our rich and diverse tradition. (The vast library of potentially relevant Christian literature alone boggles the mind.) *Talk back* to this book; don't take it as writing gospel. That process might begin in the margins of your copy, as you scribble comments and questions that our terms and claims provoke. We encourage you to share your early reflections—however tentative—with the other writers in your orbit. Test out our arguments. Raise potential objections. Make connections that we haven't ventured.

---

[33] Augustinus Hipponensis, *De Trinitate,* in *Opera Omnia S. Augustini,* vol. 3, ed. Ryan Grant (Rome: Mediatrix Press, 2015), 5. We'd like to thank our friends and colleagues Alexander Loney and Benjamin Weber for assistance with the translation.

We also recognize that you may not share our convictions or may find some of our portrayals of Christian practices strange. Worry not, reader: we do not take absolute agreement as the litmus test for the success or failure of this book. We, of course, hope that you find valuable material in these pages that you can apply in your life. Yet we believe that the book can be useful even where disagreements arise. The book may function in these cases as a mirror, revealing to you your own convictions about writing, about Christian virtues and practices, about how the pieces fit together.

A Benediction

Academics aren't the only ones who watch the threshold. Standing at the doorway has long been a pregnant image for Christians. Across the Gospels, Jesus' teaching repeatedly hangs around the door, as in his commendation to "enter through the narrow door" in Luke 13:24 and his portrayal of prayer as the act of knocking on a door in Matthew 7:7-8. And most memorably of all, Revelation 3:20 sets the Lord himself at the door: "Listen! I am standing at the door, knocking; if you hear my voice and open the door, I will come in to you and eat with you, and you with me."

Following the New Testament writers' lead, Christians have long been careful markers of thresholds. The inscriptions on or above the doors of cathedrals exemplify this with their grand presentations of Scripture (often in Latin). One frequently used expression comes from Genesis 28:17: *Domus Dei et Porta Coeli*, or "House of God and Doorway to Heaven." Churches have also long stationed saints at the door, as we see in figure 3. The saint in question is Julian of Norwich, a mystical writer at a time when it was difficult for women's voices to be heard. Her *Revelations of Divine Love* is the earliest known English book written by a woman, and it is now hailed as a spiritual classic. The statue of Julian, carved by the sculptor David Holgate, was added to the western entrance of Norwich Cathedral in 2014. Holgate's sculpture shows, once again, the deep Christian reverence for the written word. Her pose suggests that Julian is in a contemplative state, her quill ready to record a vision.

Julian of Norwich might seem like a strange person to set at the entrance. Yet we need only to spend a short time with the book that she is holding to grasp why she's a capable greeter. Julian's book is a testimony

Figure 3. David Holgate, *Julian of Norwich*

to God's charity, his self-giving love for humanity. She memorably writes, for example, "God loved us before he made us; and his love has never diminished and never shall."[34] And elsewhere, "Truth sees God, and wisdom contemplates God, and from these two comes the third, a holy and wonderful delight in God, who is love."[35] Julian is a writer full of reassurances of God's care, making her an apt symbol of Christian hospitality and a fitting presence to meet at the threshold.

Let us acknowledge, too, that books are physical spaces that have thresholds of their own. An introduction is a kind of doorway that the reader passes through on the way to the text proper. We discuss this image of Julian here as way of marking this textual passageway with a model of the kind of writing life that we seek to describe in the ensuing pages of this book—a life undertaken in pursuit of the twofold commandment to love God and neighbor. In Julian, we meet a charitable writer at the door.

With our introduction's epigraph, we have also sought to mark the entrance of this book as a welcoming one. During Epiphany, the season following Christmas, some Christians chalk the letters "C," "M," and "B,"

---

[34]Julian of Norwich, *Revelations of Divine Love*, trans. Elizabeth Spearing (New York: Penguin, 1999), 179.

[35]Julian of Norwich, *Revelations of Divine Love,* 105.

along with signs of the cross, on or above the front doorways of their homes. The Epiphany season celebrates Christ's manifestation among the Gentiles, as represented by the journey of the Magi (the "three kings" of Mt 2:1-12), whom tradition names as Caspar, Melchior, and Balthazar. But the letters have long been held to have another reference. They stand for the words of the Latin prayer *Christus mansionem benedicat*, meaning "May Christ bless this house." By marking our threshold with this sign, we offer that prayer on your behalf.

Come in, reader. May Christ be your companion here.

Part One

Humble Listening

One

Entering the Study

Let the words of my mouth and the meditation of my heart
be acceptable to you, O LORD, my rock and my redeemer.

PSALM 19:14

Before he set to work, Thomas Aquinas, a prolific author and one of the great theologians of the Christian tradition, spoke a prayer in Latin that is beloved by Christians across the denominations. This "Prayer Before Study" (*oratio ante studium*) begins by calling out to the "Ineffable Creator" who has ordered the universe. After praising God, Aquinas asks for God's help in his writing:

> Pour forth a ray of Your brightness into the darkened places of my mind; disperse from my soul the twofold darkness into which I was born: sin and ignorance.
>
> You make eloquent the tongues of infants; refine my speech and pour forth upon my lips the goodness of Your blessing.
>
> Grant to me keenness of mind, capacity to remember, skill in learning, subtlety to interpret, and eloquence in speech.
>
> May You guide the beginning of my work, direct its progress, and bring it to completion. You Who are true God and true Man, Who live and reign, world without end. *Amen.*[1]

---

[1] John Vidmar, OP, *Praying with the Dominicans: To Praise, to Bless, to Preach* (New York: Paulist Press, 2008), 49. We inserted the breaks in this version.

Aquinas was an enormously gifted scholar—it is reported that he wrote about multiple topics simultaneously, dictating to scribes like a chess master moving down a line of boards![2] Yet his prayer does not tout *his* gifts; rather, he asks for the aid of one whose thoughts are far greater than his. Moreover, Aquinas perceives that as a finite and fallen creature, he is liable to make all kinds of mistakes. Writing *well*, he recognizes, must truly be a divine blessing.

In this prayer, Aquinas models one of the aspects of *humble listening*, our first threshold concept. As we have just noted, Aquinas adopts a humble pose in relation to our Lord, acknowledging that God's wits are infinitely quicker than ours, his memory impossibly deep, and his speech the most compelling. Notice the verbs that he uses to describe God's action: "pour forth," "refine," "grant," "guide," "direct," and "bring to completion." Aquinas characterizes himself as one in need of instruction, supervision, all kinds of support. In a word, the great scholar understands himself as *God's student*. The writer's labor must be, on this account, thoroughly imbued with listening.

There is much more to say about how we can practice "humble listening" in our writing lives, as the ensuing chapters of this section will show. There are many parties or conversations to which we might turn a humble ear. By beginning with the "Prayer Before Study," however, we want to stress that all of our efforts at humble listening—as with all of the other aspects of charitable writing—must begin in relation to this prayer's audience: God. In light of all the reasons for help that Aquinas names, doesn't he seem wise to begin his work by inviting God into his study space? Shouldn't we do likewise? Thanks to Aquinas, we don't even have to come up with clever words. We can use or adapt his. And we need not look only to him: our tradition abounds with prayers asking God for humility. To give just one example, John Calvin, another great Christian theologian, emphasizes the virtue in the prayer that he wrote for students receiving religious instruction: "I entreat that thou wouldst be pleased to turn me to true humility, that thus I may show myself

---

[2]See, for example, the account recorded in Mary Carruthers, *The Book of Memory: A Study of Memory in Medieval Culture,* 2nd ed. (Cambridge: Cambridge University Press, 2008), 3.

teachable and obedient first to thyself, and then to those also who by thy authority are placed over me."[3]

The path into the study has been made smooth by the feet of the saints.

Companions in the Study

Writing is frequently understood as a task that we go off and do alone.[4] Aquinas's prayer reminds us that for Christians, however, writing need not—indeed, should not—be a solo act. We have many reasons to ask humbly that God be our companion in the study, and we may trust that he will accept our invitation.

There is a danger here, however, and we see it dramatically rendered in figure 4.[5] The image is a woodcut that the German artist Albrecht Dürer completed in 1514. Its subject is Eusebius Sophronius Hieronymus —a theologian, biblical scholar, priest, and translator whose learning earned him the title "Doctor of the Church" (an honorific also given to Saint Augustine and Thomas Aquinas). Saint Jerome, as he is more commonly known, was among the most popular subjects of medieval and early modern art. He appears, as mentioned in the opening meditation, in the Saint Luke Altarpiece, and he was often depicted as a scholar at work in his study, as we see here. Because this scene was painted over and over again, various versions of it offer fascinating windows into how different generations and particular artists imagined the scene of writing.

Dürer follows the traditional blueprint for this subject by depicting the saint's study as a retreat from the world. Dürer in fact outdoes many of his predecessors in stressing the degree of the writer's solitude. In many pictures in this tradition, Jerome's legendary companion, a lion, sits at his side, available for petting; here the lion slumbers alongside a dog. Dürer also sets Jerome against the back wall of the room—and thus at a distance from even us. "Stay back, onlooker," Dürer seems to say,

---

[3]John Calvin, *Tracts Containing Treatises on the Sacraments, Catechism of the Church of Geneva, Forms of Prayer, and Confessions of Faith*, vol. 2, trans. Henry Beveridge (Eugene, OR: Wipf and Stock, 2002), 97.

[4]Stephanie Paulsell, "Writing as a Spiritual Discipline," in *The Scope of Our Art: The Vocation of the Theological Teacher*, ed. L. Gregory Jones and Stephanie Paulsell (Grand Rapids, MI: Eerdmans, 2002), 26.

[5]In what follows, we draw somewhat on our jointly authored piece, "Companions in the Study" (forthcoming).

"saint at work here!" By depicting Jerome head-on and at an elevated writing desk, moreover, Dürer obscures the document on which the saint labors, and the artist includes no transparent clues elsewhere in the picture to tip us off to the saint's subject matter. In so many ways, then, others are closed *out* of the writing process. Dürer has rightly concluded that writing can be a deeply spiritual activity, as highlighted by the

Figure 4. Albrecht Dürer, *St. Jerome in His Study*

blazing halo around the saint's head; however, in this staging of the scene, writing appears to involve only two parties—the writer and God.[6] Now look at figure 5, a tempera painting from the 1450s by the Spanish artist Nicolás Francés. In this version of the scene of writing, the saint enjoys human company as well as that of his beastly companion. By their outfits, we can recognize that Jerome is surrounded by the members of a monastic community. Writing once again is a spiritual practice; indeed, it is now apparently a full-fledged spiritual *discipline*, an activity undertaken within the regimen of monastic life. Yet in this case that practice is imagined not as a solitary but as a conspicuously *social* pursuit.

This imagined community has another fascinating quality, which is revealed by the specific outfits worn by the monks. Their white tunics and brown scapulars and hoods indicate that the men are Hieronymites, which, as the name suggests, is a monastic order formed in commemoration of the saint many centuries after his death. Francés thus shows us not only writing's place in monastic communities in the mid-fifteenth century, when making and reading of books were profoundly communal enterprises. He also reveals writing's power to connect writers and readers from far-flung locales and separate centuries. Francés imagines a *spiritual* fellowship between Jerome and the monks who take his name, and the tie that binds them is the saint's written remains, his books.[7]

Look closely and you will see, moreover, that Francés has carefully orchestrated his readers' bodies. The middle monk's right hand slips underneath the leaning monk's book, physically supporting his brother's reading. The third figure, meanwhile, raises his left hand at such an angle that it appears (from the viewer's perspective) to touch the sheet

---

[6]For more on this topic, see Eugene F. Rice Jr., *Saint Jerome in the Renaissance* (Baltimore: The Johns Hopkins University Press, 1985), 110-12. After highlighting that Dürer has placed the crucifix and the skull in Jerome's sightline, Rice concludes, "In the end, Dürer seems to suggest, *lectio divina* and sacred scholarship must lead, like penitential discipline, to an alert consciousness of mortality and meditation on the Passion. By studying God's word the Christian scholar may achieve some small understanding of that death which assures victory over death" (112). See also David Lyle Jeffrey, *People of the Book: Christian Identity and Literary Culture* (Grand Rapids, MI: Eerdmans, 1996), 214-15.

[7]Paulsell, "Writing as a Spiritual Discipline," 17. To borrow Paulsell's observation about the monastic practice of copying works, the sort of writing that Jerome and the members of his order are doing "allows them to reach across the boundaries of geography and time to be in intimate communion with people they will never meet, but whom they hope to lead to God."

that the middle monk holds. Though the three figures digest separate texts, the artist arranges their bodies to suggest that their readings are interwoven, continuous. They read as monks are meant to live—*in community*. Francés has thus transformed Jerome's study from the standard

Figure 5. Nicolás Francés, *Saint Jerome Translating the Gospels*

scholarly retreat into a picture of generations and spiritual fellowship. Indeed, given that this piece was likely originally made for a Hieronymite community, we may even call it a *genealogical* study—a spiritual family portrait of patron saint and modern practitioners. We recognize that these matters may seem far from the present day, but we believe that there is an important lesson in these pictures about how we conceive of what we are doing when we write. Symbolically speaking, Dürer posts several "No Trespassing" signs in his rendition of Jerome's study. The writer's service to God is an exclusive affair. Francés, by contrast, opens the fellowship just as he opens Jerome's book for us to see. He offers us a Jerome who is in community with his readers, despite the gap of centuries. Francés's choice of the text on which the saint works is also suggestive: it is the Vulgate, Jerome's translation of the Bible into Latin, the literary language of Europe for centuries. The Vulgate was the book for everybody; its presence implies that the viewer has a place in the handing-down of writings, too. Dürer shows us a scene of religious writing; Francés invites us in.

Writing Is a Social Activity

Centuries before writing studies emerged as a formal academic discipline, Francés grasped one of the discipline's foundational truths: that writing is a profoundly social endeavor, whether one is writing at a table surrounded by friends or in private. We are always writing *for* an audience—perhaps even, as in Francés's picture, one that will live long after we have put down our pens for the last time. And we are always drawing *upon* the words of those who have gone before. As writing scholar Kevin Roozen puts it, "No matter how isolated a writer may seem as she sits at her computer, types on the touchpad of her smartphone, or makes notes on her legal pad, she is always drawing upon the ideas and experiences of countless others."[8] Francés depicts these realities visually in a very direct way: we see Jerome translating the words of his predecessors in the faith on behalf of his successors. Like Jerome's writing, our writing is at once a *fore*word and an *after*word: we are

---

[8]Kevin Roozen, "Writing Is a Social and Rhetorical Activity," in *Naming What We Know: Threshold Concepts of Writing Studies*, ed. Linda Adler-Kassner and Elizabeth Wardle (Logan: Utah State University Press, 2016), 17.

always writing for a future audience (even if only ourselves at a later moment) and in the wake of those who have written before us.

The scene of writing is thus profoundly social, even when we are technically alone. The words we choose, the genre conventions we invoke, the technologies—analog and digital—we use: all of these tools of the writer's trade are social goods.[9] There is no such thing as writing "on your own." This is a truth that Christians in particular have every reason to embrace, for to recognize the deeply social nature of writing is to be liberated from the unfortunately persistent cultural myth that our writing must be entirely *sui generis* (ideally, springing fully formed from our minds like Athena from the head of Zeus in Greek mythology). Writing in fact is a *dependent* activity. Looked at in the right light, our writing reveals our embeddedness in rich webs of human relationships. And "if we practice writing as a spiritual discipline," Stephanie Paulsell rightly notes, "our writing ought to deepen our life in community."[10]

---

[9]Roozen, "Writing Is a Social and Rhetorical Activity," 18.
[10]Paulsell, "Writing as a Spiritual Discipline," 27.

Two

On Humility

*When a certain rhetorician was asked what was the chief
rule in eloquence, he replied, "Delivery"; what was the second
rule, "Delivery"; what was the third rule, "Delivery"; so if you
ask me concerning the precepts of the Christian religion, first,
second, third, and always I would answer, "Humility."*

SAINT AUGUSTINE

The practice of humility should begin even before we set to work—
indeed, even before we step into the study—when we ask God to
direct our labors. Subsequent chapters will offer further reflections on
how what we're calling "humble listening" can help us as we join writing
communities. But before we proceed with such practical matters, we
ought to understand what Christians mean when we talk about humility. Humility is the virtue that allows us to see not only our finitude
and fallenness but also the goods of our communities. It allows us to
recognize that we don't have all the answers. It helps us to see the
enormous contributions of others. For the humble person, dependence
on others is not an embarrassment but a potential source of mutual
benefit. Humility, in short, makes us teachable.

As a starting point for this discussion, consider Mary. Our tradition
has long characterized Mary as a paragon of humility, pointing, in
particular, to her humble reception of Gabriel's message in Luke
1:26-38. That scene begins, as you will recall, with Gabriel's an-
nouncement that Mary is the "favored one"—she will bear the Son of

God! Initially astonished by this news ("How can this be?" she asks), Mary responds to Gabriel's assurance with these remarkable words of submission: "Here am I, the servant of the Lord; let it be with me according to your word." A few lines later, Luke records the "Magnificat" (or "Song of Praise") that Mary sings in response to the good news. Her opening words tout God's regard for her lowliness:

> My soul glorifies the Lord,
>   and my spirit rejoices in God my Savior,
> for he has been mindful
>   of the humble state of his servant. (Lk 1:46b–48 NIV)

Mary's subsequent words are a study in humility. Her song describes not her worthiness but *God's* good deeds, past and present: "He has shown strength with his arm"; "He has brought down the powerful"; "He has filled the hungry with good things"; "He has helped his servant Israel" (Lk 1:51-54). This indeed is the song of a *servant*. Mary humbly describes God as the primary actor in this story. In humility, she opens herself to his blessing. As the poet Dante memorably put it in his *Divine Comedy*, Mary at this moment "turned the key to love on high."[1]

With Mary in view, we can make our first observation about humility: it is the virtue that allows us to get out of our own sinful way and thereby embrace God's redemptive work in us. As the twentieth-century philosopher Simone Weil wrote, "Humility is the refusal to exist outside God."[2] If humility is an acknowledgment of our weakness, it is, simultaneously, an affirmation of God's strength. Humility says no to the sinful self in order to say yes to God.

Notably for present purposes, many pictures of the annunciation reaching back to the Middle Ages have depicted Mary holding a book. We see a modern example, by the artist John Collier, in figure 6. The picture is deliberately anachronistic: Collier represents Mary as a teenager living on a typical suburban street in order to help contemporary viewers recognize how shocking God's intrusion on Mary's life really was. Here Mary's face registers her surprise at Gabriel's appearance, which, in keeping with the pictorial tradition, interrupts her reading.

---

[1]Dante Alighieri, *Purgatorio*, trans. Jean Hollander and Robert Hollander (New York: Anchor Books, 2003), 213.

[2]Simone Weil, *Gravity and Grace* (New York: Routledge, 2002), 40.

Figure 6. John Collier, *Annunciation*

Medieval and Renaissance artists often, whether directly or indirectly, suggest that she is reading prophecies foretelling the Lord's birth. That detail does not, of course, appear in the Gospel accounts of the scene. Medieval artists knew that. John Collier knows that. Like Collier's choice to render Mary in modern dress, the artists' point is not historical but theological. The book in Mary's hand demonstrates her openness to the eternal Word who will, through her womb, become flesh.[3] She reads, in short, with humility. As the literary critic David Lyle Jeffrey explains, this "bookish" depiction of Mary arose at the same time that humility was touted as a primary virtue of Christian education: "Humility was regarded by medieval philosophers of education as a *sine qua non* for

---

[3]David Lyle Jeffrey, *People of the Book: Christian Identity and Literary Culture* (Grand Rapids, MI: Eerdmans, 1996), 219. See also Zina Hitz, *Lost in Thought: The Hidden Pleasures of the Intellectual Life* (Princeton, NJ: Princeton University Press, 2020), 60-63.

the serious pursuit of truth in reading."[4] In these annunciation scenes, then, Mary epitomizes the Christian ideal of humble reading.

On some occasions, artists have extended this tradition of the "bookish" Mary to depict her as a writer. We see perhaps the most famous example of this imaginative exercise—the *Madonna of the Magnificat* by the Italian Renaissance painter Sandro Botticelli—in figure 7. In the picture, Mary is shown dipping her pen in an ink pot in preparation to write the remaining words of the Magnificat, the opening words of which grace the right page of the open book. (The text of the left page, meanwhile, has been identified as the Song of Zechariah, another one of the three "canticles" at the beginning of Luke's Gospel.)

Figure 7. Sandro Botticelli, *Madonna of the Magnificat*

[4]Jeffrey, *People of the Book*, 219n11.

Some scholars have understood the Christ child on her lap as offering her encouragement, and others dictation. We are tempted to read the position of his hand as a blessing of the Magnificat itself. Either way, the scene emphasizes that Mary takes up the book in the service of humility. Yet in this case, she is a model of humble *writing*.

We believe that all of these pictures speak deep truths, for truly humility belongs among the chief virtues of our reading and writing lives. Indeed, we want to go further. We think that humility ought to be understood as the *first* writing virtue, just as humility has been traditionally considered the "first" of the Christian virtues. Theologians gave humility that title because they perceived that growing in humility enables us to pursue other virtues, since humility keeps our self-regarding (and, ultimately, self-defeating) pride at bay. As the great fourth-century preacher John Chrysostom wrote, "Humility is the mother of virtues."[5] In our epigraph above, Augustine made an analogy between the orator's first precept of eloquence, which is *delivery*, and the Christian religion's first precept, which Augustine names *humility*.[6] Our contention is that Augustine was more right than he knew. Eloquence begins with humility, too.

Defining Humility

Before discussing how humility might reshape our writing practice, we need to reflect on the meaning of the word. Consider how humility is commonly defined in our culture. The *Collins Dictionary* explains that "someone who has humility is not proud and does not believe they are better than other people."[7] Similarly, the *Merriam-Webster Dictionary* defines "humility" as "freedom from pride or arrogance." The *Cambridge Dictionary* characterizes it as "the feeling or attitude that you have no special importance that makes you better than others; lack of

---

[5]John Chrysostom, "Homily XV," in *The Homilies of S. John Chrysostom, Archbishop of Constantinople, on the Gospel of St. Matthew*, trans. Frederic Field (London: Walter Smith, 1885), 200.
[6]Quoted in John Calvin, *Institutes of the Christian Religion*, ed. John T. McNeill, trans. Ford Lewis Battles (Philadelphia: Westminster, 1960), 268-69. See also Augustine of Hippo, *The Letters of Saint Augustine*, trans. J. G. Cunningham (North Charleston: CreateSpace, 2015), 245-46.
[7]The definitions in this paragraph appear in the *Collins Online English Dictionary*, s.v. "humility," www.collinsdictionary.com/us/dictionary/english/humility (accessed July 15, 2019); *Merriam-Webster Dictionary*, s.v. "humility," www.merriam-webster.com/dictionary/humility (accessed July 15, 2019); *Cambridge Dictionary*, s.v. "humility," https://dictionary.cambridge.org/us/dictionary/english/humility (accessed July 15, 2019).

pride." All of these dictionaries define humility *negatively*, meaning that they explain what it is by what it is *not*. On these accounts, humility is the absence or avoidance of a vice, usually pride.

These definitions owe a debt to the Christian tradition. Innumerable accounts name humility as a virtue that opposes a vice, be it pride, arrogance, or vanity. Augustine, for one, famously characterized humility as the medicine that cures us of the disease of pride.[8] Yet the tradition has long preached that while humility is indeed strong medicine, it should not disable us. To cultivate humility does not mean that we must go about constantly bewailing our utter unworthiness. For when we do so, humility has ceased to be humility; it looks instead like a yielding to despair or, worse still, an exaggerated show of piety. To borrow an apt image from the friar Timothy Radcliffe, "Christian humility is not about feeling that one is a despicable worm."[9] Checking pride's vanity, humility attunes us to God's beckoning. It is a path to freedom.

C. S. Lewis recognized that humility has the potential to enrich our everyday interactions. In the third book of *Mere Christianity,* he writes the following:

> Do not imagine that if you meet a really humble man he will be what most people call "humble" nowadays: he will not be a sort of greasy, smarmy person, who is always telling you that, of course, he is nobody. Probably all you will think about him is that he seemed a cheerful, intelligent chap who took a real interest in what *you* said to *him*. If you do dislike him it will be because you feel a little envious of anyone who seems to enjoy life so easily. He will not be thinking about humility: he will not be thinking about himself at all.[10]

Notice that Lewis perceives that true humility does *not* involve constant worry about whether one is being humble. He recognizes, moreover, that someone who rattles on about his own lowliness isn't showing us what humility looks like. Quite the opposite! True humility, on this account, is seen in the humble person's endeavor to pay attention to others.

---

[8]Joseph J. McInerney, *The Greatness of Humility: St. Augustine on Moral Excellence* (Eugene, OR: Pickwick Publications, 2016), 104.

[9]Timothy Radcliffe, OP, *What Is the Point of Being Christian?* (New York: Burns and Oates, 2006), 133.

[10]C. S. Lewis, *Mere Christianity* (New York: Macmillan, 1960), 114.

Humility, to put it another way, lets the moment be about *someone else.*

Again, Radcliffe puts the point nicely: "Humility is liberation from compulsion to claim the centre of the stage, accepting to play a part in the story that one shares with others, but not necessarily always with the leading role."[11]

These remarks help us to see that there's more to the Christian understanding of humility than a simple negative definition like "the absence of pride" acknowledges. Humility frees us from excessive self-regard, thereby allowing our attention to turn elsewhere. Lewis's observation that humble people take a "real interest" in what others say to them points to a major theme of Christian thinking about what humility makes possible: humility opens us up to the world outside our own heads.

Humble Minds

The New Testament Greek word that English translators render as "humility" is *tapeinophrosynē*, which is a compound of two words. The first, *tapeinos*, means "low." The second, *phrēn*, roughly corresponds to "mind." A more direct translation in English would thus be "lowliness of mind." That "lowliness" is actually embedded in the Latin root of our "humility" too, though few see it now. *Humilitas* begins with *humus,* the Latin word for "earth" (or even "dirt"). The Greek and Latin words that we translate as "humility" thus convey a sense that the humble person isn't puffed up, doesn't have an exalted sense of self. Humility properly grounds us.

"Lowliness of mind," though, doesn't demand that we pretend that we don't have minds. It doesn't mean that we should never speak up, that we should simply assume that we have nothing new or important to say. As a virtue for the handling of ideas, humility means adopting a proper regard for our own thinking as we swim in the broad sea of ideas. As the educator Philip Dow observes, to cultivate "authentic humility" is to strive "to see ourselves as we really are."[12] "Applied to our thinking," Dow continues, "this means an uncompromisingly honest appraisal of

---

[11]Radcliffe, *What Is the Point of Being Christian?*, 134.
[12]Philip E. Dow, *Virtuous Minds: Intellectual Character Development* (Downers Grove, IL: IVP Academic, 2013), 70.

the capacities and limitations of our minds."[13] This self-assessment might seem like an invitation for you to start looking around to gauge your strengths and weaknesses as compared to those of your friends, classmates, coworkers, and so on. But it's not. As Dow points out, our pursuit of humility ought to begin by reflecting on the *ultimate* measure: "the standard of an all-knowing, infinitely intelligent and always true God."[14]

Against this backdrop, we have every reason to regard our own mental powers with the utmost humility. We have every reason, in turn, to pray prayers like that of Aquinas when entering the study. And yet, when we make God the starting point for our reflections on our thinking, we are freed to recognize that our capacities are indeed *gifts*. God has endowed us with profound capacities to learn, to ponder, to hypothesize, to reason, to understand. These powers apply to a range of fields and areas of inquiry—not least the knowledge of God himself! To recognize this is to realize that delighting in our thinking, delighting in our nimble intellects, may be a godly pursuit. To cultivate humility in regard to our ideas does not, in G. K. Chesterton's words, require that we become "too mentally modest to believe in the multiplication table."[15] Rather, such humility liberates us. As Dow observes, "Because intellectually humble people value truth over their egos' need to be right, they are freed up to admit the limits of their own knowledge. This freedom naturally produces a teachable spirit and the habit of humble inquiry that are at the heart of sustained personal growth."[16]

Humility as a Social Practice

But humility is not just a mind game for thinkers to play in solitude. Knowledge is a profoundly public affair. It grows as thinkers trade ideas in a variety of media—books, journals, blog posts, lectures, conferences, and so on. Humility, then, doesn't just play out against the background of the all-knowing God. Its domain is also our relationships with fellow pursuers of truth—whether that is our friends, classmates, fellow church members, or colleagues in an academic discipline or professional field.

[13]Dow, *Virtuous Minds*, 70-71.
[14]Dow, *Virtuous Minds*, 71.
[15]Quoted in Dow, *Virtuous Minds*, 70. See also G. K. Chesterton, *Orthodoxy* (San Francisco: Ignatius Press, 1995), 37.
[16]Dow, *Virtuous Minds*, 72.

This brings us to humility's *social* dimension.[17] The apostle Paul recognized that humility had a social role to play, and named it in multiple spots when laying out the model for Christian community. One important place he does so is Philippians 2:1-5:

> If then there is any encouragement in Christ, any consolation from love, any sharing in the Spirit, any compassion and sympathy, make my joy complete: be of the *same mind*, having the same love, being in full accord and of *one mind*. Do nothing from selfish ambition or conceit, but in *humility* [*tapeinophrosynē*] regard others as better than yourselves. Let each of you look not to your own interests, but to the interests of others. Let the *same mind* be in you that was in Christ Jesus.[18]

In English translation, humility doesn't seem quite as integral to the entire passage as it does in Greek. Recall that *tapeinophrosynē* combines two words: *tapeinos* ("low") and *phrēn* ("mind"). The latter word is the root of the other words that we have italicized: "same mind" and "one mind." Paul is calling on the members of the church at Philippi to "lower" themselves, to "regard others as better than yourselves," not because these Christians need to grovel without ceasing. Such self-absorption is, in fact, exactly what Paul is trying to defeat. Paul is laying out a program for addressing the needs of others, and thereby the establishment of a community built on mutual acknowledgment and shared understanding. The "one mind," meanwhile, is not the "hive mind" imagined by science fiction writers but the mind of Christ. As commentators down through the ages have argued, Paul is calling on his fellow Christians to imitate their Lord's example of humility, which is the way of self-giving, of loving service.

Paul's aim here is to lay out a model for building specifically Christian communities. In such a context, *everyone* should be striving to practice "lowliness of mind," with the end of growing together in the traits that

---

[17]The division between "humble minds" and "humility as a social practice" in this chapter is inspired by discussions among moral philosophers about the *epistemic* and *social* aspects of intellectual humility. For more on intellectual humility, see Robert C. Roberts and W. Jay Wood, *Intellectual Virtues: An Essay in Regulative Epistemology* (Oxford: Oxford University Press, 2007); and Ian M. Church and Peter L. Samuelson, *Intellectual Humility: An Introduction to the Philosophy and Science* (London: Bloomsbury, 2017).

[18]Emphasis added.

Paul enumerates at the start of the passage: love, compassion, sympathy, joy, and the sharing of the Spirit. Paul's instructions have an obvious application in local writing communities whose members are Christians. "Lowliness of mind," let us underscore, does not require us to brush aside disagreements that are rooted in careful research and reflection. Rather, it provides an animating spirit for a community of service—in which we seek to aid one another in making the best case for the positions that we adopt while also striving to do justice to alternative views.

Moreover, humility's social scene does not extend only to Christians. The tradition has, in fact, often promoted the cultivation of a humble disposition toward *all of our neighbors*, be they Christians or not. Recall Lewis's picture of the humble person as a "cheerful, intelligent chap who took a real interest in what *you* said to *him*." Lewis doesn't limit the humble person's range of interest to his or her fellow churchgoers. Humility is a disposition that can—and we may hope, will—animate our daily passage through the world.

With that lesson in mind, we can return productively to a point made above: humility's place among the primary virtues of writing. In the twelfth century, Hugh of Saint Victor, a theologian who cared deeply about teaching and learning, wrote about the meaning of humility for students in his *Didascalicon de studio legendi* (*On the Study of Reading*). Hugh names humility as "the beginning of discipline."[19] He then argues that while humility teaches many lessons, three are of the utmost import for students: "first, that he hold no knowledge and no writing in contempt; second, that he blush to learn from no man; and third, that when he has attained learning himself, he not look down upon everyone else."[20] Later in the same chapter, he adds: "The wise student, therefore, gladly hears all, reads all, and looks down upon no writing, no person, no teaching."[21] On this account, humility not only makes us teachable. By helping us to get over our blinding pride, humility also helps us to acknowledge the numerous teachers in the world around us. Arguing in the same vein, philosophers Robert C. Roberts and Jay Wood observe that "the humble inquirer has more potential teachers than his less

---

[19]Hugh of Saint Victor, *The Didascalicon of Hugh of Saint Victor: A Medieval Guide to the Arts,* trans. Jerome Taylor (New York: Columbia University Press, 1991), 94.

[20]Hugh of Saint Victor, *Didascalicon,* 94-95.

[21]Hugh of Saint Victor, *Didascalicon,* 95.

humble counterparts."[22] Once again, humility is not only a negative habit—the suppression of pride—but also an opening for the writer into a world of possibilities.

Jerome as Humble Writer

We have suggested that Aquinas's "Prayer Before Study" (or some other invocation, offered in the same spirit) provides a good starting place for our writing practice. But once we have made such a prayer, are we done with humility? Can we move on from the "first" virtue to others? The answer to both questions is, of course, no. Humility doesn't just help us to make a start: it needs to be our constant companion as we write. Hugh of Saint Victor clearly grasped this truth. Notice how his threefold scheme for the practice of humility makes it both the novice's virtue and the expert's. Perhaps humility is even *more* necessary to the scholar who has "attained learning," since as we "master" a subject the temptation only grows to hold our noses up high. Prideful scholars are, on Hugh's account, not only insufferable; they're also *bad* scholars, since pride narrows their pool of possible teachers.

We must, then, hold humility before us *throughout* the writing process. This truth takes a particularly vivid form in a diptych (or "bifold") by the fifteenth-century Italian painter Benedetto di Bindo (see figure 8). The subject on the right is already familiar to you, since we reviewed two examples of this scene in the previous chapter: here is Benedetto's take on Jerome at work in his study. Once again, medieval and Renaissance artists weren't aiming for historical accuracy in their Jeromes. Instead, these pictures depict the *spiritual* nature of scholarly practices such as reading and writing. They testify to the Christian tradition's reverence for what goes on within the study.

Benedetto's diptych pairs the studious Jerome with a panel in which Mary and the Christ child sit.[23] The arrangement of that second scene

---

[22]Roberts and Wood, *Intellectual Virtues*, 253. Nicole Mazzarella makes a similar point in "Facing the Blank Page" (Wheaton College TowerTalks, January 13, 2017), www.wheaton.edu/academics/faculty/towertalks/facing-the-blank-page. After highlighting C. S. Lewis's passage on the "humble man" (which we quote earlier in the chapter), Mazzarella observes, "When I think about people who are intellectually curious, I think of them as people who recognize that they can learn from many different people."

[23]In what follows, we again draw on our jointly authored piece, "Companions in the Study" (forthcoming).

tells us that Benedetto has a particular lesson in mind. The image is organized according to the conventions of the so-called Madonna of Humility picture, which, as the name suggests, celebrates Mary's exemplification of that virtue. We began this chapter with Scripture's portrayal of Mary's humility. Artists like Benedetto sought to translate Scripture's written messages into visual symbols. Notice, for example, that here Mary is seated on a cushion on the floor, bringing her closer to the *humus* at the heart of humility. She expresses humility, moreover, by providing sustenance and care to the infant Christ. Behind Mary sit spools of thread—a sign of her attention to her daily chores—and an open book. Her reading is also a token of her humility, as we saw in Collier's annunciation picture. Earlier we noted that the book served as a pictorial sign of Mary's receptivity to the eternal Word. Here we see the other side of that story: cradling the Word itself, she sets aside her reading for the moment.

By pairing Jerome with the Madonna of Humility, Benedetto invites us to look for humility in this studious saint's labors. There are many suggestive elements, but let us focus now on two. The first is Jerome's

Figure 8. Attributed to Benedetto di Bindo, *Virgin of Humility and Saint Jerome Translating the Gospel of John*

attire. Benedetto wraps him in the red robes of a cardinal, one of the highest positions in the hierarchy of the Catholic priesthood. The official position of cardinal didn't exist in Jerome's day; the garb was borrowed by artists to symbolize Jerome's stature in the church's memory. Draped in a cardinal's robes, the saint could be (as he is in other "Cardinal Jerome" pictures) a towering figure. Benedetto, though, seats him at a writing desk. The artist brings the saint low through the act of writing—in alignment with the lowly Mother and Child in the left panel.

The second point relates to Jerome's text. Draw very close to the diptych, and you can discern that the upper book, the one Jerome reads, is in fact gibberish. Art historians tell us that Benedetto is imitating the Greek alphabet that he can't read. Meanwhile, the lower book displays John 1:1-7 in Latin. Benedetto thus depicts Jerome at work on the same task that Francés sets out for his Jerome: working on the Latin Bible translation known as the Vulgate. The artist's choice of the opening of John's Gospel as Jerome's text is suggestive. It, too, is about humility—that of the Creator who entered his creation. This is the same person whom we see in the left panel as a fragile infant, one dependent on his mother for life.

Indeed, perhaps we can say that we look with Jerome at the infant, for Benedetto arranges the scene so that Jerome appears to look *through* the Greek text to Mary and Jesus.[24] The picture thus depicts Jerome not only as one who enacts humility through the gestures we have noted above; he is also one who, like us, contemplates lessons in humility. His efforts as a translator, moreover, make Jerome a transmitter of humility —for thanks to his Vulgate, future generations would be able to read of how Mary and Jesus lived out the lowly virtue.

To close, let us stress that we offer these images not because we think that the practice of charitable writing requires that you station diptychs or icons around your workspace (though we know people who do so). Rather, we bring Benedetto to your attention because the artist makes exactly the connection between writing and humility that we have been articulating throughout this chapter. He saw clearly that humility isn't

---

[24]As we observed in an earlier note, in his book *Jerome in the Renaissance* (Baltimore: The Johns Hopkins University Press, 1985), Eugene F. Rice Jr. points out that Albrecht Dürer "positioned skull and crucifix" in Jerome's sightline, which, Rice suggests, is a commentary on "that death which assures victory over death" (112). Benedetto uses sightlines as well, though his focus is on incarnation, not crucifixion.

just a virtue that gets us in the door; it is an *abiding* writing virtue, a deskmate. Finally, Benedetto is exemplary for present purposes because he possesses the kind of *imagination* that we have been encouraging you to cultivate. In looking for models of humility, he turned to the resources that we have commended: Scripture and tradition. His diptych performs a translation whereby the humility of the left panel infuses the scholarly activity of the right. *That's* the practice that we are advocating —the practice of keeping traditional patterns of humility in view while you write. Some readers will find inspiration in paintings, others the printed page. The medium is not the point. Recall James K. A. Smith's argument about growth in virtue: "We learn to be virtuous by imitating exemplars of justice, compassion, kindness, and love."[25] Our tradition bears abundant witness to humility. The saints stand at the ready; it falls to you to *listen in.*

---

[25]James K. A. Smith, *You Are What You Love: The Spiritual Power of Habit* (Grand Rapids, MI: Brazos Press, 2016), 18.

Three

Humble Listening in Local Writing Communities

Christian life is a listening life.

Rowan Williams

Listen in. *Listen up. Listen closely. Stop, look, and listen.* These and other familiar expressions speak to the distinct state that is listening: it requires that we press in, wake up, draw close, stop whatever else we are doing. Listening places heavy demands on mind and body alike. It is hard work. For this reason, numerous commentators over the ages have argued that few people truly listen well. Most of us, most of the time, do it poorly, barely, and perhaps not at all. In a radio broadcast titled "Listen to This," the American writer Alice Duer Miller remarked, "People love to talk but hate to listen. . . . Listening is not merely not talking, though even that is beyond most of our powers; it means taking a vigorous, human interest in what's being told us."[1] Miller then encapsulated her lesson in a memorable image: "You can listen like a blank wall or like a splendid auditorium where every sound comes back fuller and richer."[2]

Even though (and perhaps because) listening is so taxing, Scripture is deeply invested in it. The Old Testament often enjoins careful listening, as in Isaiah 28:23: "Listen, and hear my voice; Pay attention, and hear my

---

[1]Quoted in Henry Wise Miller, *All Our Lives: Alice Duer Miller* (New York: Coward-McCann, 1945), 124.
[2]Quoted in Miller, *All Our Lives*, 125.

speech." Proverbs 18:13, to cite another example, counsels: "If one gives answer before hearing, it is folly and shame." The New Testament similarly fixates on listening, as in God's command at our Lord's transfiguration: "This is my Son, the Beloved; listen to him" (Mk 9:7). The book of James offers a kind of echo of these words: "You must understand this, my beloved: let everyone be quick to listen, slow to speak, slow to anger" (Jas 1:19). *Listen, listen, listen*: this is Scripture's constant refrain.

Why does Christianity prioritize listening to such a great extent? One reason may be listening's close connection to humility. Notice that C. S. Lewis's picture of the humble person highlights this connection: "a cheerful, intelligent chap who took a real interest in what *you* said to *him*."[3] Listening, as Lewis recognized, means concentrating on what others say rather than rushing to assert your own take on things. Listening is a significant part of humility's repertoire; it is one way we see humility in action.

In light of this close association between humility and listening, our threshold concept "humble listening" has an almost redundant ring. We like the phrase, however, because it emphasizes that listening, like so many of the routine activities of our day, is a training ground for virtue. Humble listening, as we're defining it, involves paying careful attention to our neighbors and their ideas; such attention is born out of our love for them and for learning itself as well as an acknowledgment of our fallenness and finitude.[4] Other attributes of humble listening will emerge over the next

---

[3]C. S. Lewis, *Mere Christianity* (New York: Macmillan, 1960), 114.

[4]See Jeffrey M. Ringer, "The Dogma of Inquiry: Composition and the Primacy of Faith," *Rhetoric Review* 32, no. 3 (2013): 349-65; Kathleen Fitzpatrick, "Listening," *Generous Thinking: The University and the Public Good*, accessed August 13, 2019, https://generousthinking.hcommons. org/2-on-generosity/listening. Our reflections on humble listening have been informed, in part, by Ringer's concept of *humble dogma* and by Fitzpatrick's comments about listening in her "generous thinking" project. Ringer defines humble dogma as "the basic beliefs that allow for and even prompt reflection into one's own beliefs, research into unfamiliar topics, or exploration of various sides of a debate" (350). And of listening, Fitzpatrick writes that "we need to understand more fully what it is to listen, even—or perhaps especially—to those with whom we will never agree. [Communication scholar Lisbeth] Lipari notes that while 'listen' and 'hear' appear to us to be synonyms, they in fact describe very 'different ways of being in the world. Etymologically, "listening" comes from a root that emphasizes attention and giving to others, while "hearing" comes from a root that emphasizes perception and receiving from others' (99). Listening, then, is not just an act of taking-in, but a practice of generously giving one's focus to another." Fitzpatrick goes on to note that "generous listening is the necessary ground for generous thinking." We agree (and encourage you to explore Fitzpatrick's entire project in more detail), but we also want to add that a necessary prerequisite for such generosity is the virtue of humility.

two chapters. At the outset, though, we should recognize one of its most important qualities: *humble listening declares itself.* While listening is sometimes associated with pious silence, humble listening is like Miller's auditorium. It doesn't just take another's words in; it offers them back "fuller and richer." Humble listening receives in order to respond, and responds in order to receive still more. It is an art of enrichment.

In this chapter, we discuss humble listening in the local writing community. Our focus is on the routines of the residential college classroom (our own habitat), but many of the practices that we discuss are pertinent to other contexts and communities in which writing is shared.[5] Following the example of Thomas Aquinas, we argued in chapter one that humble listening should begin before we set to work—perhaps before we even step in the door—with the invitation that is prayer. Yet, as we also stressed in that same chapter, writing is not a solitary activity—something that we only do with God—but a social one. This chapter explores how humble listening can enrich the social dimensions of writing.

Humble Listening as Community Art

As in previous chapters, we want to offer you an image that serves at once as an illustration of the matter before us and an opportunity for continued meditation as you read the rest of this chapter. It is a mosaic titled *The Luminous One,* found on the campus at Wheaton College, where we work (figure 9). The image that you see suggests something of the beauty and delicacy of the mosaic's design, but it doesn't clearly convey its enormous size or range of colors. The work measures fifteen feet by seven and a half feet, nearly filling a wall floor-to-ceiling. It is composed of more than 63,000 shards—or tesserae—of glass, ceramic, and stone, including magnificent blues, golds, reds, and greens.[6]

---

[5]In online writing courses, many of the practices we recommend can be emulated through digital tools. We've found that discussion threads, video conferences, screen sharing software, and cloud-based collaborative word processing are particularly helpful in this regard. If you are in an online course, we recommend you have a conversation with your classmates about specific techniques you can use to ensure effective communication with one another. Such techniques need not be complex. For example, when listening to a classmate's comments during an online video conference, you may want to provide more visual cues, such as nodding, than you would during an in-person discussion. Doing so signals that you are listening actively. Being intentional about how you provide feedback to one another can vastly improve the online learning experience.

[6]Our description of the mosaic's design, symbolism, and construction in this section is largely adapted from "The Luminous One," Wheaton College website, accessed April 8, 2020, www.wheaton.edu/academics/programs/art/the-presidents-art-commission/the-luminous-one.

Figure 9. Jeremy Botts et al., *The Luminous One*

The centerpiece of the image is the meeting of Jesus and the Samaritan woman at the well in John 4. Of their chief influences, the creators explain as follows:

> In Orthodox tradition the Samaritan woman's name is *Photini,* meaning "the one who brings light" or "the brilliant one," and she gives our mosaic its name. In the story, Jesus reveals himself as the source of the good news of boundless community, and Photini in turn, becomes an evangelist herself.

The creators have surrounded the two figures with a range of symbols, including the peacock (an ancient symbol of eternal life), the goose (a Celtic symbol for the Holy Spirit), and the sheep (signifying Jesus's role as the Lamb of God). The stone well and the olive tree suggest the West Bank. The wheat and wildflowers celebrate the Midwestern context in which the piece resides. The piece also intentionally gestures to the academic disciplines of the building in which it hangs, including archeology, biblical and theological studies, crosscultural communication, and psychology.

The Luminous One is in so many ways a model image for us in this book. It is interdisciplinary. It ranges across time. In both its material form and its content, the mosaic gathers little pieces of assorted shapes and colors into a large, harmonious whole. Our book responds to the Christian tradition in exactly the same spirit. Indeed, perhaps we can say that in assembling our polyptych, we too are making a mosaic, our subject being the virtues of the writing life.

Yet we call on *The Luminous One* now not just because of what it says but also *how it was made.* The mosaic is an example of community art, meaning art created *with* members of a local community *for* the community. As we have talked with the artists involved, we have been struck by the fact that it didn't just require manual labor (many, many hours' worth). To assemble such a monumental work required an incredible amount of *listening.* That began when the lead designers, Jeremy Botts (who did the original drawing) and Leah Samuelson (who led the piece's construction), spoke with community members, and those who work in the building that houses it in particular, about their disciplines, their values, their inspirations. In planning the composition, Botts listened to Scripture and tradition for ideas, harvesting the symbols mentioned above.

The actual assembly of the piece required the coordinated efforts of two separate classes of students as well as other volunteers, many of whom received special training (let's call it "hands-on listening") from instructors at the Chicago Mosaic School. Those same students and volunteers were then responsible for not only assembling the tesserae according to Botts's schematic: they were also the ones individually shaping the thousands of pieces using special tools and mixing the mortar in which those pieces would set. Patience was required: one three-hour work session might result in nine square *inches* of mosaic. All of this work also required careful collaboration, which meant that contributors were in constant communication (perhaps a bit like a basketball team calling out to one another on defense). If one person stopped listening, hours—if not an entire day's labor—might be lost. As this rundown of listening sessions makes clear, the designers and volunteers were no ordinary listeners: they were humble ones, attending closely to others' words in order to create a piece that would not only speak to its audience but speak *for* many—the artists, the volunteers, the community whom they represent.

As we have pondered *The Luminous One* and its origins story, we have come to realize that local writing communities at their best work in much the same way. Someone or some small group has an idea. They situate that idea against the background of a larger community, usually a discourse community (see chap. 4). They bring their plans to trusted readers and ask them to share in the labor of constructing it. Charitable writing, we've realized, bears many resemblances to the process of assembling a mosaic, except in this case we piece together not tesserae but words.

As we walk through the stages of humble listening in the remainder of this chapter, we urge you to keep an eye on *The Luminous One*. Think of how its designers went about their work. Consider the parallels between the volunteers' labors of cutting and arranging and those of your peers who read your work. Listen to the mosaic. Let your writing be community art.

Meeting Your Peers

On the first day of writing classes, we have often asked our students what they hope to get out of the course. Many students tell us that they want to learn how to write more effectively or efficiently, fulfill a general education requirement, or, speaking bluntly but also perhaps more honestly, get an "A." A few sometimes admit that they just want to make it through the semester unscathed. In our many years of teaching writing at the college level, though, we have never heard a student remark that he or she hoped to forge a writing community—let alone a "charitable" one. And we can't recall a single instance in which a student has expressed as an initial goal the hope to support her fellow classmates as writers. Indeed, at the start of the semester, we've never heard a student express the hope that the skills developed in the class will support *anyone else* at all.

The reason for this self-focus is not difficult to discern. Most of us are trained from an early age to think about our educations in individualist (and often consumerist) terms. The idea that our educations should serve the common good is one to which most of us would give ready assent, but we imagine that payoff taking place somewhere down the line—usually after our schooling has ended. The writing classroom challenges those assumptions, since its success or failure hinges on participants' abilities (and, frankly, willingness) to serve one another. Writing classes demand that we view fellow participants not as *competitors* but as *peers*, people from whom we can learn and with whom we will collaborate in the process of developing our work.

What is more, your fellow participants are not simply *peers* but your *neighbors*. To recognize them as such brings with it an obligation, for, as our Lord teaches, we must love our neighbors. In the setting of the local writing community, that love can take many forms, but one of its primary (and ongoing) expressions should be that of humble listening. Giving your classmates your full attention is a means of practicing charitable writing. They will benefit greatly from such attention—as will you. Recall Roberts and Wood's claim that "the humble inquirer has more potential teachers than his less humble counterparts."[7]

Before anything else can happen, though, a simple task must be completed: you need to listen carefully to your peers' names and commit them to memory so that you can address them personally. This basic act of recognition reduces the strangeness of the setting for everyone. The practice of calling one another by name may also be a profound

---

[7]Robert C. Roberts and W. Jay Wood, *Intellectual Virtues: An Essay in Regulative Epistemology* (New York: Oxford University Press, 2007), 253.

blessing for your classmates, especially for those who lack confidence or have been silenced in the past. To address a peer by name is to invite her speech. It is the first step to humble listening. There is no community among the anonymous.

Participation in Discussion

In a well-regarded article titled "Barn Raising: Collaborative Group Process in Seminars," education scholars Don McCormick and Michael Kahn observe that many seminar classes are conducted according to the logic of the "Free-for-All."[8] They describe this style, and its fallout, as follows:

> There is a prize to be won, whether it's the instructor's approval or one's self esteem. There is no other goal but to win. If fighting fair won't win, then one fights in whatever way will win. One wins not simply by looking smart, but by looking smarter. Thus, important as it is to look smart, it is equally important to make the others look dumb.[9]

McCormick and Kahn argue that there is a better way to lead a seminar, and we will return to their alternative proposal later in this book. At present, we simply want to acknowledge how pervasive the "Free-for-All" mentality is, not just in our classrooms but also in our society at large. Many of us unthinkingly operate according to this model, since we assume that speaking up is the only way to earn points.

The implications of the "Free-for-All" model for a writing community—especially as it is beginning to take shape—are easy enough to perceive. Those who are comfortable joining the fray will compete for airtime (and thus the prize of esteem), while those who are not will be effectively silenced. We acknowledge that the most vocal rarely assert themselves out of ill intent; they are simply playing according to what they understand to be the rules of the game. Yet regardless of what participants intend, this dynamic often results in resentment all around. Eventually, everyone in the classroom hardens into Alice Duer Miller's "blank walls," unable to provide one another with sufficient meaningful feedback (either because they haven't stopped talking long enough to

---

[8]Don McCormick and Michael Kahn, "Barn Raising: Collaborative Group Process in Seminars," *Exchange: The Organizational Behavior Teaching Journal* 7, no. 4 (1982): 17.
[9]McCormick and Kahn, "Barn Raising," 17.

hear from others or because they *have* had a chance to talk but haven't developed the skills to do so effectively). Rather than serving as auditoriums with magnificent acoustics, gatherings become echo chambers of a select few—which, as far as learning is concerned, might just as well be empty rooms.

We recommend humble listening as a preventive measure against this kind of disaster. Here we can add another quality of humble listening to our definition above, rooted in Hugh of Saint Victor's teaching that humble students should "blush to learn" from *no one*.[10] Humble listening entails giving *everyone* a hearing.

For the most assertive members of the group, this means keeping in mind the advice of the philosopher Zeno: "The reason . . . we have two ears and only one mouth is that we may listen the more and talk the less."[11] Assertive group members will need to practice self-discipline, choosing their strongest points for general review. They must also be challenged to consider how comments can serve as means (to facilitate an ongoing conversation with others) rather than ends (to score points). The best contributions to class discussions are often questions.

For the community's quieter members, the call to humble listening is, seemingly paradoxically, a call to speak up. If others build an auditorium for you, you do them a disservice if you fail to sing. As we noted above, humble listening must declare itself: you are simply not listening well if you don't talk back. When your peers speak, they need to hear from you. At the very least, they need to know that they have been properly understood, and they often need to receive your comments and criticisms so that they can improve their ideas and arguments. The same is true when you speak up. In his "Prayer Before Study," Aquinas reminds us that we have been born into the "twofold darkness" of "sin and ignorance."[12] As limited creatures who are prone to error, we *all* need to hear from others.

These practices can transform a writing community. Where humble listening flourishes, participation is liberated from the exhausting

---

[10]Hugh of Saint Victor, *The Didascalicon of Hugh of Saint Victor: A Medieval Guide to the Arts*, trans. Jerome Taylor (New York: Columbia University Press, 1991), 94-95.

[11]Quoted by Diogenes Laertius, *Lives of Eminent Philosophers*, vol. 2, trans. R. D. Hicks (Cambridge, MA: Harvard University Press, 1931), 135.

[12]John Vidmar, OP, *Praying with the Dominicans: To Praise, to Bless, to Preach* (New York: Paulist Press, 2008), 49.

routines of one-upmanship. You no longer need to worry about speaking a certain number of times per session, getting your two cents in, or saying your piece. The mantra of humble listening is, *it's not all about you.* Rather, participation becomes more about "taking part in," and hopefully building up, community—a community of writers and, if the central argument of our book is right, a richly *Christian* community. Participation is transformed from saying your piece into *sharing in the peace of Christ.*

As a reminder of these larger aims, we'd like to recommend that you and your classmates "pass the peace" with one another, regularly or occasionally. Growing out of Jesus' words of greeting to his followers as well as the opening of many of Paul's letters, the passing of the peace is a common practice in many churches, and we've found it to be a meaningful one in the writing classroom as well. In our church contexts, the practice typically involves a handshake between two parishioners, accompanied by the following brief exchange:

Greeting: "The peace of the Lord be always with you."

Response: "And also with you."

Christ's peace, which flows from the cross and makes us and our broken world whole, may be one of the very best things you can share with another person, and it is almost certainly so in the inaugural meetings of a writing group. We urge you, though, not to see the passing of the peace as merely a preliminary exercise. We encourage you to see yourself as giving and receiving Christ's peace alongside, or even through, *all* of your words. The liturgical formula isn't just a conversational nicety. It's a charter for your writing community.

Viewing class participation as an opportunity to pass the peace of Christ liberates us from the struggle to puff ourselves up at the expense of others (Mt 23:12). We are free to build up our classmates in love, using our words not as swords for cutting others down but as plowshares for creating fertile spaces where they can thrive (to borrow metaphors from Is 2:4). When we agree with what our classmates have said, we can say so and—even better—validate their ideas by affirming and extending them. When we disagree, we can express our convictions with sensitivity, mindful of Paul's exhortation to be "tenderhearted" to one another (Eph 4:32). And when we do hurt each other, as inevitably happens when we live and work in community, we will be more willing to apologize and, perhaps, even quicker to show mercy.

Workshopping Writing

What makes a writing community distinct from other sorts of learning communities is, of course, that not just conversation but writing is shared. Writing communities entail workshopping. That practice can take various forms, but all involve the circulation of work between members for the purpose of receiving feedback. This activity can be uncomfortable for many of us. Allowing others to view and comment on our work requires us to be out there, on display—in a word, vulnerable.

Many of us recoil from *this* kind of attention. Sometimes, pride tells us that we don't need to listen to peers' advice. We don't need to revise; we're better than that. In fact (pride whispers), we're better than *them*. So we resist feedback, either by responding defensively to criticism or by haughtily ignoring it when it is offered. At other times, it is not pride but despair that cripples us. Taking criticisms too much to heart—that is, mistaking criticisms of our work for attacks on ourselves—we buckle at the knees and give up. Suggestions for revision seem far too daunting to do, so we ignore them. As in the case of pride, we learn nothing from despair. Both hinder our ability to hear the instructive words coming from outside ourselves. This is true not only of criticism but also of praise, which we often can't see clearly. What's lost in the process is the chance to build on what is working and to improve what isn't. This situation is disastrous for your improvement as a writer and, in all likelihood, for your growth as a disciple. We are *all* in need of correction and encouragement, both as writers and as followers of Jesus Christ.

Perhaps humble listening is needed at this stage of the writing community's work most of all. To practice humble listening is to approach the workshop with the kind of "honest appraisal" of our own abilities that we discussed in the last chapter.[13] This humility, once again, does not equate to utter self-doubt. Rather, exactly by confronting us with our limitations, humility allows us to turn to others to discover what insights they may offer. It allows us to view workshopping and revision

---

[13]Philip E. Dow, *Virtuous Minds: Intellectual Character Development* (Downers Grove, IL: IVP Academic, 2013), 70-71.

hopefully. We are liberated to receive criticism without throwing up our hands in despair, and to receive praise without letting it go to our heads.

Humble listening doesn't just apply to receiving feedback; it's also a posture that we can adopt when it is our turn to review our peers' work. In this case, the "listening" that we do is not to others' spoken words (as they usually come in discussion or when we receive comments about our own writing) but to their *written* words. This is listening in the metaphorical sense of reading with great care—as when we describe reading the Bible as "listening to the Word."

How do you listen humbly to a text? To begin, it requires that you give your peers' writing your time. This kind of reading can't be rushed through. It also involves seriously entertaining your peers' positions, not in the hopes of winning arguments but with the goal of helping them to state their claims more clearly, more powerfully, more persuasively. Like hosts who open up their home to strangers in a gesture of hospitality, you must make space for your peers' views amidst your own. This doesn't mean that you won't eventually voice disagreements or concerns about what they've written; however, before you take issue with an idea, it's best to make sure you've got the point right. Carl Rogers—a psychotherapist whose ideas about communication have been adopted by some in the field of writing studies—offers advice to help ensure that you sufficiently understand the content of a peer's argument: try to paraphrase her ideas in ways that satisfy her before sharing your own views.[14]

After you've successfully grasped the argument's content (what it says) through paraphrase, turn to a consideration of the argument's form (how it says) and function (what it does).[15] Don't *evaluate* at this stage; instead, attempt to *describe* how the argument is constructed and what the argument's parts—its paragraphs, sentences, and word choices—accomplish. By paraphrasing your peers' ideas and describing the form and function of their arguments, you'll be better equipped to offer them evaluative feedback and suggestions for

---

[14]Carl R. Rogers, "Communication: Its Blocking and Its Facilitation," in *Rhetoric: Discovery and Change*, ed. Richard E. Young, Alton L. Becker, and Kenneth L. Pike (San Diego: Harcourt Brace Jovanovich, 1970), 286.
[15]These suggestions are adapted from Richard Bullock, "Thinking About How the Text Works: What It Says, What It Does," in *The Norton Field Guide to Writing*, 2nd ed. (New York: W. W. Norton, 2009), 358-60.

improvement when it is time to do so. Humble listening, we are suggesting, begins the process of offering feedback not with a summary judgment about the success or failure of this or that. It opens like Alice Duer Miller's "splendid auditorium where every sound comes back fuller and richer." In humility, we can respond by simply offering back what we heard—describing what the writer said, how the writer went about saying it, and for what purposes. Giving your peers' writing back to them in this way will almost certainly be a revelatory experience for them, and for you.

To be clear, we are not saying that you should avoid evaluative feedback altogether. If you and your colleagues want to become more effective writers, you'll have to judge writing as effective (or not) at some point. However, keeping such comments anchored to description lends legitimacy to your judgments, enhances their usefulness, and helps to ensure that they will receive a hearing. When you do offer judgments (as you must), be sure to give attention to explaining both why what works is successful and how what doesn't work might be improved. We have noticed that students often skip the first step—noting what works—because they take for granted that their peers already know where the piece is solid. That is frequently *not* the case. (For many of us, the strengths and weaknesses of a piece of writing are hard to ascertain when we are still in the thick of the writing process.) As many writing teachers will tell you, it is also a missed opportunity to provide the writer with an exemplary model (of her own making!) to build on elsewhere, whether in troublesome spots in the same document or in other writing contexts.

Finally, in keeping with Hugh of Saint Victor's teaching, we encourage our students either to end their peer review sessions by articulating what they learned by reading their peers' work. This last step is important for two reasons. First, it provides a reminder that the purpose of the entire enterprise isn't simply to serve an instrumental goal (such as getting a good grade) but to engage in the shared pursuit of knowledge. Second, it provides an opportunity for mutual expressions of thanks: the writer for the reviewers' care, the reviewers for new insights. Gratitude is a traditional companion of humility, making such words of thanks a fitting end to the humble listening of all participants.

The Luminous One

What does it mean to listen humbly in the context of a local writing community? This chapter has made a number of claims. Humble listening, we have argued, declares itself, which is to say that it makes itself known through the body language of careful attention and the spoken language of questions, paraphrase, description, encouragement, evaluation, and gratitude. Humble listening checks the impulses of those accustomed to the free-for-all mentality and its companion, the rush-to-judgment. But if humble listening requires self-discipline for those accustomed to getting the first and last word in, it also asks for courage from those who tend to retreat from peer engagement, whether it be in the context of discussion, workshopping, or perhaps even the ice-breaker at the first meeting. Humble listening animates the reading that a peer reviewer undertakes for the writer's benefit, and the writer's response to his peer's honest appraisal of the work (which is not an appraisal of the writer's *person*).

We sometimes regard listening as an individual activity. Yet we can never do it alone: one must always be listening to something, to someone else. What we have proposed here takes the social dimension of listening further still. Humble listening is a communal practice. It doesn't work if just one member of the group, or even a handful, decides to do it. Just as one person cannot set up a monopoly on speech, there can be no silent partners in this enterprise. This kind of community can't be assembled by fiat; it must be constructed together by the participants. That is why seemingly small community-building gestures like passing the peace matter so much, for they recall the deeper nature of the connection that we have with our peers. These people are our neighbors, our fellow children of God.

Let's return to *The Luminous One* for one last reminder about the need for humility in the local writing community, as in all of our endeavors. The Gospel of John recounts the story behind the mosaic as follows:

A Samaritan woman came to draw water, and Jesus said to her, "Give me a drink." (His disciples had gone to the city to buy food.) The Samaritan woman said to him, "How is it that you, a Jew, ask a drink of me, a woman of Samaria?" (Jews do not share things in common with Samaritans.) Jesus answered her, "If you knew the gift of God, and who it is that is saying to you, 'Give me a drink,' you would have asked him, and he would have given you living water."

The woman said to him, "Sir, you have no bucket, and the well is deep. Where do you get that living water? Are you greater than our ancestor Jacob, who gave us the well, and with his sons and his flocks drank from it?" Jesus said to her, "Everyone who drinks of this water will be thirsty again, but those who drink of the water that I will give them will never be thirsty. The water that I will give will become in them a spring of water gushing up to eternal life." The woman said to him, "Sir, give me this water, so that I may never be thirsty or have to keep coming here to draw water." (Jn 4:7-15)

Granting the request that the woman makes at the end of this passage involves a twofold revelation. First, Jesus brings her wrongdoing to light, revealing, the woman later admits, "everything I have ever done." Then Jesus reveals himself to be the Messiah. Here, standing before her, is the one with the power to forgive sins, the source of living water, "the Savior of the world." This double revelation leads to another: the woman leaves her water jug behind and returns to town to tell her fellow Samaritans about Jesus' living water. Her testimony prompts many of them to believe and seek Jesus out (Jn 4:16-42).

The wisdom of the mosaic's depiction of the encounter flows from the many ways it invites us into the scene. One of the most obvious of these is that Jesus directs his gaze at us, reminding us that we are all of us like the woman, in need of the living water. More subtly, the mosaic asks us to see ourselves in its missing figures. We are like the other Samaritans who, on hearing the woman's testimony, come to Jesus to hear his account for ourselves. It is likely for this reason that the artists inserted—in golden tesserae, just to the right of the figure of Jesus—a version of the Samaritans' words: "We have heard for ourselves this is true." (The last three of these words have been written backward in the tiles, suggesting that *we* may be the ones uttering them.) In the mosaic, then, we are reminded that Christians are a listening people: we hear the good news from other disciples, and we seek after Jesus, in Scripture and in prayer, to hear it from the source. Listening to this message requires humility. To truly hear it—to hear it as the truth—we must acknowledge our faults and recognize Jesus as the Messiah.

The lessons of the mosaic for writers are many, for those with ears to hear. What image is your local writing community creating together, and how? How might *you* become the luminous one?

Four

Humble Listening in Discourse Communities

If you don't want to live in a one-person universe (which is the worst of all fates), then seek humility, because humility is the door to all communion.

BERNARD BONOWITZ

For whom do you write? For all of us, there isn't a single answer to this question. We write for a variety of audiences, in a variety of contexts, and with a variety of ends in view. Ancient rhetoricians recognized this fact, and they developed a thick stock of terms and techniques to help their students navigate the diverse settings in which they would need to make a persuasive case. Contemporary writing scholars confront the same problems concerning the settings in which we write. However, they frame the problem for their students as the identification and analysis of the "discourse community" in which one's exchange takes place—whether in person, on paper, or via social media. This may sound like a heady academic concept, but it is actually a useful tool for thinking about the distinct ways that we communicate in the many spheres of our lives.

Brian Paltridge, a TESOL scholar, provides this useful definition of a discourse community, which makes its wide application clear:

> A discourse community is a group of people who share some kind of activity. Members of a discourse community have particular ways of communicating with each other. They generally have

shared goals and may have shared values and beliefs. A person is often a member of more than one discourse community. Someone may be a university student, a member of a community volunteer organization and a member of a church group, for example. The ways in which they communicate in each of these groups and the values and beliefs that are most prominent in each of these groups may vary. There may also be discourse communities within discourse communities. Academic departments, for example, may differ in the ways that they do things and the beliefs and values that they hold, as indeed may other parts of the university.[1]

Other commentators emphasize that a discourse community need not be site-specific—in contrast to the kind of local writing community that we discussed in the last chapter. One can imagine a university student, for instance, transferring colleges and still knowing, generally speaking, how to communicate with other students and professors. The same is true of members of religious groups. Fly halfway around the world and you'll still be able to identify particular features of a worship service— even if you are not fluent in the language in which the service is conducted. This is even true of a number of volunteer organizations. Volunteer for a few weeks with Habitat for Humanity, and you'll learn not only construction skills but also ways of communicating within a construction crew that can be translated to other job sites.

Discourse communities, then, are not necessarily bound up with places but with shared activities, ways of using language, and goals. You recognize a fellow member of a discourse community not solely by where she stands (though that can be a tip-off, as in the case of a college classroom or a church sanctuary); rather, her identifying traits have to do with what, how, why, and with whom she communicates.

To recognize these features of discourse communities makes plain why we are so concerned about listening. Listening is one of the main practices that allows us to join discourse communities. To become a member of a discourse community, we need to listen in the literal sense—paying attention to spoken words or, as in the case of church communities, hearing certain phrases, songs, or passages repeated so many times that they become ingrained in our minds. In addition to

---

[1]Brian Paltridge, *Discourse Analysis* (New York: Bloomsbury Academic, 2012), 16.

listening in the literal sense, we also need to listen in the metaphorical sense discussed in the last chapter: listening as reading with great care.

We establish ourselves as members of academic discourse communities by listening (in the literal sense) to how our teachers speak from behind the lectern, at the seminar table, and in office hours. We listen to how more advanced students speak during discussions. But we also listen (in the metaphorical sense) to the texts that the discipline in question uses to advance knowledge—such as scholarly books and articles, book reviews, abstracts, and more. Such listening requires that we pay attention not only to *what* these texts say but *how* they say it. To use the language of the field of writing studies, we must learn to attend to *genre conventions,* the recurring features of a text type, which members of a discourse community use, adapt, and exchange. Genre conventions inform large-scale writing practices, such as how we organize arguments, as well as subtler elements, such as the style of footnotes. Lab reports, legal briefs, and lyric poems not only sound different when we read them aloud; they also all look different on the page! Listening in the metaphorical sense takes note of these differences.

We have already said a good deal about listening in this chapter, but we haven't yet mentioned humility. Humility's role in all of this is likely already apparent; indeed, to be confronted with the conventions of a new discourse community or genre is, for most of us, quite *humbling.* (You may, in fact, find your inability to successfully navigate the barrage of new material not just humbling but also *humiliating.*) But humility is precisely what you need to enter into a new discourse community. Trappist contemplative Bernard Bonowitz makes a similar point in a book about the medieval church leader and theologian Bernard of Clairvaux:

> [Bernard] says that humility is the door to all communion. If you want to live in relationship with other persons, if you don't want to end up in existential solitude and isolation, if you don't want to live in a one-person universe (which is the worst of all fates), then seek humility, because humility is the door to all communion and pride is the condition of all alienation. Pride is what distances us finally even from our own selves, but also from God and from our neighbor.[2]

---

[2]Bernard Bonowitz, OCSO, *Saint Bernard's Three-Course Banquet: Humility, Charity, and Contemplation in the* De Gradibus (Collegeville, MN: Liturgical Press, 2013), 7.

Bernard of Clairvaux would have us see that humility not only enables community; it keeps us in community. Even after we've successfully entered a discourse community, we need humility to keep pride at bay, to continue to listen to those around us, and to recall that we are not— nor should we strive to be—self-sufficient.

Perils and Possibilities for Christian Writers

The concept of the discourse community is especially important for Christian writers because it helps to bring into focus certain tendencies and temptations that writing presents for us. Recall, first of all, Paltridge's observation that a university is one kind of discourse community, while a church is another. Paltridge's point, once again, is that a single person can participate in both discourse communities, in addition to still others, such as a sports team, a political party, or a workplace. Throughout our lives (indeed, often throughout an average day), all of us move among these various discourse communities, and we adjust our patterns of communication according to the group that we are currently addressing, often without thinking. Thus, we text our friends with truncated phrases and half-expressed inside jokes, but when the time comes to write to the professor or the boss, we lay out our sentences with care and perhaps slip in a few SAT words for good measure.

Our ability to alter our writing for different discourse communities is easy enough to do when we are seasoned community members. However, this can be extremely difficult when one is still new to a discourse community. As the writing teacher David Bartholomae observed in his well-known piece "Inventing the University," the challenges of doing so as a college student can be acute:

> Every time a student sits down to write for us, he has to invent the university for the occasion—invent the university, that is, or a branch of it, like History or Anthropology or Economics or English. He has to learn to speak our language, to speak as we do, to try on the peculiar ways of knowing, selecting, evaluating, reporting, concluding, and arguing that define the . . . discourses of our community, since it is in the nature of a liberal arts education that a student, after the first year or two, must learn to try on a

variety of voices and interpretive schemes—to write, for example, as a literary critic one day and an experimental psychologist the next, to work within fields where the rules governing the presentation of examples or the development of an argument are both distinct and, even to a professional, mysterious.[3]

The challenges described here are often further amplified at Christian colleges and universities, where the lines between ecclesial and academic discourses are sometimes blurred (often productively but, at times, confusedly). Members of Christian colleges are members of the church, yet they are also participants in the global endeavor that is higher education.

In our time teaching at a Christian college, we have seen two recurring missteps, which we believe are instructive.[4] Let's call the first "the misdirected sermon." In this case, students are asked to write using the conventions of an academic discipline and genre, yet they respond with papers that share more with preaching than academic writing. These papers can have numerous virtues: they are often passionately written, they often incorporate a good deal of evidence—typically from Scripture—in support of their claims, they often have sturdy argumentative architectures. However, students who write them have not considered how the conventions of argument vary by situation and context.

To members of the academic discourse community in which the student writes, the passion seems inappropriate, the evidence doesn't count, and the structure fails to account for other scholarly voices. *The student hasn't really listened.* She hasn't seized an opportunity to try out a new genre for engaging the world, missing a chance to connect with a new discourse community. If such a paper were delivered at an academic conference or sent to an academic journal, it would fail to persuade its audience because it does not speak the language of its target community. To use the language of Gerald Graff and Cathy Birkenstein's

---

[3]David Bartholomae, "Inventing the University," *Journal of Basic Writing* 5, no. 1 (1986): 4.

[4]Though we focus here on common pitfalls, it is important to acknowledge a growing body of literature that explores the resources that religious (and, in particular, evangelical) students bring to the writing classroom. See, for example, Michael-John DePalma, "Re-envisioning Religious Discourses as Rhetorical Resources in Composition Teaching: A Pragmatic Response to the Challenge of Belief," *College Composition and Communication* 63, no. 2 (2011): 219-43; and Jeffrey M. Ringer, *Vernacular Christian Rhetoric and Civil Discourse: The Religious Creativity of Evangelical Student Writers* (New York: Routledge, 2016).

well-known writing guide, the writer of the misdirected sermon hasn't listened to what "they say," or how.[5]

We've dubbed the second issue "the dis-integrating paper." In this case, we are not-so-subtly referencing one of the mantras of Christian higher education in our times: "the integration of faith and learning." On this view, the goal of education is to grow in faith as one grows in learning, rather than seeing these pursuits as unrelated activities. Unlike the misdirected sermon, the dis-integrating paper may invoke the proper conventions of the assignment's discipline and genre. The student has heard and approximated the language. The trouble in this case is not procedural, then. The trouble is that the student's heart just isn't in it. The paper is nothing more than paper-pushing—yet another assignment to ace, hoop to jump through, or box to check off on the road to graduation. While we cannot see or measure the motivations of others, we know that the dis-integrating paper is a common problem because our students have talked with us about their motives for writing—and because we know our own hearts. We have written dis-integrating papers, too.

Students who complete assignments in this manner fail (or refuse) to see that their writing is always a spiritual activity. These students, we might say, are *hearing effectively* but are not *listening humbly*. They have failed to honor Hugh of Saint Victor's first charge to the humble student: that he or she "hold no knowledge and no writing in contempt."[6] We recognize that some assignments will feel like busywork, and that sometimes (and for numerous reasons) we may not be able to rouse ourselves to approach each and every assignment with alacrity. Sometimes work simply must get done. Yet we urge you to guard against the spiritual malaise that produces dis-integrating papers. They represent not just hollow work but lost opportunities to develop as disciples.[7] The writer

---

[5]Gerald Graff and Cathy Birkenstein, *They Say/I Say: The Moves That Matter in Academic Writing*, 4th ed. (New York: W. W. Norton, 2018).

[6]Hugh of Saint Victor, *The Didascalicon of Hugh of Saint Victor: A Medieval Guide to the Arts*, trans. Jerome Taylor (New York: Columbia University Press, 1991), 94.

[7]To be clear, we're not advocating for anything resembling perfection with respect to our attitude toward academic work. Given our many commitments as well as our own finitude and fallenness, we shouldn't hold one another to unattainable standards, and there is grace for us when we fall short. That said, we ought to encourage one another to resist the temptations of apathy and cynicism, which can become habitual. Unchecked over time, a negative feedback loop often emerges: students' failure to recognize the significance of their writing leads to greater apathy and cynicism, which, in turn, undermines their ability to view their academic work as significant, and so on.

may catch the *form* of academic discourse, but she misses out on the chance for Christian *formation*.

A Model Listener: Pandita Ramabai

The misdirected sermon and the dis-integrating paper are both negative examples. Where might we turn for a positive one? The Christian tradition provides us with many model writers capable of communicating effectively with multiple discourse communities. A number of figures mentioned in this book, in fact, might be cited for their success in this regard. Several of the ancient Christian writers that we have named—such as Augustine and Jerome—weren't just scholars of the ivory-tower variety; they wrote numerous other kinds of documents—sermons, epistles, and, in Augustine's case, an autobiography—that were aimed at other audiences, even specific local ones.

C. S. Lewis, another prolific author, wrote for his fellow academics as well as the wider modern reading public. His discourse communities included, among others, scholars of medieval and early modern literature, science fiction and fantasy fans, philosophers, and educators. And Victor Turner, an anthropologist who laid the conceptual foundation for the scholarship on threshold concepts that we mentioned in the introduction, wrote for multiple discourse communities. A titanic figure in the field of anthropology, Turner's scholarly writings are still widely cited decades after his death. Yet Turner was also a Christian. Though he entered the field as a committed secularist Marxist, Turner's experiences led him (and his wife and fellow anthropologist, Edith) to convert to Catholicism in 1958.[8] In later years, he would write explicitly as a Christian for his fellow believers in venues such as *Worship,* a Benedictine journal, and *Concilium,* a Roman Catholic theology journal.[9]

There are many more writers' stories that we could tell, but we wish to concentrate now on a figure that is less well-known, at least among modern Western readers—Pandita Ramabai, a social reformer in India in the late nineteenth and early twentieth centuries. Ramabai's early life marked her out for an unusual path. Her father and mother taught

---

[8]We are grateful to our friend and colleague Timothy Larsen for this example. See Timothy Larsen, *The Slain God: Anthropologists and the Christian Faith* (Oxford: Oxford University Press, 2014), 174-220.

[9]Larsen, *The Slain God*, 198.

Pandita to read Sanskrit, the language of the Hindu scriptures, despite cultural prohibitions against that kind of female learning.[10] Arriving in Calcutta as an adult, Ramabai's linguistic abilities astonished observers. As the historians Mark Noll and Carolyn Nystrom observe, Ramabai soon "became a celebrity":

> Her massive learning and understanding of ancient Sanskrit texts earned newspaper headlines, invitations to speak and two titles bestowed by scholars: "Pandita" (a wise person) and "Saraswati" (goddess of learning). Although she at first declined these titles, she would later be known as "the Pandita" or simply "Pandita."[11]

Ramabai would use this newfound fame to advocate for women's rights in India, her primary targets being childhood marriage and the mistreatment of widows. In line with her parents' educational goals for her, she also supported literacy initiatives for women.

What happened next in her life is particularly important for us. After traveling to England for further study in 1883, Ramabai lived among the women of an Anglican religious community and was moved to become a Christian. However, after her baptism, Ramabai didn't renounce her Indian heritage, despite pressure from some of her fellow Christians to do so. "A Christian by belief and a Hindu by culture," Ramabai now occupied—and would remain committed to—two worlds, and she would attempt to address both regarding the issues that were important to her through her writing.[12] Aided, no doubt, by her immense knowledge of languages, Ramabai's reach extended to audiences in the West and the East. In the words of one commentator, she was able to occupy "the position of a traveler between cultures, a sort of 'bridging writer' who experiences both 'strains of thought' and who seems willing to explain to both 'hemispheres' the reasons for their cultural attitudes and the misunderstandings that can derive from them."[13]

---

[10]Pandita's father, Anant Shastri Dongre, taught her mother, Lakshmibai Dongre, to read Sanskrit. Some accounts credit Pandita's father for her language education; some, her mother. We've chosen to acknowledge both of Pandita's parents here.

[11]Mark A. Noll and Carolyn Nystrom, *Clouds of Witnesses: Christian Voices from Africa and Asia* (Downers Grove, IL: InterVarsity Press, 2011), 130.

[12]Noll and Nystrom, *Clouds of Witnesses*, 128.

[13]Arianna Maiorani, "Pandita Ramabai (1858–1922)," in *Great Women Travel Writers: From 1750 to the Present*, ed. Alba Amoia and Bettina L. Knapp (New York: Continuum, 2005), 119.

Like most writers, Ramabai's career had multiple phases. For present purposes, we only need to focus on a few moments from her writing life. The first is the late 1880s, when Ramabai was living in the United States. Writing in English, she educated American audiences about the suffering of widows in India, raising support to establish a school for Hindu women. Her book *The High Caste Hindu Woman* was well received in the English-speaking world, and modern scholars credit Ramabai for her ability to be "impassioned and critical" of Indian society yet nonetheless retain "a profound sympathy for [her] Hindu culture."[14] Meanwhile, she wrote a book in Marathi, the language of her native region, called *Conditions of Life in the United States*, which is about the social position of American women and religious practices in the United States. Like the other figures we mentioned above, Ramabai was adept at navigating multiple discourse communities.

She was also skilled at writing in different genres. In addition to her book-writing abilities, Ramabai was an effective letter writer, with correspondents on three continents. This skill was an essential quality for the leader of philanthropic activities such as Mukti Mission, an organization that she founded in the 1890s to provide refuge and education for child-widows and orphans.

Ramabai would remain an active writer until her death in 1922, and we could spend several more paragraphs discussing the variety of audiences she addressed. But we want to highlight one final project—which she labored on right up to her death—because it shows another important side of her writing life that bears on our discussion of discourse communities. Though Ramabai wrote for an international readership during her lifetime, this last project was much closer to home, geographically and spiritually. It grew out of her observation that the Marathi translation of the Bible created by missionaries in the mid-nineteenth century used an idiom that only the educated could grasp.[15] In the final decades of her life, she thus undertook an initiative to translate the Bible into the common language of the village men and women around her.

---

[14]Barbara Celarent (pseudonym for Andrew Abbott), "Review of *The High Caste Hindu Woman* by Pandita Ramabai Sarasvati; *Pandita Ramabai's America: Conditions of Life in the United States* (*United Stateschi Lokasthiti ani Pravasvritta*) by Pandita Ramabai Sarasvati, Kshitija Gomez, Philip C. Engblom, and Robert E. Frykenberg," *American Journal of Sociology* 117, no. 1 (2011): 354.

[15]Clementina Butler, *Pandita Ramabai Sarasvati: Pioneer in the Movement for the Education of the Child-Widow of India* (New York: Fleming H. Revell Company, 1922), 81.

In order to produce *that* book, Ramabai had to create others, including "an interlinear translation of five different versions of the words and idioms of the Old Testament."[16] Notably, the printing for many of the stages of this process was done by the Indian women who had come to live at Mukti Mission.[17] As a publisher "owned and operated" by women, Mukti Mission Press was remarkable not only in early twentieth-century India; such a press was rare even in the West. One of Ramabai's biographers observes of this effort, "When one thinks of the multifarious characters, Roman, Marathi, Greek and Hebrew type used in the typesetting, the greatness of this achievement becomes almost incredible."[18] The biographer continues, "Not seventy translators"—as in the legend of the ancient Greek translation of the Old Testament known as the Septuagint—"but Ramabai alone with her students made this version! And she did it well!"[19]

We have chosen Ramabai for special consideration in this section not only because she trained herself to use the conventions of discourse communities in New York, London, and Calcutta. She is also a model humble listener because she listened to the humble around her. Equally remarkable, her grand endeavor to translate Scripture drew on the talents of those near to her—including those women whose abilities Indian society at the time tended to discount. In earlier chapters, we observed several pictures of Jerome in his study, working away at his translation of the Bible, the Vulgate. Figure 10 offers us a modern equivalent to that scene. It shows us Pandita Ramabai seated on the floor with a writing desk on her lap in some quiet corner, presumably on the grounds of Mukti Mission. Her text is, perhaps, the "People's Book" (which is what the "Vulgate" means) for her time and place, a more colloquial Marathi translation of the Bible. This image offers another panel for the polyptych that we have been building across this book. It serves, moreover, as a useful reminder that the high drama of Christian writing has no necessary costume or set design. What unites the panels of Jerome and Ramabai is not their props but their purpose. Each strove to be a servant of the Word.

---

[16]Butler, *Pandita Ramabai Sarasvati*, 81.
[17]Butler, *Pandita Ramabai Sarasvati*, 81.
[18]Butler, *Pandita Ramabai Sarasvati*, 81-82.
[19]Butler, *Pandita Ramabai Sarasvati*, 82.

Figure 10. Ramabai at work on her translation of the Bible into popular Marathi

Testimony in Another Key

There is one further lesson that we can derive from Pandita Ramabai's writing life. It is, in fact, a lesson that echoes across the writing lives of the other authors that we have mentioned here, including Turner and Lewis. That lesson is this: a Christian writer is not duty bound to write from an explicitly Christian standpoint all the time. To put it another way, every document you write does not need to be a variation on your personal testimony. There are times when we are called to use our studies to speak to the church explicitly, as in preaching or writing about our learning in layman's terms. Yet our studies would suffer from such a unilateral understanding of their function: our learning benefits tremendously from exchanges with fellow scholars at institutions that do not have religious affiliations. Christian institutions would suffer, for example, if they failed to keep up with the latest developments in DNA research. This is also true of our understandings of the American Civil War, international trade, the plays of William Shakespeare, black holes, urbanization, and the daily life of ancient Israel. To write about these topics in ways that promote learning in academic discourse communities is to share our testimony in another key.

The playwright and novelist Dorothy L. Sayers offers a helpful perspective on these matters. For her, our vocations, or callings, ought to determine the form that our faith takes in our professional lives. She writes:

> Let the Church remember this: that every maker and worker is called to serve God *in* his profession or trade—not outside it. The Apostles complained rightly when they said it was not meet they should leave the word of God and serve tables; their vocation was to preach the word. But the person whose vocation it is to prepare the meals beautifully might with equal justice protest: It is not meet for us to leave the service of our tables to preach the word.[20]

Sayers's remarks remind us that *all* of the ways we are called to serve carry with them a special dignity. And no matter the station or vocation, our service can itself be a kind of testimony: we bear witness to the work of the One who made all things simply by doing what we have been called to do. Academic and professional work is no exception. "For believers to be studying created things," historian Mark Noll reminds us, "is to be studying the works of Christ."[21] So even if your writing doesn't explore the intersections between faith and your chosen area of study or work explicitly, conducting careful research can testify to the truth, beauty, and goodness that Christ has inscribed in creation and, thus, to the Creator himself.

You may, of course, find yourself in a situation where you simply can't embrace the norms of an academic or professional discourse community *and* remain true to your convictions. Such situations are uncommon, at least within the daily business of academic life. However, if they do occur, your commitment to Christ ought to take precedence. Should you find yourself in such a situation, we urge you to recall the virtue at the heart of this first section of the book: humility. Humility resists our knee-jerk reactions. It forestalls the rush to judgment. It requires listening.

---

[20]Dorothy L. Sayers, "Why Work?," in *Letters to a Diminished Church: Passionate Arguments for the Relevance of Christianity* (Nashville: Thomas Nelson, 2004), 133.
[21]Mark A. Noll, *Jesus Christ and the Life of the Mind* (Grand Rapids, MI: Eerdmans, 2011), 25.

Loving Argument

Five

The Law of
Charitable Writing

"You shall love the Lord your God with all your heart, and
with all your soul, and with all your mind." This is the
greatest and first commandment. And the second is like
it: "You shall love your neighbor as yourself." On these two
commandments hang all the law and the prophets.

MATTHEW 22:37-40

C haritable writing, as we noted in the introduction, is writing that
embodies the distinctive Christian understanding of love, which
used to go by the name "charity" in English (*caritas* in Latin and *agapē*
in Greek). In part two of our book, we aim to reflect on this distinctive
understanding of love and discuss its implications for our approach to
writing. Along the way, we use as our test case a seemingly loveless
genre: argumentative writing.

Charity has long been esteemed as the *highest* of the Christian virtues,
the virtue to which all the others tend and, in the ideal, the animating
spirit of our daily affairs. Humility, meanwhile, has long been understood as the *foundation* on which love builds. That architectural metaphor—which reaches back at least as far as Augustine in the fourth
century—is reflected in the structure of this book.[1] We, too, have

---

[1]Joseph J. McInerney, *The Greatness of Humility: St. Augustine on Moral Excellence* (Eugene, OR:
Pickwick Publications, 2016), 75-76, 85-86. See Augustine, "Sermon XIX," in *Saint Augustin:*

begun with humility, whose listening eyes and ears lay the groundwork for the writing that Christian writers then undertake.

The chapters of part two thus represent the second stage of the writer's work, when our attention turns from listening to responding. Here, we argue, love must play a particularly conspicuous part in our efforts. These chapters constitute the heart of the book and, taken together, make up the longest of its three main sections. In light of love's place among the other virtues, we believe this is fitting. Yet we also recognize that humble listening is itself an expression of Christian love. (Consider for a moment how well-attuned humble listening is to Paul's characterization of *agapē* love in 1 Cor 13.) So too is keeping time hopefully, our emphasis in part three. In other words, "charitable writing" isn't a step in the writing process: it *is* the writing process as we've reimagined it.

The Double Commandment

In the introduction, we highlighted the biblical imperative to which our writing lives must answer, the so-called double commandment of Matthew 22 (seen in the epigraph above). Now, an attentive reader will notice that at no point in the speech does Jesus mention writing. He demands that we love God, and then there is the second command to love our neighbor. Apparently, writing research papers didn't make Jesus' list of priorities when it came to describing love.

But this doesn't mean we're exempted from following the law of love when we write—any more than we're exempted when playing sports, paying a parking fine, or receiving a text from a peeved friend. The trouble with searching for exemptions is Jesus' final sentence. Our friend and mentor Alan Jacobs explains, "Since the ordinances of the law cover the whole range of human interactions with one another and with God, it follows that there can be no realm of distinctly human activity in which Jesus' great twofold commandment is not operative."[2] In other words, the twofold commandment is universal: it applies to *every* interaction, *every* "realm of distinctly human activity." There is no action too great or too small for this commandment, and neighbors are found everywhere we turn—as is God.

Sermon on the Mount, Harmony of the Gospels, Homilies on the Gospels, trans. R. G. MacMullen, Nicene and Post-Nicene Fathers 1.6 (New York: Christian Literature Company, 1888), 315.

[2] Alan Jacobs, *A Theology of Reading: The Hermeneutics of Love* (New York: Westview Press, 2001), 10.

That this commandment had something important to say to Christians whose work is with words was already apparent to Augustine. In *On Christian Teaching*, the saint placed the labor of interpreting Scripture under the government of the double commandment. Specifically, he made the promotion of love the sign of bona fide interpretation: "Whoever . . . thinks that he understands the divine Scriptures or any part of them in such a way that it [i.e., his interpretation] does not build up the double love of God and of our neighbor does not understand [the Scriptures] at all."[3] Augustine's argument here speaks to the scope of Jesus' words in Matthew 22. Jesus argued that the whole of the law and the prophets hang on the commandments to love God and neighbor. Augustine bears out that reasoning, arguing that we ought to be encouraged in those loves wherever and whenever we read Scripture.

On Christian Teaching was written with preachers particularly in view, and that point is worth dwelling on for a moment. It helps us to see that Augustine wasn't imagining charitable Bible reading as a personal practice; reading is meant to "build up the double love" within the reading community of believers. Love is a way—indeed, the *true* way—of gathering around the biblical text, and, in turn, going out together into the world.

But is the Bible the only book to which the double commandment applies? Jacobs has argued that Augustine's loving approach to Scripture doesn't go far enough. In keeping with the universal nature of Jesus' double commandment, he would have us bring the *whole* of our reading lives under love's rule:

> We need not shy away from evaluating *any* everyday pursuit according to what the fourteenth-century English theologian Richard Rolle (along with many others) calls "the law of love." "That you may love [Jesus Christ] truly," says Rolle, "understand that his love is proved in three areas of your life—in your thinking, in your talking, and in your manner of working."[4]

Jacobs observes that Rolle's three "proofs"—thinking, talking, and working—have a particular claim on those engaged in academic (and,

---

[3]Quoted by Jacobs, *A Theology of Reading*, 10. For another translation, see Augustine, *On Christian Teaching*, trans. R. P. H. Green (New York: Oxford University Press, 1997), 27.
[4]Jacobs, *A Theology of Reading*, 10.

we would add, professional) pursuits since "our thinking (including reading) and talking (including writing) pretty much *are* our 'manner of working.'"⁵ Augustine's charitable Bible reading thus offers a model for our handling of *all* texts—whether, to borrow examples from Jacobs, they are "epic poems or national constitutions."⁶ Always and everywhere, our duty is to read with love.

In titling our book *Charitable Writing*, we mean to register our debts to Augustine and to Jacobs. This book might be said to represent a translation, since our ambition is to apply their insights about charity's role in reading to the sphere of writing. And, as we have already seen Jacobs point out, writing represents one of the clear contexts in which those engaged in academic and professional labors—those whose working *is* thinking and communicating—should seek to fulfill the "law of love."

Augustine Writing by Heart

Augustine himself is an exemplary model in this regard. Like Jerome, Christian artists down through the ages have frequently depicted Augustine at work in his study. These images capture a deep truth about the saint, for no less than Jerome, Augustine's spiritual life was bound up with his reading and writing lives. There is something distinctive about how Augustine-the-scholar has been rendered, though, and it is on display in figures 11 and 12: he holds his heart in his hand!⁷

To understand the significance of this motif, let us begin with the first of these images. Here Augustine's heart has been pierced by an arrow, which might seem to be a very strange symbol to insert into a picture of a bishop holding a book. But in fact the image derives from the book in hand. In a famous passage from his spiritual autobiography, *The Confessions*, Augustine writes, "With the arrows of your charity you had

---

⁵Jacobs, *A Theology of Reading*, 10.
⁶Jacobs, *A Theology of Reading*, 10.
⁷A key difference between figures 11 and 12 is worth mentioning as well. As the theologian Justo L. González explains in *The Mestizo Augustine: A Theologian Between Two Cultures* (Downers Grove, IL: IVP Academic, 2016), Augustine had "a Roman father and a mother who was probably of Berber origin" (18). He was, therefore, a mestizo, "a person in whom two cultures, two legacies, two world visions clashed and mingled" (9). "To be a mestizo," González notes, "is to belong to two realities and at the same time not to belong to either of them" (15). Given Augustine's background, figure 11 is likely a much more accurate representation of him.

pierced our hearts, and we bore your words within us like a sword penetrating us to the core."[8] The Latin word that Augustine uses for "charity" is *caritas*, that special word that theologians have used to designate God's unique kind of love. Augustine borrows the image of the "arrows

Figure 11. Sheldon and Lucy Rose Till-Campbell, *Augustine of Hippo*

[8] Augustine, *The Confessions*, trans. Maria Boulding, OSB (New York: Vintage, 1998), 171.

of love" from pagan myths (think of Cupid and his bow), yet he gives it a striking new spin in this and other writings. The Christian God is now the archer, yet rather than enflaming us with erotic love (as Cupid would do), our God kindles in our hearts love for *him*.[9] Engagement with Scripture is an occasion for divine archery: it "builds up" the reader's love for God.

Figure 12 shows us an alternative rendition of Augustine's heart. Now it is not pierced by arrows but set ablaze. The lesson, though, is the same: God's love is a force to be reckoned with! The painter, Philippe de Champaigne, attends to a different aspect of Augustine's life in the study. Other than the saint's fiery heart, the most conspicuous element of the scene is the light of *veritas*, or "truth," that shines above the book on the left—which is, of course, the Bible. Augustine the writer, we might say, follows truth's lead.

More subtly, yet no less important for our purposes, the painter seems to call attention to the art of rhetoric in his rendering of the saint's head and hands. In the wake of the Renaissance, we need to recognize, European painters began to conceive of their trade in light of the traditional liberal arts, and many works from this period make subtle and not-so-subtle allusions to the practice of rhetoric. Such an allusion appears in the isosceles triangle stretching between Augustine's head and two hands. The arrangement recalls the famous "rhetorical triangle" that rhetoricians have been expounding since antiquity. This is the concern for "logos," "pathos," and "ethos." In brief, those three terms address the orator's (or writer's) concerns for speaking reasonably, engaging the audience's imagination and feelings, and, finally, presenting oneself as a credible authority.

Philippe aligns these three concepts with Augustine's appearance. Augustine's head has been set ablaze by *veritas*, his left hand holds his fiery heart, and his right hand holds the pen. Within this triangle of head and hands, meanwhile, lies Augustine's colorful robe, which is decorated with images of Jesus and the apostles, several of the latter clutching books. Augustine is wearing the Christian tradition. Augustine's writing, the artist suggests, grows from the coordinated efforts of head, heart, and tradition—or, to use the terms noted above, logos,

---

[9]Robin Lane Fox, *Augustine: Conversions to Confessions* (New York: Basic Books, 2015), 300.

Figure 12. Philippe de Champaigne, *Saint Augustine*

pathos, and ethos. This allusion to rhetoric isn't simply an interesting side note. It helps to spell out the painting's lesson about that fiery heart. Remember that Philippe is here playing on the pictorial tradition that uses Augustine's heart to symbolize the saint's receptiveness to God's love. In the present picture, *writing* has become the event in which Augustine experiences *caritas*. Yet the suggestion of the picture is not that Augustine only receives love by writing. By stationing Augustine's heart over the book, Philippe portrays the text as a vehicle through which Augustine's heart is expressed. *Caritas* spills onto the page.

We have dwelled on Philippe's allusion to the rhetorical triangle not only because it helps illustrate the painting's concern for the double commandment. Calling attention to rhetoric's presence in this picture raises a second issue, one that we flagged at the start of this chapter: the seemingly obvious tension between *argument* and *love*. It is easy enough to see how many kinds of writing might fulfill the law of love, such as writing a birthday card for a friend or collecting get-well notes for a sick coworker. But making arguments seems more at odds with the law of love. Questions quickly mount: Isn't arguing really attacking? Is that kind of self-assertion, in which you put *your* view forward as superior to others', really *loving*? And doesn't arguing for *your* point seem to undermine the cultivation of our other favored virtue, humility? One can see why, practically speaking, most proceed as if love has nothing whatsoever to do with our argumentative practices.[10] Argument seems to belong to another spiritual universe entirely.

In the following chapters, we seek to address the chief hindrances to the application of the law of love to our writing. The first issue, addressed in chapter six, has to do with cultural views about argument. Many people understand "argument" in terms of winning and losing, victory and defeat. The problem is a deeply rooted one: it lies at the conceptual level, with the unexamined metaphors that govern how we go about the business of arguing. But the trouble isn't just with our views about argument; many Christians also have an impoverished understanding of our tradition's distinctive notion of love. We cannot argue with love if we don't know what love is! To that issue we turn in chapter seven. Chapter eight then lays out our proposal for a metaphorical framework that honors the law of love as well as other Christian ethical priorities, including hospitality. Finally, in chapter nine, we consider some difficulties that our proposal raises.

The structure of these chapters follows the basic structure of an argument as defined by many scholars of writing studies: we begin by identifying a problematic aspect of our status quo (our argument culture); we then clarify terms (what is argument? what is charity?); we

---

[10]One notable exception is Jim W. Corder, "Argument as Emergence, Rhetoric as Love," *Rhetoric Review* 4, no. 1 (1985): 16-32.

offer our own position or "claim," which we support with reasons and evidence; and, finally, we acknowledge and respond to potential problems. We hope that you find this argument persuasive. More important, we hope that you find it loving.

Six

On Argument

*We need to use our imaginations and ingenuity to find different ways to
seek truth and gain knowledge through intellectual interchange, and
add them to our arsenal—or, should I say, to the ingredients for our stew.*

DEBORAH TANNEN

Argument and love make for an odd couple in most people's esti-
mations. We can easily enough call to mind other genres in
which love is not only in the air but the explicit purpose of writing: the
Valentine's Day card, the love poem, and the wedding vow and its ac-
complice, the wedding sermon. But argumentative writing seems a
strange candidate to include in the category of "loving genres." This
seeming strangeness speaks to our misguided assumptions about both
argument and love alike. What follows is our attempt to right the course.
In the present chapter, we explore the metaphor that often governs how
most of us go about arguing and, in turn, point to alternatives suggested
by concerned observers. In the next chapter, we examine what Scripture
and theology mean when they talk about the distinctive character of
Christian love. Through these investigations, we set the table for the
union of argument and love in the remaining chapters of part two.

How Should We Then Argue?

You will immediately recognize that we didn't title this section,
"What Is Argument?" That question is easy enough to answer, at least
within an academic context. Nearly all writing guidebooks—and

many philosophy textbooks, too—define argument according to a basic formula, though the specific terms used may differ. The formula runs like this: an argument seeks to persuade an audience to adopt a position (also known as a "thesis," "conclusion," or "claim") using solid evidence and sound (or "logical") reasoning. Take, for example, *The Craft of Research*, a popular textbook in composition courses. *The Craft* defines argument in terms of five constituent parts: "You make a *claim*, back it with *reasons*, support them with *evidence*, *acknowledge and respond* to other views, and sometimes explain your *principles of reasoning*" (these are sometimes referred to as "warrants").[1]

The Craft's authors note that these steps vary somewhat depending on the disciplinary community for which one writes (for example, anthropologists work with very different kinds of evidence than physicists).[2] Yet they also rightly stress that argument as they've laid it out is entirely commonplace: "There's nothing arcane in any of [the five parts of an argument], because you do it in every conversation that inquires thoughtfully into an unsettled issue."[3] Where should we eat lunch? Who should win the NBA MVP award? Which class should I take to satisfy the lab requirement? Which software should we buy? The answers to all of these questions are *arguments* in the sense that *The Craft*'s authors invoke. Arguments, on this account, are part of everyday life: we are always making and responding to them. As one textbook's title memorably puts it, *Everything's an Argument*.[4]

We hardly need to explain where the trouble with arguing comes in, since our historical moment is rife with examples of arguments gone awry. Your newsfeed offers daily examples of people engaged in behavior that gives argument a bad name. The problem isn't simply with the definition of argument that is being used (though the explanation of the "parts of argument" that we find in *The Craft* may help us to spot missing pieces in these debates). The problem also won't be solved by gently encouraging the participants to lower their voices because, ultimately, the issue isn't volume (though volume does matter). The main

---

[1]Wayne C. Booth, Gregory G. Colomb, and Joseph M. Williams, *The Craft of Research*, 3rd ed. (Chicago: University of Chicago Press, 2008), 108-9.

[2]Booth, Colomb, and Williams, *The Craft of Research*, 119.

[3]Booth, Colomb, and Williams, *The Craft of Research*, 108-9.

[4]Andrea A. Lunsford, John J. Ruszkiewicz, and Keith Walters, *Everything's an Argument: With Readings*, 7th ed. (Boston: Bedford/St. Martin's, 2016).

problem is the conceptual framework in which we conduct arguments in our culture. The problem is that "ARGUMENT IS WAR."[5]

Consider the following familiar expressions:

- Your claims are *indefensible*.
- He *attacked every weak point* in my argument.
- His criticisms were *right on target*.
- I *demolished* his argument.
- I've never *won* an argument with him.
- You disagree? Okay, *shoot!*
- If you use that *strategy*, he'll *wipe you out*.
- He *shot down* all of my arguments.

This list was assembled by the cognitive linguist George Lakoff and the philosopher Mark Johnson in their classic study *Metaphors We Live By*.[6] Lakoff and Johnson compiled the list to illustrate the kind of metaphors mentioned in their title: metaphors that don't just ornament our writing but structure the way we think and affect the way we conduct ourselves.

Through this catalog, then, Lakoff and Johnson don't just want to show us that the metaphor ARGUMENT IS WAR has come to permeate our language. They want us to see that the war metaphor shapes how we understand and go about the business of arguing:

> We don't just *talk* about arguments in terms of war. We can actually win or lose arguments. We see the person we are arguing with as an opponent. We attack his positions and we defend our own. We gain and lose ground. We plan and use strategies. If we find a position indefensible, we can abandon it and take a new line of attack. Many of the things we *do* in arguing are partially structured by the concept of war. Though there is no physical battle, there is a verbal battle, and the structure of an argument—attack, defense, counter-attack, etc.—reflects this. It is in this sense that the ARGUMENT AS WAR metaphor is one that we live by in this culture; it structures the actions we perform in arguing.[7]

---

[5]George Lakoff and Mark Johnson, *Metaphors We Live By* (Chicago: University of Chicago Press, 2003), 4. We adopt Lakoff and Johnson's formatting here.

[6]Lakoff and Johnson, *Metaphors We Live By*, 4. Alan Jacobs, whose work we cite throughout this chapter, discusses the same section of Lakoff and Johnson's book in *How to Think: A Survival Guide for a World at Odds* (New York: Currency, 2017), 96-98.

[7]Lakoff and Johnson, *Metaphors We Live By*, 4.

Lakoff and Johnson contend that war has become so deeply entrenched in our notion of argument that we can hardly recognize it as a metaphor. Not surprisingly, then, many of us have great difficulty thinking about arguments in any other way. Again, our friend Alan Jacobs is a helpful commentator. Writing about the same passage from Lakoff and Johnson, he wryly observes: "The identification of argument with war is so complete that if you try to suggest some alternative way of thinking about what argument is . . . you're almost certainly going to be denounced as a wishy-washy, namby-pamby sissy-britches."[8] Jacobs calls attention to the fact that opting out of this framework is difficult because it is so ingrained: militant arguers will try to bait you back into the war zone.

Let's stick with Jacobs a moment longer. After the words that we've just quoted, he offers a troubling assessment of the interpersonal consequences of war's reign over our argument culture:

> But there's another side to this story: what is lost not *in* an argument but *through* passive complicity with that militaristic metaphor. Because there are many situations in which we lose something of our humanity by militarizing discussion and debate; and we lose something of our humanity by dehumanizing our interlocutors. When people cease to be people because they are, to us, merely representatives or mouthpieces of positions we want to eradicate, then we, in our zeal to win, have sacrificed empathy: we have declined the opportunity to understand other people's desires, principles, fears. And that is a great price to pay for supposed "victory" in debate.[9]

Jacobs's remarks force us to confront what we might call the "human" costs of (unthinkingly) conducting our arguments under the banner of war. As Jacobs points out, those with whom we disagree become less than people: they become mere types rather than distinct, complicated individuals. We fail to see them as creatures formed, like us, in the image of God. At the same time, we *dehumanize ourselves*, since we sacrifice our unique human capacity to empathize, to "understand people's desires, principles, fears." By arguing as if we are at war with others, moreover, we rob ourselves of opportunities to grow in the virtues that Christ models and commands.

---

[8]Jacobs, *How to Think*, 97.
[9]Jacobs, *How to Think*, 98.

Alternative Frameworks

Lakoff and Johnson invite us to pause and consider the consequences of calling for a ceasefire. They invite us to step for a moment onto the dance floor:

> Try to imagine a culture where arguments are not viewed in terms of war, where no one wins or loses, where there is no sense of attacking or defending, gaining or losing ground. Imagine a culture where an argument is viewed as a dance, the participants are seen as performers, and the goal is to perform in a balanced and aesthetically pleasing way. In such a culture, people would view arguments differently, experience them differently, carry them out differently, and talk about them differently.[10]

On this account, substituting a new metaphor wouldn't just clear the air. It wouldn't just change our expectations about what making an argument entails. It would fundamentally change both the *purpose* and *procedure* of making arguments, and thereby transform the *relationships* of those involved. Directed by the dance, arguments would no longer be zero-sum affairs with clear winners and losers. There would be no attacks, demolitions, or shots fired, whether on target or not. Indeed, there would be no targets (or weak points, or defenses) at all. To formulate an argument would be more readily identifiable as *making* something. Moreover, it would be a means of connection and collaboration (rather than destruction). Arguers would be artists, and argument, at its best, a beautiful performance. Readers and previous commentators could be welcomed as fellow performers rather than greeted suspiciously as potential antagonists. Argument could become, in turn, the art of circling and separating, but always keeping time together.

Lakoff and Johnson originally put forth the dance metaphor simply as a thought experiment. At the time, they didn't believe that dance was likely to outstrip war in the collective imagination, given how deeply embedded war is in our culture's conception of argument. Subsequent commentators, however, have recognized the same state of affairs and posited that academic and professional communities are capable of conceiving of argument in other terms. Linguist Deborah Tannen, to cite a

---

[10]Lakoff and Johnson, *Metaphors We Live By*, 4-5.

notable example, has been an outspoken advocate for the reimagining of argument since the publication of her book *The Argument Culture*.[11] In a *USA Today* article adapted from the book, Tannen writes,

> We need to find metaphors [for argumentation] other than sports and war. Smashing heads does not open minds. We need to use our imaginations and ingenuity to find different ways to seek truth and gain knowledge through intellectual interchange, and add them to our arsenal—or, should I say, to the ingredients for our stew. It will take creativity for each of us to find ways to change the argument culture to a dialogue culture.[12]

Notice that Tannen begins to follow her own advice: she tests out a culinary metaphor ("ingredients for our stew") as a replacement for the militaristic metaphor ("our arsenal"). The connection between cooking and arguing is not difficult to grasp. Like cooking, arguing involves working with, and ultimately combining, various "ingredients"—our data, our analyses, previous scholarly findings—in order to produce a new whole. It is also labor-intensive and time-consuming to do it well.

In a subsequent piece in the *Chronicle of Higher Education*, Tannen praises the sociologist Kerry Daly's likening of a theory's development to "bread dough that rises with a synergetic mix of ingredients only to be pounded down with the addition of new ingredients and human energy."[13] As Tannen notes, the benefit of this metaphor is that it frees us from conceiving of arguments as "static structures to be shot down or falsified" (and then thrown out). They become, instead, "sets of understandings to be questioned and reshaped." Under these terms, we can more readily grasp that arguments develop over multiple stages, *improving* as a result of revision, addition, and constructive critique. Arguments, on these terms, progress through waves of "rising" and "pounding down." Let's also recognize that these culinary metaphors

---

[11]Deborah Tannen, *The Argument Culture: Stopping America's War of Words* (New York: Ballantine Books, 1998).

[12]Deborah Tannen, "How to Turn Debate into Dialogue: Why It's So Important to End Americans' War of Words and Start Listening to One Another," *USA Today Weekend*, February 27–March 1, 1998.

[13]Deborah Tannen, "Surviving Higher Learning's Argument Culture," *Chronicle of Higher Education*, March 31, 2000, www.chronicle.com/article/Surviving-Higher-Learnings/18745; Kerry J. Daly, *Families and Time: Keeping Peace in a Hurried Culture* (Thousand Oaks, CA: SAGE Publications, 1996), xv.

change the writer's relation to other writers and readers. While some chefs do cook competitively (as in television shows like *Top Chef*), the cooking that most of us do is not part of a contest. Rather, we labor to nourish our bodies and those of others. Dinner is not won. It is served. In that same *Chronicle* piece, Tannen discusses a second metaphor that is worthy of our attention here. It appeared in Don McCormick and Michael Kahn's article about the style of seminar classes, which we introduced in chapter three.[14] McCormick and Kahn, too, recognize that the war metaphor has had a smothering hold on us, which, they rightly note, "makes idea-conversation so unpleasant that students do their best to avoid it, in college and afterwards."[15] They perceive, too, how anxieties about conflict can prevent students from engaging directly with each other's suggestions. Thus, if some classrooms are combative "free-for-alls," others look more like "beauty pageants" or "distinguished house tours," involving the mere display of ideas rather than working together to refine or to advance them through elaboration, clarification, and productive disagreement.[16]

McCormick and Kahn propose a new metaphor and attendant set of communal practices: barn raising. The metaphor recalls a once-familiar event in our country (though it is still practiced in some Amish communities):

> In frontier America when a family needed a barn but had limited labor and other resources, the entire community gathered to help them build the barn. The host family described the kind of barn it had in mind and picked the site. The community then pitched in and built it. Neighbors would suggest changes and improvements as they built.[17]

Notice that the starting point here is an acknowledgment of human limitation: the family needing the barn doesn't have the hands and tools to construct a barn on their own. McCormick and Kahn would have us see, though, that the final product is not worse for the outside help; rather, the structure will be stronger thanks to the mental and manual

---

[14]Don McCormick and Michael Kahn, "Barn Raising: Collaborative Group Process in Seminars," *Exchange: The Organizational Behavior Teaching Journal* 7, no. 4 (1982): 16-20.

[15]McCormick and Kahn, "Barn Raising," 16.

[16]McCormick and Kahn, "Barn Raising," 17.

[17]McCormick and Kahn, "Barn Raising," 17.

efforts of other contributors. The community's help, moreover, brings with it a reciprocal responsibility: the receiving family is now expected to pitch in when another family is in need of the same support, which we may imagine they will be glad to do. Gratitude is paid forward. This is how McCormick and Kahn urge us to think about academic argument—as a communal activity in which ideas are shared. When argument is understood as barn raising, they observe, your ownership of your ideas is productively undermined:

> You are not the lonely defender of [your] idea but part of a task-force whose job is to develop it to its fullest potential, to make the best possible case for it. It is not your idea anymore; it belongs to the seminar. The energy which might have gone into conflict, or into polite challenge-and-defense, now is directed toward a common goal.[18]

McCormick and Kahn's proposed metaphor does not abolish disagreement.[19] Disagreement is, in fact, "built into" the metaphor insofar as posing alternative ideas and highlighting potential weak points are imperative to raising a sturdy barn. Yet disagreement is transformed here by the way that ideas are disentangled from isolated selves. Within the conversational space of McCormick and Kahn's classroom, ideas become communal goods rather than individual possessions. Under this model, arguments are to be experienced as construction sites rather than battlefields, fellow writers seen as colaborers rather than rivals.

Argument as Conversation

We could go on listing thought-provoking alternative metaphors for some time. The rhetorician Barbara Tomlinson, for example, has unearthed eight common metaphors that writers use for thinking about revision, including refining ore, sewing, and sculpting.[20] And the Christian philosopher Nicholas Wolterstorff, who is the son of a woodworker, has likened writing a philosophical argument to the art of joining pieces of

---

[18]McCormick and Kahn, "Barn Raising," 18.
[19]McCormick and Kahn, "Barn Raising," 17.
[20]Barbara Tomlinson, "Tuning, Tying, and Training Texts: Metaphors for Revision," *Written Communication* 5, no. 1 (1988): 58-81.

wood together.[21] But let us acknowledge now that within the field of writing studies one metaphor enjoys preeminence: *conversation*.[22] Once more, *The Craft of Research* illustrates the point. In their discussion of academic research, the authors encourage readers to embrace

> a kind of argument that is less like a prickly dispute with winners and losers and more like *a lively conversation with amiable colleagues*. It is a conversation in which you and your imagined readers cooperatively explore an issue that you both think is important to resolve, a conversation that aims not at coercing each other into agreement, but at cooperatively finding the best answer to an important but challenging question.[23]

It is important to recall how *The Craft* defines argumentation. Once again, it consists of advancing a claim (a position) with the support of the other "parts" of argument, beginning with reasons and evidence. That process, the authors stress, does not have to play out as a "prickly dispute." It needn't be a battle. People who share the same interests do this all the time, often without recognizing that what they are doing is trading arguments: What do you make of the new polling numbers? How do you interpret that difficult passage? What is the best statistical model to apply to that data set? What do you make of the new ruling? When colleagues exchange ideas in this way, they are engaging in *argument as conversation*.

Our passage from *The Craft* bears out an important consequence of writing within this metaphorical framework. Understanding argument as conversation reshapes our conception of the other parties affected by our work, beginning, of course, with the reader. She is not to be treated as a skeptic or rival needing correction but an "amiable" conversation partner. But our reader isn't the only one with whom we "converse." Our "sources"—those whose words we quote and work we cite—are conversation partners, too. The popular textbook *They Say/I Say* foregrounds

---

[21]Nicholas Wolterstorff, "It's Tied Together by Shalom," *Faith and Leadership*, March 1, 2010, www.faithandleadership.com/qa/nicholas-wolterstorff-its-tied-together-shalom.

[22]See, for example, Stuart Greene, "Argument as Conversation: The Role of Inquiry in Writing a Researched Argument," in *The Subject Is Research*, ed. Wendy Bishop and Pavel Zemliansky (Portsmouth, NH: Boynton/Cook, 2001), 145-64.

[23]Booth, Colomb, and Williams, *The Craft of Research*, 105-6. We have changed the italicized elements of this passage to emphasize our own point.

this aspect of the conversational metaphor with its title, and—like many scholars working in the field of writing studies—the textbook's authors borrow an image from the rhetorician Kenneth Burke to emphasize the point.[24] Burke compared our position to that of a guest entering a parlor in which an animated conversation is taking place—indeed, has been going on for some time.[25] Our arguments, this metaphor emphasizes, don't come out of nowhere: they build on past arguments, some quite ancient. "Every argument you make," the writing and literacy scholar Stuart Greene summarizes, "is connected to other arguments."[26] To argue is to keep the conversation going.

Along with the metaphor of conversation, the field of writing studies also emphasizes the possibility of writing as *inquiry* and *discovery* rather than simply the expression of one's previously held positions. *The Craft*'s authors speak in this vein when they describe research writing as a joint *exploration* with readers.[27] To research is to venture out into new terrain, previously unknown to us. To write, in turn, is to compose a scholarly travel narrative designed to aid future (fellow) travelers. There is space in such an account to discuss the routes taken by past explorers—where they arrived, what they found, and what they made of their findings. But the exploration metaphor also emphasizes the need to lay out clearly the steps that led to our conclusion.

Viewing writing as exploration means that you don't have to have it all worked out before you begin. We find just such a sentiment modeled by Augustine. Responding to a criticism of his book on free will, he wrote, "I endeavor to be one of those who write because they have made some progress, and who, by means of writing, make further progress."[28] Similarly, the twentieth-century Catholic writer Flannery O'Connor admitted, "I have to write to discover what I am doing. Like the old lady, I don't know so well what I think until I see what I say; then I have to say it over again."[29] Simply stated: we may write *to learn what we think.*

---

[24]Gerald Graff and Cathy Birkenstein, *They Say/I Say: The Moves That Matter in Academic Writing*, 4th ed. (New York: W. W. Norton, 2018), 15-16.

[25]Kenneth Burke, *The Philosophy of Literary Form* (Berkeley: University of California Press, 1967), 110-11.

[26]Greene, "Argument as Conversation," 147.

[27]Booth, Colomb, and Williams, *The Craft of Research*, 105-6. See also 14, 187.

[28]Saint Augustine, *The Letters of St. Augustine*, trans. J. G. Cunningham (North Charleston, SC: CreateSpace, 2015), 293.

[29]Flannery O'Connor, *The Habit of Being: Letters of Flannery O'Connor,* ed. Sally Fitzgerald (New York: Farrar, Straus and Giroux, 1988), 5.

Recognizing that Augustine and O'Connor share the views of writing studies experts is notable for another reason. It reminds us that our own tradition can offer guidance in our search for an alternative framework for writing. We have now amassed several metaphors for this purpose, including dancing, adding ingredients to a stew, bread making, barn raising, woodworking, conversing, and exploring. As our review of these options above has suggested, we find each of these metaphors attractive and useful. Yet the task before us now is not to decide which ones please us or seem easiest to put into practice. Our task is to discern a metaphor for argument that helps us fulfill the twofold commandment. *What metaphorical framework will help us to honor the law of love?* In order to answer this question, we need to reflect on the love that Jesus commands, which is, in many ways, different than what contemporary English speakers normally mean when they speak of "love." We need to define charity.

Seven

On Charity

Beloved, let us love one another, because love is from God.

1 JOHN 4:7

In the previous chapter, we considered metaphors that shape how we understand and practice argumentative writing. This chapter addresses the other conceptual issue we must confront when trying to understand how to argue in accordance with the law of love: What is this love that we are commanded to offer to God and to our neighbors?

Which Love?

In the English-speaking world, talk about "love" is muddled by our tendency to squeeze many human types of love into a single syllable. C. S. Lewis recognized this problem sixty years ago, prompting him to compose a little book titled *The Four Loves*.[1] The four on which Lewis concentrates all enjoy classical pedigrees: affection, friendship, romantic love (which he calls "eros"), and charity. Unsurprisingly, Lewis gives his highest praise to the last member of the group, which he presents as the distinctly Christian form of love. This is the form that answers the Lord's call to love God and neighbor. Lewis argues, however, that the other three loves bring great benefits to our lives as well. It is good to be affectionate, to have friends, to be "in love." Yet the Oxford don saw that none of these loves is, from a Christian perspective, "self-sufficient."[2] "If the feeling is to be kept sweet," affection, friendship, and

---

[1]C. S. Lewis, *The Four Loves,* repr. ed. (New York: Harcourt, 1991).
[2]Lewis, *The Four Loves,* 116.

romance must be anchored elsewhere.[3] Charity is the spring from which all other loves flow. In focusing our attention on charity in this chapter, we cut to the chase, since it is above but also, ideally, within all other loves.

Yet before turning fully to the topic of charity, we want to acknowledge that another love on Lewis's list, friendship, may grow in the midst of our writing lives, too. In Lewis's account, "Friendship arises out of mere Companionship when two or more of the companions"—notice that the number is open—"discover that they have in common some insight or interest or even taste which the others do not share and which, till that moment, each believed to be his own unique treasure (or burden)."[4] Regarding this commonality between friends, Lewis explains:

> It may be a common religion, common studies, a common profession, even a common recreation. All who share it will be our companions; but one or two or three who share something more will be our Friends. In this kind of love, as Emerson said, *Do you love me?* means *Do you see the same truth?*—Or at least, "Do you care about the same truth?" The man who agrees with us that some question, little regarded by others, is of great importance, can be our Friend. He need not agree with us about the answer.[5]

Lewis concludes the next paragraph with a memorable image: "We picture lovers face to face but Friends side by side; their eyes look ahead."[6]

No great stretch of the imagination is required to see how this model of friendship might apply to the Christian writing life. A fellow Christian pursuing the same course of study, a fellow Christian who loves the same books, a fellow Christian who is pondering the same big questions: all of these commonalities, Lewis would have us see, provide rich soil for friendship to grow. We ourselves have seen many friendships arise in our writing courses as our students discover not just mutual interests but, as Lewis describes it, a shared desire to get at the truth of something. In the same way, the book you hold in your hands is a testament to friendship: we became friends while working together

---

[3]Lewis, *The Four Loves*, 116.
[4]Lewis, *The Four Loves*, 65.
[5]Lewis, *The Four Loves*, 65-66.
[6]Lewis, *The Four Loves*, 66.

at a Christian college. But the writing of this book has deepened our love for each other.

Let's note now, too, that in Lewis's paradigm friendship does not prohibit argument. His friends need agree only on *the question*; they do not need to reach the same answer. Surprisingly enough, friendship here appears as an ideal context in which to argue because the common pursuit of truth is the aim of the exercise. We may even *enjoy* arguing with friends because the back-and-forth addresses topics that give us delight regardless of whether our friends ultimately find our positions convincing. To play on Lewis's image, we might say that friendly arguers point ahead rather than at each other.

In friendship, we catch a first glimpse of an argumentative process propelled by love. In fact, Lewis's model of friendship gives us a two-loves-in-one bargain, since the love for the friend is initiated by the shared love of a topic. So charming is this picture that we may be tempted to stop here, making friendly argument our ideal for writing. *The Craft of Research*'s authors make such a move when they depict academic argument as "a lively conversation with *amiable* colleagues."[7] Argument as amiable conversation is a laudable goal—certainly an improvement on argument as war. But Christians are called to something higher and richer. Following Lewis's analysis, we believe that the sweetness of friendly argument is, like friendship itself, ensured only by regular infusions of charity.

What Is Charity?

The concept of charity—which, as we've already noted, goes by *caritas* in Latin and *agapē* in Greek—has had a storied career in Christian literature. This begins with its distinctive role in the New Testament's discussions of love. When Jesus issues the law of love, his word for both commands is *agapēseis* ("you shall love," Mt 22:37-39). In his call to love our enemies, he says *agapate* (Mt 5:44). And *agapē* is the word that Paul uses in his famous discourse on love (1 Cor 13). However, before the New Testament writers employed *agapē* in these ways, it had been a rarely used word with an imprecise meaning. It had been, the

---

[7]Wayne C. Booth, Gregory G. Colomb, and Joseph M. Williams, *The Craft of Research*, 3rd ed. (Chicago: University of Chicago Press, 2008), 106, emphasis added.

theologian Karl Barth observed, "a relatively colorless word."[8] The New Testament brought *agapē* to life.

The fine points of this love have been much debated among theologians ancient and modern, but there is consensus among commentators on a number of its qualities. First of all, *agapē* love is not merely a feeling, nor is it simply an act. It is a virtue. Virtues, once again, are "good moral habits."[9] That definition rightly emphasizes that charity doesn't come naturally to us. We must practice it regularly, and our hope is that over time it will become a stable part of our character.

But to say that charity is a virtue doesn't get us far enough; it doesn't help us to see it clearly as distinct from other virtues. Of its particular qualities, the theologian J. I. Packer offers a magnificent summary.[10] For the sake of ease of reading, we present his list of characteristics in bullet points:

- First, it has as its purpose doing good to others, and so in some sense making those others great. *Agapē* Godward [that is, directed toward God], triggered by gratitude for grace, makes God great by exalting him in praise, thanksgiving, and obedience. *Agapē* [humanward], neighbor love as Scripture calls it, makes fellow humans great by serving not their professed wants, but their observed real needs. Thus, marital *agapē* seeks fulfillment for the spouse and parental *agapē* seeks maturity for the children.

- Second, *agapē* is measured not by sweetness of talk or strength of feeling, but by what it does, and more specifically by what of its own it gives, for the fulfilling of its purpose.

- Third, *agapē* does not wait to be courted, nor does it limit itself to those who at once appreciate it, but it takes the initiative in giving help where help is required, and finds its joy in bringing others benefit. The question of who deserves to be helped is not raised; *agapē* means doing good to the needy, not to the meritorious, and to the needy however undeserving they might be.

---

[8]Quoted in Josef Pieper, *Faith, Hope, Love* (San Francisco: Ignatius Press, 1997), 156. Cf. Karl Barth, *Church Dogmatics IV: The Doctrine of Reconciliation, Part 2*, ed. G. W. Bromiley and T. F. Torrance, trans. G. W. Bromiley (New York: T&T Clark, 2004), 736.

[9]James K. A. Smith, *You Are What You Love: The Spiritual Power of Habit* (Grand Rapids, MI: Brazos Press, 2016), 16.

[10]J. I. Packer, *Revelations of the Cross*, repr. ed. (Peabody, MA: Hendrickson, 2013), 126. All of the following bullet points are direct quotations from a single passage.

- Fourth, *agapē* is precise about its object. The famous *Peanuts* quote, "I love the human race—it's people I can't stand," is precisely not *agapē*. *Agapē* focuses on particular people with particular needs, and prays and works to deliver them from evil.

Packer concludes the passage with one last overarching observation, which we believe warrants its own bullet point:

- In all of this [*agapē*] is directly modeled on the love of God revealed in the gospel.

With this last point, Packer highlights that *agapē* is the traditional term for God's love for us, as we see, for example, in 1 John 4:7-8. Here are those verses, with all of the uses of *agapē* in brackets: "Beloved [*agapētoi*], let us love [*agapōmen*] one another, because love [*agapē*] is from God; everyone who loves [*agapōn*] is born of God and knows God. Whoever does not love [*agapōn*] does not know God, for God is love [*agapē*]."

These verses are supersaturated with *agapē*. John addresses his readers as those who are loved in the specifically Christian way. He calls on them to do likewise ("let us love"). He cites the presence of this love as the sign that they are Christians ("everyone who loves has been born of God"). And he is clear that God is the source of all this love, for he is *agapē*. John's point is that Christians are capable of the love that we are calling "charity" only because God first loves us. Charity thus moves according to the logic of the gift in this passage. As we have received it—are receiving it right now—we must endeavor to pass it on. Charity isn't ours to keep. John himself models this by calling his readers "beloved," *agapētoi*. John is a charitable writer!

Now, your mind may already be brimming with ideas about how we might reboot our writing under these guidelines. But before we suggest some of the implications that we see, we want to make a few further observations about the New Testament's model of charity. The first concerns love's place among the virtues. In a number of passages, but in Colossians 3:12-14 most explicitly, Paul presents *agapē* as the virtue that orders the other virtues (the list here including "compassion, kindness, humility, meekness, and patience") and "binds everything together in perfect harmony." To recall Smith's apt phrase, Paul portrays *agapē* as "the big belt that pulls together the rest of the ensemble."[11] Paul's point

---

[11]Smith, *You Are What You Love*, 16. See also Gal 5:22-23.

echoes our theme: the law of love applies always and everywhere. In our acts of kindness, in our attempts at patience, in our efforts to forgive, we must be led by love.

But love is, in Paul's account, not simply the culminating virtue. Take, for instance, how Paul explains *agapē*'s nature in 1 Corinthians 13:4-10, which we offer here in a revised version of the famous KJV rendering. We have made changes in order to track more closely where *agapē* appears in Paul's sequence of clauses:

Charity [*agapē*] is patient, is kind. Charity [*agapē*] is not envious. Charity [*agapē*] is not boastful, is not puffed up, does not dishonor others, is not self-seeking, is not easily angered, does not keep a record of wrongs, does not delight in evil, but rejoices with the truth. It always protects, always trusts, always hopes, always perseveres.

Charity [*agapē*] never fails. But where there are prophecies, they will cease; where there are tongues, they will be stilled; where there is knowledge, it will pass away. For we know in part and we prophesy in part, but when completeness comes, what is in part disappears.

The repetition of *agapē* at the beginning of this passage suggests Paul's awareness that he and his fellow early Christians are giving the formerly "colorless" word a vibrant new life. Notice how within this expansive explanation of what *agapē* is Paul goes beyond the "big belt" metaphor of Colossians 3. Here, *agapē* love *is* patient, *is* kind, *is not* envious, boastful, or prideful, and so on. (In other words, charity is humble, generous, forgiving, etc.) Love in this case is not just the crowning piece of the outfit. Paul's description suggests that these other virtues form parts of love's character. That seems imperative to the task that Packer sets out for love: to respond to particular people's particular needs at particular times. Charity must be nimble; charity must be versatile. Love is a way of life.

Agapē at the Table

Let us make one final observation about the practice of *agapē* in the early church's life that will be important to our thinking in the next chapter: *agapē* was a concept closely associated with table fellowship. Consider the little book of Jude. In the twelfth verse, Jude addresses bad influences that have slipped into the nascent Christian community. He worries that such people are becoming "blemishes on your love-feasts [*agapais*]" (Jude 12). This is the lone verse that uses the term *love-feast* in the New Testament, but the event in question is referred to elsewhere in Scripture as well as in other early church documents. "The *agapē*" as it was sometimes called for short, was the meal that Christians shared in keeping with the general practice of close-knit communities throughout the Mediterranean world, Jews and Gentiles alike. It was, commentators note, the original context of Christian worship, including the celebration of Communion.[12]

First Corinthians 13 is pertinent here as well. Paul's beautiful words on love were likely provoked by ugly table manners. Two chapters earlier, Paul responds to reports that rich participants in what he refers to as the "Lord's supper" have ceased to share (1 Cor 11:17-22). This supper encompassed both the ritual celebration of the Lord's death (our Communion) and a communal meal—a time for eating, drinking, and conversation. Like Jude, Paul is so concerned about the corruption of the supper because he views the communal meal as a foretaste of the revolutionary society that the church is called to be, one in which rich and poor are equally valued, equally loved. At several turns, including the scenes of Jesus at dinner parties, the New Testament suggests that the *agapē* way of life found both a model in and nourishment at the banquet table.

Signs of the Christian banqueting tradition linger in the late third- and fourth-century frescoes that decorate the catacombs in Rome, where early Christians were buried and, in times of persecution, re- treated. Figure 13 offers an example: Christian banqueters call to a female figure bearing the allegorical name Agape, asking her to mix more wine. The banquets were not limited to men. In other frescoes from this era, women break bread and mixed companies share food and drink. The suggestion of these scenes is that love presides over the table. All of these details from Scripture and early Christian art are significant for present purposes because they reveal that in the early Christian imagination *agapē* wasn't just a personal virtue. It was also a communal practice—and, as these frescoes suggest, a *convivial* one!

---

[12]Thomas M. Finn, "Agape (Love Feast)," in *The Encyclopedia of Early Christianity*, ed. Everett Ferguson (New York: Routledge, 1999), 24-25.

Figure 13. *Eucharistic Love Feast*, Marcellinus Catacomb, Rome

Not surprisingly, later generations of Christians have sought to revive this beautiful practice. One notable revival occurred in the eighteenth century, first among the Moravians and then among the Methodists. For John Wesley, who founded Methodism, the love-feast illustrated a model Christian society that eliminated considerations of sex and rank. In comments that appear in his journal, Wesley observed, "The very design of a love-feast is a free and familiar conversation, in which every man, yea, and woman, has liberty to speak whatever may be to the glory of God."[13] The Moravians and Brethren continue to hold love-feasts to this day (in the Moravian case often featuring citrusy sweet buns and coffee), as do some Methodist, Catholic, and Orthodox groups. As the writer Martha Johnson Bourlakas testifies, the practice remains a potent one, "a symbol of the bounteous hospitality of God and the infinite possibilities for our own hospitality toward others."[14] What this symbol might mean for writers is the subject of the next chapter.

---

[13]Quoted in Karen B. Westerfield Tucker, *American Methodist Worship* (Oxford: Oxford University Press, 2001), 80.

[14]Martha Johnson Bourlakas, *Love Feast: Together at the Table* (New York: Morehouse Publishing, 2016), 8. Bourlakas's book includes a recipe for love-feast sweet buns, which we'd encourage you to try (10-11).

Eight

Charitable Writing as Love's Banquet

Charity is a good dish.

BERNARD OF CLAIRVAUX

W e have seen that arguments don't have to be wars, and we have amassed a number of other metaphorical candidates that might provide frameworks for our writing, including dancing, cooking, bread making, joining furniture, barn raising, conversing, and exploring. Each of these suggestions has some appeal. But now we need to take up the question that we left open at the end of chapter six. Which metaphor is best suited to help us to pursue the law of love in our writing lives?

Let's quickly recap the distinctive qualities of the Christian love that we have by turns called charity, *caritas,* and *agapē.* This love, once again, is not just a passing feeling or a one-off good deed. It's a cultivated habit, a virtue. Following J. I. Packer, we observed that such love involves giving of oneself and what one has, freely and without consideration of merit, to meet the actual needs of specific people and promote their greatness; it seeks to imitate God's love for us as revealed in Scripture, the Gospels above all.[1] In 1 John 4:7-8, we witnessed many of these characteristics in action: John addresses his audience as "beloved," identifies *agapē* love as the marker of Christians, and names God as *agapē's*

---

[1]J. I. Packer, *Revelations of the Cross,* repr. ed. (Peabody, MA: Hendrickson, 2013), 126.

wellspring. John, in fact, goes so far as to define God in terms of *agapē* in the letter's famous pronouncement that "God is love."

What metaphor could measure up to *that*? What metaphor can reach such heights?

Reflections on Choosing a Metaphor

The answer to these questions must be: none. At least, that must be our answer in an ultimate sense. God's love is simply too great to be captured in a single image. This is a truth written all over Scripture, which, as you've likely noticed, assembles a menagerie of metaphors to describe God and his lovingkindness toward us. God is our King, Shepherd, Rock, Sun, Father, and Potter (Rev 19:16; Ps 23:1; Ps 18:2; Ps 84:11; Rom 8:15; Jer 18:6). In the prophetic books, God's relation to Israel is likened to a marriage (often in need of repair), a mother giving birth, and a farmer tending his vineyards (Is 54:5-8; 42:14; 5:1-7). The book of Psalms is a treasury of metaphors unto itself, including the recurrent image of God as a mother bird providing shelter "under the shadow of thy wings" (as the King James Bible memorably puts Ps 17:8). That image is recycled by Jesus when he describes his longing to "gather [Jerusalem's] children together as a hen gathers her brood under her wings" (Mt 23:37; Lk 13:34). As Robert Farrar Capon observes of the parables (another stockpile of metaphors and similes), Jesus' images are radical, yet his technique is traditional: "Speaking in comparisons and teaching by means of stories are, of course, two of the oldest instructional techniques in the world."[2]

The lesson of Scripture from this is a hopeful sort of humility. That no metaphor is adequate does not pose a problem; rather, this fact should offer us encouragement. The kingdom of God is a topic whose richness we can never exhaust. So we need not worry now about nailing down *the* definitive metaphor for translating charity into argumentative writing. On this topic, we readily grant that more will remain to be said after this chapter's conclusion. Other metaphors surely await discovery. But while we can't claim to have found the final image, we do believe that we've discerned a principle by which we can sift hearty metaphors from dry husks.

---

[2]Robert Farrar Capon, *Kingdom, Grace, Judgment: Paradox, Outrage, and Vindication in the Parables of Jesus* (Grand Rapids, MI: Eerdmans, 2002), 5.

That principle is this: *start with Scripture and tradition*. As we have just observed, these resources are not only deep and wide; Scripture itself models the process of returning to, and often refreshing, images as the generations turn. As the biblical scholar Luis Alonso Schökel observed, Scripture is "a vast collection of interwoven images."[3] And generations of faithful Christians have added to this immense metaphorical storehouse, leaving to us a great many resources that might help us write more charitably.

We believe that we ought to share these resources with one another in order that we might "build up each other" in love (1 Thess 5:11). While no single metaphor can fully capture the love of God, specific metaphors may help us on our journey together as disciples and writers. In that spirit, allow us to share one metaphor that has been particularly helpful to us. We hope you find it to be helpful as well.

An Invitation

We would like to invite you to join a feast. Yet let there be no confusion: we are not the hosts. As suggested above, we set out to find a metaphorical framework in which to practice charitable writing, yet our explorations revealed that what we needed was already waiting for us at home. Scripture and tradition laid out the fare. The image is, of course, the banquet. As we noted at the conclusion of the last chapter, the early church's practice of banqueting already unites many of our concerns. The table was for Christians—as it was for Jews, Greeks, and Romans in antiquity—a forum for thoughtful conversation. But it was loaded with additional theological significance for the church. The banquet was to be an occasion when *agapē* was made manifest.

Yet the image does not merely come down to us from Scripture. We are, moreover, the beneficiaries of the church's later ruminations (from the Latin *ruminatio,* meaning "to chew over") on the connections between charity and feasting. It has been judged a ripe metaphor by many past Christian writers, including the thirteenth-century theologian Bernard of Clairvaux, whose banquet metaphor serves as one of our book's epigraphs. Here are those words again:

---

[3]Quoted by Nancy L. deClaissé-Walford, "Psalms," in *Women's Bible Commentary*, 3rd ed., ed. Carol A. Newsom, Sharon H. Ringe, and Jacqueline E. Lapsley (Louisville, KY: Westminster John Knox, 2012), 224.

Charity [*caritas*] is a good dish, set in the middle of Solomon's banquet. With the sweet scent of its many virtues, like a medley of fragrant spices, it refreshes those who hunger and delights them as they are refreshed. It is seasoned with peace, patience, kindness, long-suffering, and joy in the Holy Spirit; and if there are any other fruit of truth or wisdom, they are mixed in, too. Humility's course is part of the spread, the bread of suffering and the wine of remorse. Truth offers these first to beginners, to whom it is said: *Rise up after you have eaten, you who eat the bread of sorrow.* Contemplation brings the solid food of wisdom, made of the finest flour. Served with wine, it makes the human heart glad. To this food Truth invites the mature, saying: *Eat, my friends, and drink and take your delight, my best-beloved.*[4]

Bernard was an abbot, the head of a monastic community, and these words' first audience was likely his "companions in the spiritual life."[5] The book in which these words are found, *The Steps of Humility and Pride*, was probably meant as a guide for his fellow monks. That context helps to explain Bernard's choice of imagery. Among many other activities, monks ate together. Consequently, the original audience would not have interpreted the banquet laid out here as a party of one, as if each Solomon were to be seated at his own table. Dining—and above all, *feasting*—was a communal affair. The courses, Bernard's original readers understood, are to be shared. Love is served family style.

Yet, as Bernard surely knew when he wrote these words, monks are not the only ones in need of humility, love, and contemplation. As one commentator has observed, *The Steps of Humility and Pride* lays out a "path" that "naturally [pertains] to every person who, like the monastic novice, 'truly seeks God.'"[6] That path runs right through the present book. In fact, the structure of *Charitable Writing* follows Bernard's meal plan. We, too, began with humility—in Jerome's language, the first of

---

[4]For a Latin version of the text, see Bernard of Clairvaux, *Liber de gradibus humilitatis et superbiae*, in *Sancti Bernardi Opera*, vol. 3, ed. Jean Leclerq, C. H. Talbot, and H. M. Rochais (Rome: Editiones Cistercienses, 1957–1971), 13-59. We'd like to thank our friend and colleague Benjamin Weber for assistance with the translation.

[5]Gillian Rosemary Evans, *Bernard of Clairvaux* (Oxford: Oxford University Press, 2000), 39.

[6]Simeon Leiva, OCSO, "Editor's Foreword," in Bernard Bonowitz, OCSO, *Saint Bernard's Three-Course Banquet: Humility, Charity, and Contemplation in the* De Gradibus (Collegeville, MN: Liturgical Press, 2013), xi.

the Christian virtues—in the book's opening section. We have now proceeded to the banquet's main dish, charity. Contemplation, meanwhile, awaits us in the third and final section. Equally important, we have joined Bernard in characterizing charity as not just one virtue among many. It is the *virtue of virtues*—not only the highest virtue but the virtue at the heart of all other Christian virtues. Other virtues like patience and kindness are, as Bernard puts it, the fragrant seasoning of love's meat (or for our vegan readers, tofu).

Our nomination of the banquet as the overarching metaphor for our writing—and not just our immediate concern of argumentative writing but *all* of our writing—is not only determined by the image's traditional pedigree. We also suggest it because the banquet seems to us an ample metaphor, one roomy enough to accommodate the many stages of the writing process that the individual metaphors we've surveyed only catch in piecemeal fashion. So bountiful is the banquet that we need not pick it over the earlier metaphors that we have entertained. Many are, in fact, built-in features of the feast.

To illustrate this point, consider a depiction of the wedding feast at Cana by the Mexican-Swedish-American painter John August Swanson (figure 14). The picture's most obvious attribute is its abundance. This isn't just one scene; it's three.[7] In the foreground, we observe Jesus performing his first miracle, turning water into wine, which in addition to displaying the Lord's powers was a blessing on the banquet itself. The hosts had run out of wine, threatening to conclude the party prematurely. Through the miracle, Jesus-the-guest becomes Jesus-the-cohost: it is his provision that keeps the feast alive.

In the background on the left, feasters enjoy an array of flavors at the table. According to Swanson, the banquet includes "wine, fish, corn on the cob, bean soup, squash, asparagus, small Mexican breads, beans, peaches, fried croquettes, peas, cabbage rolls, and golden turnips."[8]

---

[7] In Swanson's artist's notes about the painting, he describes how he created a tripartite, yet unified, scene: "There is an unusual design that unites and yet creates three different spaces. This design is on the tiles of the floor. They are almost like semicircles around each activity: the meal at the wedding table, the dancing, and the excitement around the wine jars. Somehow one can look at them as being separate rooms or one large room with these tiles—separating and yet uniting them. The three pillars help create this framework as well," Chris Romano (artist assistant and office manager, the Studio of John August Swanson), email correspondence with James Beitler, May 22, 2020.

[8] Romano, email correspondence, May 22, 2020.

Figure 14. John August Swanson, *Wedding Feast*

(Bernard would be well pleased with the fragrances wafting from this meal!) Notice the servers there, too, who arrive with full platters, suggesting that the kitchen remains busy. The guests are free to linger at the table, conversing. But if they are ready to move, they can also get up and dance. We see dancing in the back right, where a circle turns in swift motion, propelled by violinists and a pipe player. Its shape gives us fresh eyes to recognize that the table opposite is circular, too, and the symmetry reinforces the communal nature of both activities. Through these multiple scenes, Swanson's painting reminds us that a banquet flourishes through the union of several complementary parts—like the dishes of the meal that its guests are served.

To stage a successful banquet, then, isn't simply to do one thing; it is to do many things under one banner. It entails many preparatory labors: the host must plan the meal, buy the ingredients, organize the room, set the tables, gather a team of helpers. Then, of course, follows the work of preparing the meal. To recall Kerry Daly's discussion of bread making, cooking isn't a one-step operation.[9] It is the art of combination and, through the addition of heat and human energy, transformation. It involves following templates but also, as we master those recipes, improvisation (a dash of paprika!). But food isn't the banquet's only fuel; no banquet can take place without *guests*. Hosting involves deciding on a guest list and issuing invitations. On the evening of the event, guests must be welcomed, preferably at the threshold. They also need to be conducted through the banquet's stages. The typical procession, as Swanson's picture displays so well, begins with the meal consumed at a pace that encourages conversation but ultimately opens to dancing. "The Wedding Feast," Swanson writes in his artist's notes about the painting, "is a celebration. A celebration of life now lived and life to come. The new couple want all to share in their joy. They invite all to the wedding feast. They bring together the village community. The guests celebrate the wedding couple, the expected promise of new life in the fruitfulness of love and the mystery of life itself. They wine and dine with gusto."[10]

---

[9]Deborah Tannen, "Surviving Higher Learning's Argument Culture," *Chronicle of Higher Education*, March 31, 2000, www.chronicle.com/article/Surviving-Higher-Learnings/18745; Kerry J. Daly, *Families and Time: Keeping Peace in a Hurried Culture* (Thousand Oaks, CA: SAGE Publications, 1996), xv.

[10]John August Swanson, email correspondence with the authors, May 22, 2020.

Reframing Argument

How might adopting this new metaphor as our framework change our writing and, more specifically, our argumentative writing? Recall our earlier discussion of Lakoff and Johnson's dance experiment. We argued that the move to the dance floor would fundamentally change the *purpose* and *procedure* of making arguments, and thereby transform the *relationships* of the participants in the argument. Let's reflect on each of those issues in relation to the banquet.

The *purpose* of a banquet is not to win. Banquets are celebrations; ideally, all participants benefit by joining in. Those benefits aren't simply material—as in a good meal or a nice souvenir—but intellectual and relational. Once again, in the ancient world, the banquet was the ideal setting for the exchange of ideas *and* companionship. And as we see in Swanson's picture, a banquet provides abundant opportunity for conviviality. Similarly, a piece of writing can be an opportunity to draw readers in, to help them feel welcome.

Procedurally, a banquet is not a singular event; it involves multiple elements, including some that may take place simultaneously. For all of their strengths, many of the other metaphors we've discussed tend to isolate individual aspects of the writing process—say, working in the ingredients of our argument (soup making), or orienting us properly toward our scholarly sources and readers (conversation). The banquet metaphor is a bigger tent; it entails a longer and more variable sequence of events. In this way, it more closely resembles the barn-raising framework suggested by Don McCormick and Michael Kahn, which traces the movement of an idea from its conception to its collaborative refinement and, in the best of cases, communal ownership.[11] (Let us here acknowledge that the two metaphors meet. In nineteenth-century practice, once the barn's frame was raised, a feast commenced, followed by dancing.)

Moreover, the banquet metaphor well captures the fact that the stages of the writing process overlap. Conversation flows as the food is refreshed, keeping the kitchen busy, and party members slide between the table and the dance. So it is when we write. The process of making

---

[11]Don McCormick and Michael Kahn, "Barn Raising: Collaborative Group Process in Seminars," *Exchange: The Organizational Behavior Teaching Journal* 7, no. 4 (1982): 16-17.

sense of our evidence often leads us to adjust our hypotheses. We revise our research question as we come into contact with new scholarly publications. Our arguments change (even specific words change) as we receive feedback from peers. Neither writing nor a banquet is a simple sequence, though each operates according to a general timetable.

Finally, we come to the participants' *relationships*. We have pitched the banquet metaphor as an ideal tent in which to bring our uniquely Christian convictions about love to bear on our writing. Consider now how the banquet allows us to reframe our relationships with the multiple parties that we discussed earlier in the book. First, recall one of the chief lessons of part one: writing is a social practice. Our point, once again, was that though we may be seated alone while we write, we are in fact participating in a larger and ongoing enterprise; our work always relies on others' previous labors. Under the terms of the banquet, we may recognize now that we are not simply playing the part of *host* of the affair. When we write, we need to recognize ourselves as *guests*, too, who owe debts of gratitude to those who have come before us and out of whose provision we build our arguments.

Our responsibility, then, involves—to adapt Packer's language—making others' work great, even in contexts where we disagree with our fellow writers' positions. The novelist Robin Sloan has offered a memorable description of the sort of back-and-forth that we have in mind here.[12] The catalyst to Sloan's words is his experience witnessing debates held by the Long Now Foundation, in which a debater cannot present a counterargument until he has summarized the other debater's argument "to her satisfaction." When the second debater's argument concludes, then the first must do the same: summarizing his argument "to *his* satisfaction."[13] Sloan calls this the "steel man" argument, playing on the familiar notion of a "straw man argument" in which a debater mischaracterizes her opponent's argument, usually by making it more

---

[12]The episode is described in Alan Jacobs, *How to Think: A Survival Guide for a World at Odds* (New York: Currency, 2017), 108-9. See Robin Sloan, "The Steel Man of #GamerGate," *The Message*, September 5, 2014, https://medium.com/message/the-steel-man-of-gamergate-7019d86dd5f5.

[13]This debate style is consistent with Carl R. Rogers's recommended approach to argumentation, which we introduced briefly in chapter three. See Carl R. Rogers, "Communication: Its Blocking and Its Facilitation," in Richard E. Young, Alton L. Becker, and Kenneth L. Pike, *Rhetoric: Discovery and Change* (San Diego: Harcourt Brace Jovanovich, 1970), 286.

extreme or oversimplifying it, in order to make it easier to refute. When making a steel man argument, by contrast, one makes the best possible case for the alternative position prior to offering a response. Sloan claims that what he saw at the Long Now Foundation is "dangerous," which he explains as follows:

> This kind of writing is dangerous because it goes beyond (mere) argumentation; it becomes immersion, method acting, dual-booting. To make your argument strong, you have to make your opponent's argument stronger. You need sharp thinking and compelling language, but you also need close attention and deep empathy. I don't mean to be too woo-woo about it, but truly, you need love. The overall sensibility is closer to care-giving than to punditry.[14]

In an earlier chapter, we noted Jacobs's astute observation that the *argument as war* metaphor has the tendency to dehumanize not only our "opponents" in argument but also ourselves. What Sloan beheld at the Long Now Foundation might be called the *re*humanizing of argument. He saw a style of argumentation that involved listening so deeply to another's thinking that one becomes able to grasp her logic, speak his language. That listening process entails, of course, our first virtue, humility. As Sloan recognized, the act of rearticulating another's argument *to her satisfaction* requires something more than humility. It demands the boldness of self-giving love.

Setting a Hospitable Table

The other participants in our arguments, of course, are readers. How might the banquet framework change our relationship to them? Our thinking in this case has been influenced by our colleague Alison Gibson's reflections on the place of hospitality in the writing classroom. As Gibson has observed, hospitality has been part of the ethics of the Judeo-Christian tradition from the beginning—the importance of treating guests well is a prominent theme of Genesis, just as it is in the Gospels.[15] Paul's concern for the disruption of table fellowship

---

[14]Sloan, "The Steel Man of #GamerGate"; also quoted in Jacobs, *How to Think*, 109.

[15]Alison Gibson, "Welcoming the Student Writer: Hospitable Christian Pedagogy for First-Year Writing" (faculty paper, Faith and Learning Program, Wheaton College, January 4, 2018). For

referenced in chapter seven is, moreover, about the *breakdown* of hospitality. Hospitality is so vital to the Christian tradition because it is so obviously tied to the second half of the double commandment to love: you cannot love your neighbor at a distance!

To recognize that writing not only can be but also *should* be a hospitable practice has profound implications for Christian writers. To write hospitably requires that we use words and genre conventions that our reader will recognize and understand. To write hospitably requires that we take the time to edit our writing so as to make it approachable. To write hospitably requires that we actually think about who our readers are in the first place. Above all, to write hospitably requires that we recognize writing as a *gift.* "And yet," Gibson writes, "I know of few students who describe their academic papers as gifts. As 'work' or 'products' or 'achievements' or 'projects'—but not as gifts."[16] As Gibson perceives, our educations form us to understand our writing first and foremost in terms of *our* personal productivity or success. It's about us. That, of course, is not how a banquet functions. A banquet succeeds when the hosts and guests enjoy themselves together.

But who is the guest here? And who the host? One of the striking qualities of the Greek word that the New Testament uses in discussions of hospitality, *xenos,* is that it can in fact mean "a home host or alien guest."[17] That "semantic fluidity" is notable now because it reflects the fact that we actually take turns playing these different roles in our writing.[18] Recall the dynamics of the local writing community discussed in chapter three. We observed there that in the peer-review process humility goes both ways: it is a quality required of the writer whose work is under review just as it is essential to the reviewer. Those roles, of course, flip at certain point, the writer becoming the reviewer, the reviewer the writer. Both play the parts of guest and host.

That same mindset, we want to argue to close this chapter, is helpful in conceiving of our relationship with the reader. Following the "law of love," we must seek to be gracious hosts, our writing marked by the

---

more on hospitality and the classroom, see Richard Haswell and Janis Haswell, *Hospitality and Authoring: An Essay for the English Profession* (Logan: Utah State University Press, 2015).

[16]Gibson, "Welcoming the Student Writer."

[17]Richard Haswell and Janis Haswell, *Hospitality and Authoring,* 16.

[18]Amy G. Oden, ed., *And You Welcomed Me: A Sourcebook on Hospitality in Early Christianity* (Nashville: Abingdon Press, 2001), 51; Gibson, "Welcoming the Student Writer."

qualities discussed above. In the ideal, our writing would be a feast, welcoming and enlivening to our readers. Yet we must recognize that a reader is also a kind of host. Readers *receive* our writing, bringing it into their homes, giving it their time and attention. The challenge of charitable writing, then, isn't simply to be a good host. It is, at the same time, to be a good guest. Our aspiration must not be simply to love others through our writing, as if we are all-sufficient. With all humility, we may earnestly hope that our writing will be an occasion to be loved.

Nine

Beastly Feasting

*Therefore let us keep the Festival, not with the old
bread leavened with malice and wickedness, but with
the unleavened bread of sincerity and truth.*

1 Corinthians 5:8 (NIV)

W e have offered the feast to you as an ideal (and even *idealized*)
"metaphor to write by." In the previous chapter, we enu-
merated what we see as the chief virtues of the banquet metaphor, our
most pressing point being that adopting this framework will help us to
fulfill the double commandment to love. Now comes the moment when
we acknowledge how very difficult it is to honor the law of love at all
times in our writing, how very difficult it is to keep the feast. We (the
authors included) get tired. We get cranky. We get overwhelmed. We
recoil from (what we see as) the repugnant thoughts and deeds of other
people. We are treated as enemies, and we respond in kind. Our words
become weapons despite our intentions to speak truth with grace.
Meanwhile, all of these scenarios are playing out in others' writing lives,
too—across the globe, across campus, perhaps across the table from us.
Sometimes the law of love will seem onerous, sometimes an impossible
standard, sometimes an inconvenience that we'd rather set aside. Sometimes we'd rather savor "victory" in the free-for-all than the "charitable"
meal that Bernard of Clairvaux tasted.

Our choice of the feast metaphor has in part been motivated by these
considerations. The difficulties of table fellowship are not new, and we
need look no further for examples than the pages of Scripture. Both the

Israelites and the early church struggled to embrace those in need at the table, and they were firmly and repeatedly rebuked for it. In the book of Ezekiel, for example, the prophet rails against Israel's so-called shepherds for gorging themselves—a false feast, if you will—on the very ones who they ought to be feeding: "You eat the fat, you clothe yourselves with the wool, you slaughter the fatlings; but you do not feed the sheep," Ezekiel declares (Ezek 34:3). The lowly members of the flock are traditionally interpreted as the needy members of the society: the poor, the sick, widows, and orphans. Ezekiel continues: "So they [the sheep] were scattered, because there was no shepherd; and scattered, they became food for all the wild animals" (Ezek 34:5). In the ensuing verses, the prophet explains that God has taken away the leadership of society from the powerful for their misconduct. Ezekiel's remarks here are intended to rend the heart. The final image of the lowly "sheep" being consumed by "wild animals" is despairing, yet it is in fact only a continuation of their experience. Their leaders—those with the power to speak and be heard—had already become beasts.

The image of the cannibalizing shepherd is important for our purposes because it recurs elsewhere in Scripture, including in Jude's discussion of the love-feast mentioned in chapter seven. In his brief letter, Jude warns against "worldly people, devoid of the Spirit, who are causing divisions" in the church (Jude 19). These people include the "grumblers and malcontents" who "indulge their own lusts" and "are bombastic in speech, flattering people to their own advantage" (Jude 16). Echoing Ezekiel, Jude describes such people as "shepherds who care only for themselves" (see NRSV note on Jude 12). But he doesn't stop there, amplifying his rebuke with a string of potent metaphors: "They are waterless clouds carried along by the winds; autumn trees without fruit, twice dead, uprooted; wild waves of the sea, casting up the foam of their own shame; wandering stars, for whom the deepest darkness has been reserved forever" (Jude 12-13). Remember that Jude's concern is the corruption of the love-feast. These metaphors help us to see what's wrong with these false shepherds: like fruitless trees and waterless clouds, their words provide no *nourishment* to others. Because of their selfishness and slander, their concern with their "own lusts" and their "own advantage," Jude suggests that these people deserve no part in the love-feast. These so-called shepherds are actually "intruders" in the church and "blemishes" on the banquet (Jude 4, 12).

As we noted in an earlier chapter, the church at Corinth was also divided at the table, and Paul berates those who use the table to flaunt their advantages:

> When the time comes to eat, each of you goes ahead with your own supper, and one goes hungry and another becomes drunk. What! Do you not have homes to eat and drink in? Or do you show contempt for the church of God and humiliate those who have nothing? What should I say to you? Should I commend you? In this matter I do not commend you! (1 Cor 11:21-22)

Paul is deeply concerned about these bad table manners because the table is the living symbol of the new kind of society that the church is supposed to be inaugurating. The meal was being used, instead, to exalt the powerful and shame the lowly. Though the pretense of the gathering was to celebrate Communion, the church's feasting had strayed far from the practice that Jesus Christ had instituted on the night he was betrayed. "When you come together," Paul laments, "it is not really to eat the Lord's supper" (1 Cor 11:20).

For Ezekiel, Jude, and Paul, the table is simply no place for selfishness and discord. At the table we are called to a higher standard.

Keeping the Feast as a Communal Problem

In chapter three, we observed that humble listening isn't simply an individual practice—something that we do *for* other people. It only "works" if the members of a writing community commit to undertaking its various disciplines together. If a small cohort dominates conversation and another retreats, the humble enterprise collapses. Like humble listening, loving argument is a *communal* practice—an activity that we undertake *with* our peers.

Such a community cannot be brought about on command, but as a first step, we suggest that you join with the other members of your local writing community in a discussion of the strengths and weaknesses of the metaphors that we have essayed across the preceding chapters—beginning with argument as war. The next step is to discuss together what metaphor or metaphors might govern your community. This might seem like a strange suggestion, given that we have just spent an entire chapter trying to convince you to adopt our metaphor. Let us be clear that, while we hope our metaphor will be of service to you, the metaphor of the feast may not, in the end, catch certain characteristics of charity that other frameworks productively bring to the forefront. What is more, a different metaphor may serve your own unique context better.

To help choose a metaphor, we have used a "fill in the blank" approach, sending our students off individually or in small groups with prompts such as "A good conversation is like _____" and "A loving argument is like _____." (You may also want to explore prompts that reveal the consequences of the breakdown of these goods, as in "A loveless argument is like _____.") It is important at this step to articulate the *virtues* that are embedded in the metaphor. We have concentrated in this book on humility and charity, but we have also mentioned others such as peace, patience, kindness, and generosity. After everyone reconvenes, the last step is to choose the metaphor or metaphors that clearly and vividly express the community's shared commitments —to the "law of love" above all.

The metaphor(s) that your writing community elects—along with the enumeration of the virtues that it expresses—can then function as a kind of mission statement. It offers a homegrown description of what the community values and, thereby, a compact for community conduct. As time passes, as nerves become frayed, as deadlines loom, as members become tired or overwhelmed, the framework may provide a reminder not only of the community's principles but also of what is at stake in forgetting or intentionally abandoning them—the free-for-all, the war zone, beastly feasting.

This brings us back to our own metaphor and what we've pitched as the communal problem of *keeping* the feast. This language may be familiar to readers whose churches include the phrase "Therefore let us keep the feast. Alleluia!" in their Communion liturgies.[1] Yet that phrase is itself borrowed (as is much of the liturgy) from Scripture. Specifically, it appears in 1 Corinthians 5, immediately following Paul's admonishment of the church in Corinth for the community's failure to deal correctly with a member's immoral relationship. Paul writes:

> Your boasting is not good. Don't you know that a little yeast leavens the whole batch of dough? Get rid of the old yeast, so that

---

[1] "The Holy Eucharist: Rite Two," in *The Book of Common Prayer and Administration of the Sacraments and Other Rites and Ceremonies of the Church* (New York: Church Publishing Incorporated, 2007), 337.

you may be a new unleavened batch—as you really are. For Christ, our Passover lamb, has been sacrificed. Therefore let us keep the Festival, not with the old bread leavened with malice and wickedness, but with the unleavened bread of sincerity and truth. (1 Cor 5:6-8 NIV)

Paul's metaphor here plays on the practice of purging the home of leaven, the agent that makes bread dough rise, during the religious festivals of Passover and Unleavened Bread (Ex 12:1-28). He likens that purging here to the *communal* turn from vice (malice and wickedness) to make room for the *community* to enjoy the metaphorical new bread, packed full of virtues.

We emphasize the words *communal* and *community* because that is the important lesson in the present context. As Paul recognized, a feast can't be celebrated alone. It's something that a group must bring about together. When the feast thrives, all enjoy its fruits. When a feast flounders, meanwhile, it is rarely the fault of a single party. It is, rather, the result of multiple breakdowns. Accordingly, when love falters in your writing community, we urge you to avoid looking for a specific culprit. Instead, you should call one another to reflect on the metaphor that you envisioned at the beginning of your journey together. Talk about that metaphor, particularly about what your subsequent experiences have revealed about its strengths and weaknesses. If need be, make modifications to your "mission statement." *Only then* should you consider together where *the community as a whole* has failed to live up to the standards that you crafted for yourselves. At that point, without listing other members' deficiencies, ask the members of your writing community what you can do individually to renew the feast. You might also revisit Paul's and Packer's portraits of charity—which, for most of us, even on our best days, is a very humbling thing to do.

Keeping the Feast as a Personal Problem

With those last remarks, we have already begun to narrow our scope. We must recognize that while keeping the feast is a communal responsibility, its vitality and longevity also hinge on members' willingness to evaluate themselves against the community's—and, more important, our Lord's—standards. Above all, we must strive to be faithful to the law of love, which, as we have been stressing throughout this book, is a burden that we carry with us throughout our days and into all the spheres in which we move. The law is universally binding. Striving to write under that law is not always easy, especially at moments when it serves to remind us that our writing practice has strayed from our ideals. To put the matter bluntly, sometimes this kind of reflection reveals that *we* have become beastly feasters.

This may happen in relation to one's local writing community, and in that case the proper response is simple: repentance. This need not take the form of an elaborate (and potentially melodramatic) confession. On more than one occasion, each of the writers of this book has either written to a student asking for forgiveness or, in more egregious situations, publicly addressed the class in request for corporate forgiveness for an errant word or deed. This, we should note, has almost always had positive effects, and we have noticed that the tone of our communities often improves in the aftermath.

Our experience has shown us, though, that our individual transformations into "beastly feasters" is more often a problem in relation to the neighbors whom we can't see—the people whose work precedes and perhaps specifically prompts our decision to make an argument. It is in situations where we feel that some distant author (and probably someone with real influence) has erred gravely that we are most likely to revert to the gladiatorial mode of argument. Indeed, at such moments we may hardly realize that we have abandoned our principled commitments to argue with fairness, empathy, and love. In short, sometimes our arguments go feral.

One of the most poignant accounts of this degeneration appears, in fact, in the writings of the Christian scholar whom we named among our chief influences on the law of love: Alan Jacobs. Following his discussion of the "charitable" debate format at the Long Now Foundation, Jacobs reports on an important moment of reckoning in his own writing life.[2] The context, he explains, was a blog post that he had read denouncing the Archbishop of Canterbury, Rowan Williams. It was, Jacobs reports, a total takedown. Not only did the post's author hold "Williams largely to blame for the rise of pro-homosexual views within

---

[2] Alan Jacobs, *How to Think: A Survival Guide for a World at Odds* (New York: Currency, 2017), 109-10.

the Anglican world," he also claimed that Williams's views on sexuality revealed that he "didn't believe in the Bible at all, held no orthodox theological positions, and may not have even believed in God."[3] Jacobs knew that Williams's *many* books on Christian faith and practice attested to his commitment to Scripture, his orthodoxy, and his belief in God. He found the author's claims "an outrageous set of assertions, and defended Williams's orthodoxy, even though I had at best mixed views about his theology of sexuality."[4]

What happened next is of vital importance to our present concerns. Jacobs continues, "Before long I had come to a series of conclusions about the writer's own exercise in bad logic and bad faith, and was hammering out in some detail the views he *really* held but lacked the courage and honesty to state explicitly."[5] You can see what was beginning to happen here. In his anger, Jacobs had ceased to view the blog post writer as his fellow Christian, his fellow Anglican, his *neighbor*. The writer had become, instead, his opponent, and in keeping with the free-for-all mindset of the battlefield, Jacobs's argument had strayed from the original topic (Williams's positions) to his adversary's character. Jacobs had begun his own takedown. But then, he tells us, "in the midst of what would surely have been an irresistibly powerful assault," Jacobs *paused*. He explains:

> I didn't pause because I realized that I was in-other-wordsing with the worst of them. I didn't pause because I realized that I was treating debate as war and was desperately eager for victory. I paused because my hands were shaking so violently I couldn't type accurately. That's how angry I was. So I *had* to "give it five minutes"; I didn't have a choice. And during that enforced break I *did* start to realize what I was doing—what I was becoming. I wasn't offering "close attention and deep empathy"; my sensibility did not overlap with "caregiving" at any point. Now, it may very well have been true that the person I was arguing with didn't practice any of these virtues either. But he was beyond my control. I had a problem of my own that I needed to address. So I deleted the comment I was writing and shut down the computer and walked away.[6]

---

[3]Jacobs, *How to Think*, 109.
[4]Jacobs, *How to Think*, 109.
[5]Jacobs, *How to Think*, 109-10.
[6]Jacobs, *How to Think*, 110.

There are many possible lessons to take away from Jacobs's honest account of how this argument almost got away from him, but we want to focus now on two. The first is a word of encouragement. If Jacobs—someone who has spent years thinking about charitable scholarship—can experience such momentary lapses, then we novices shouldn't be surprised when we experience our missteps. We say this not to encourage you to take such moments lightly; rather, our point is to see that all of us on the road to sanctification are prone to error. The key is to *respond* appropriately, which in Jacobs's case was to recognize that he needed to stop writing. The law of love in this case operated as a check on his argument. Perhaps someone else could have written a loving reply, but Jacobs realized in this moment that he couldn't. We may find ourselves in similar positions, where we speak our love best with silence.[7]

The second lesson pertains to the medium in which Jacobs was reading and writing: the blog. Blogs are notably "frictionless" writing environments. Little stands in the way of our disseminating our thoughts. All Jacobs needed to do to was type up his response and hit "post," and then the original post's writer and a host of other readers would have been able to reply in turn. And of course, we can easily imagine what the *tone* of that original post writer's response would have been—followed by Jacobs's reply to that, and the reply to that, and so on. Arguments in frictionless media environments have a perilous tendency to snowball into personal attacks. That tendency gives us a good reason not only to follow Jacobs's example and acknowledge the need to pause (even when our hands aren't shaking). It also reminds us of the value of surrounding ourselves with others who will read our work and who can help us to see whether the law of love is really operative in our writing. Later, in our book's third part, we will make the case that charitable writing is often "slow writing." At present, let us simply recognize that slowing down can allow us the chance to step back from our writing to assess what it is that we are doling out. Is our writing, we should pause to ask ourselves, "the old bread leavened with malice and wickedness"? Or is it the new, "unleavened bread of sincerity and truth"? What kind of table are we setting?

---

[7]C. S. Lewis's response to John A. T. Robinson's book *Honest to God* offers another example of this sort. See James E. Beitler III, *Seasoned Speech: Rhetoric in the Life of the Church* (Downers Grove, IL: IVP Academic, 2019), 46-47.

Ten

Making Space at the Table

The very best writing emerges from generosity, the desire to
meet and nourish another. No matter how inadequate our
words may seem to us, in our struggle to find the right ones,
we make room for others to find words of their own.

STEPHANIE PAULSELL

W e have seen how attending to Scripture's feasting metaphors might enrich our attempt to provide an alternative framework for our writing. The "beastly feast" was a negative example, however. It shows us how *not* to approach our writing communities and, more personally, our relationships with writers who don't enter into our immediate presence. In the present chapter, we turn to another biblical meditation on feasting that we see as offering more positive guidance about how we should write.[1] In the passage, which comes from the Gospel of Luke, Jesus tells a parable about a wedding banquet.

As with all of the parables, the setting in which Jesus relates this one is important. Luke begins by reporting that "Jesus was going to the house of a leader of the Pharisees to eat a meal on the sabbath" (Lk 14:1). He then continues: "they were watching him closely." Jesus' relationship with the Pharisees is already quite fraught at this point in Luke's Gospel, and Luke's note that Jesus was being closely watched is particularly telling. It suggests that Jesus was not shown the warm, welcoming

---

[1]One of our guides in this chapter is the Christian philosopher Nicholas Wolterstorff. See, in particular, his *Justice: Rights and Wrongs* (Princeton: Princeton University Press, 2008), 122-29.

hospitality commended by both the Old and New Testaments. Characteristically, however, Jesus turns the tables on those who attempt to trip him up: he begins to watch his watchers (Lk 14:7). After noticing "how the guests chose the places of honor," he offers this parable:

> When you are invited by someone to a wedding banquet, do not sit down at the place of honor, in case someone more distinguished than you has been invited by your host; and the host who invited both of you may come and say to you, "Give this person your place," and then in disgrace you would start to take the lowest place. But when you are invited, go and sit down at the lowest place, so that when your host comes, he may say to you, "Friend, move up higher"; then you will be honored in the presence of all who sit at the table with you. For all who exalt themselves will be humbled, and those who humble themselves will be exalted. (Lk 14:8-11)

The parable is a thinly veiled rebuke of not only the immediate behavior of the dinner party's members but also their root assumptions about how a banquet ought to work and what social functions a banquet performs. The table, Jesus is observing, is for these guests all about seeing and being seen. Feasting is ranking. His remarkable last words offer a different picture of table etiquette and, with it, an alternative ethical program. *Lower yourself*, Jesus argues; a good host—someone like our Lord—won't forget you.

But Jesus isn't finished. Next, he turns to his host and encourages him to rethink how he composes a guest list:

> When you give a dinner or a banquet, do not invite your friends or your brothers or your relatives or rich neighbors, lest they also invite you in return and you be repaid. But when you give a feast, invite the poor, the crippled, the lame, the blind, and you will be blessed, because they cannot repay you. For you will be repaid at the resurrection of the just. (Lk 14:12-14 ESV)

Notice the last member of Jesus' first list of invitees: "*rich* neighbors." The not-so-subtle point here is that the typical banquet is in fact a means of social advancement for the *host*. Like his guests, the host is using the banquet to promote his own interests; he, too, is looking to be honored. It is exactly for this reason that Jesus' suggested guest list is so shocking. Those people aren't honorable companions for such a prominent member of society! Their fellowship wouldn't serve his interests; they couldn't pay him back in the social coin in which he trades. Yet Jesus' words can't be, for an observant Pharisee, summarily dismissed, for once again Jesus' seemingly radical new ethics is really the remembrance of what the Hebrew Scriptures time and again enjoin: caring for the down-and-out in society. Jesus is reminding the assembled parties that one does not work one's way up in God's kingdom by rubbing shoulders with the rich and famous. To the guests he says, *get low*. To the host he says, *go get the lowly*—"the poor, the crippled, the lame, the blind." In both cases, he's calling them all to follow his example.

Jesus' Feast and Our Writing Feasts

What does this have to do with writing? We have three suggestions. The first is perhaps the most obvious: that our Lord's instructions apply to our writing feasts just as much as they do to banqueting practices in ancient Israel. Parables are provocative because, while they *begin* with Jesus' immediate context, their implications don't *stop* there. They invite us to reconsider our own implicit assumptions about how the world works.

Does this mean we should now start jockeying for the "lowest" position—the seat, to use the example from our own context, at the far back of the lecture hall? Perhaps. However, while there may be some very practical suggestions to be gleaned here, on our view the chief lesson concerns the mindset that we bring to the writing table. It is, in fact, quite easy to see the parallel between the ranking exercise going on among the guests beneath the polite veneer of the party and the often unspoken ranking that goes on in writing communities, especially ones that arise in classrooms and workplaces. The parable thus offers an occasion to recall one of the chief messages of part one: pride makes our world smaller, closing our ears to the truths that "humbler" tongues may offer. But our reflections on charity can now enrich that message: humble listening strives to let someone else's voice be great; and it opens us, in turn, to others' efforts to make our writing great. As Bernard taught us, humility prepares the way for charity at the feast.

Making Space

To introduce the second lesson, let us read the writing on the wall—and we mean that quite literally. The book you hold in your hands was largely written at Blackberry Market, a café not far from the college where we work. Blackberry's virtues are many (including its delicious cinnamon rolls), but chief among them is its ethos of hospitality. On the brick wall opposite the table where we have often written together we read these words in bold, backlit cursive: *make space at the table.* This is Blackberry's mantra, and it is obviously related to the spirit of the banquet that we have been exploring.

But the phrase—presented as an imperative for the café's staff and patrons—is far more difficult to put into practice than it may seem at first. Making space at the table unsettles us. It requires that we get up, move over, or squish together. We have to share, or even abandon, the place we've reserved for ourselves. And such minor inconveniences only scratch the surface of the ways that Blackberry's motto challenges us. When we try to take these words seriously in other areas of our lives (not just in the coffee shop), we confront additional, far more troubling difficulties. We face the question that Jesus raised for his host in Luke 14: *Who is invited?*

This is the second challenge of Jesus' words to us. We must look around and be mindful of who is at the table, and how the table functions. Do our local writing communities really operate according to the quid pro quo whereby the savviest trade favors as they ascend the social ladder? Do our discourse communities?

What we mean to call attention to here is that those *with* a place at the table—those who, culturally speaking, have capital—often fail to see the people who don't have a seat. Those on the periphery are often barely visible, if not invisible, to those in the center. People on the bottom rungs of the social ladder (to switch metaphors for a moment) are often concealed from those high in the clouds. Meanwhile, those *without* a place at the table—those who lack cultural capital—face numerous barriers, visible and invisible, blocking the way to a seat. The obstacles facing the have-nots are typically perpetuated by the haves, often unconsciously. Consider the problem of poverty. In addition to the obvious financial hurdles that academic and professional advancement pose to the poor, they are also victims of familiar cultural stereotypes. "In depicting the poor, whether in literature, journalism, painting, or photography, representations swing between imaging the impoverished as dangerous, intemperate, low-life street thugs, or as helpless victims," writing teacher Diana George notes.[2] Neither image empowers the impoverished to join the feast.

Many of the readers of this book, we recognize, will be students who, at least early in their academic careers, do not choose their writing communities. They are *assigned*. Those in such a position may well protest at this moment that they are powerless to bring new guests to the party, since they don't have the power to manage the guest list! That is a fair complaint, of course, yet it only applies to one's *present* circumstances. A writing group formed *outside of class*, as we have sometimes seen students do, faces no such limitation. Furthermore, Jesus' proposed "guest list" faces us with difficult questions about *whom our writing serves*. Our writing must not simply be another tool that those with means use to scale the social ladder. We need to write in ways that bring others to the feast.

One of our own guides in this endeavor is the composition scholar Anne Ruggles Gere, the author of this book's foreword. In a celebrated article on the history of writing studies, Gere highlighted the limited scope of histories of the field, which rarely ventured beyond the familiar settings of schools and college campuses.[3] Gere saw that if the field continued to focus on academic writing practices, it would miss (and, thus, fail to learn from) many important voices—especially those of women, people of color, and members of the working class.[4] To hear those voices, Gere suggested, scholars needed to pay attention to "the extracurriculum of composition."[5] She used this phrase to describe writing practices that took place "in living rooms, nursing homes, community centers, churches, shelters for the homeless, around kitchen tables, and in rented rooms."[6] By looking at "kitchen tables and rented

---

[2] Diana George, "Changing the Face of Poverty: Nonprofits and the Problem of Representation," in *Popular Literacy: Studies in Cultural Practices and Poetics,* ed. John Trimbur (Pittsburgh: Pittsburgh University Press, 2001), 240.

[3] Anne Ruggles Gere, "Kitchen Tables and Rented Rooms: The Extracurriculum of Composition," *College Composition and Communication* 45, no. 1 (1994): 76.

[4] Gere, "Kitchen Tables and Rented Rooms," 86.

[5] Gere, "Kitchen Tables and Rented Rooms," 76.

[6] Gere, "Kitchen Tables and Rented Rooms," 76.

rooms," Gere countered the myopia of the field's way of accounting for itself. She sought a more panoramic view of writing lives. She shows us, in turn, what a more spacious writing studies table might be.

Listed among Gere's exemplary writers is Josephine St. Pierre Ruffin (figure 15).[7] If Gere offers us a model of an established writer who is concerned to make space, Ruffin provides the corresponding figure who recognizes and then resists her exclusion. A black American living

Figure 15. Josephine St. Pierre Ruffin

around the same time as Pandita Ramabai, Ruffin combated slavery and championed women's rights through her writings, speeches, and publishing efforts. Ruffin was a skilled organizer, instrumental in establishing several clubs and organizations that advocated for civil rights. In 1894, for example, she founded the Woman's Era Club—one of the first of its kind for black women.

Another first for black women was the club's newspaper, *The Woman's Era,* which Ruffin established and edited. "The format for the paper evolved over time," one scholar has noted, "but one constant element . . . was the page or two of editorials that appeared in the middle of the publication. These dealt almost exclusively with civil rights issues and illustrate the belief of Ruffin and her coeditors that their publication was a serious journal in which women could engage with difficult issues that affected African Americans."[8] Ruffin's reaction to *Plessy v. Ferguson*—the 1896 Supreme Court ruling declaring racial segregation constitutional—well illustrates

---

[7]Gere, "Kitchen Tables and Rented Rooms," 84. See also Anne Ruggles Gere, *Intimate Practices: Literacy and Cultural Work in U.S. Women's Clubs, 1880–1920* (Chicago: University of Illinois Press, 1997), 93, 99, 162, 165-66.

[8]Teresa Blue Holden, "A Presence and a Voice: Josephine St. Pierre Ruffin and the Black Women's Club Movement," in *Bury My Heart in a Free Land: Black Women Intellectuals in Modern U.S. History,* ed. Hettie V. Williams (Denver: Praeger, 2018), 61.

the point: "If laws are unjust," she argued, "they must be continually broken until they are killed or altered. . . . The world is turning a callous ear to appeals for justice; it is evident that the only way to get what we want is to take it even if we have to break laws in getting it."[9] Sometimes, Ruffin would have us see, charitable writing must demand justice. In this, too, charitable writing is a social enterprise. Ruffin was not alone; she was part of a larger social movement. The origin of the image of Ruffin that we see in figure 15 bears witness to this fact. It comes to us from a scrapbook held at the Museum of African American History in Massachusetts. According to Cara Liasson, the museum's collection manager, the scrapbook is full of newspaper clippings, photographs, and other artifacts from 1883 to 1919 that feature African Americans who were involved in the antislavery and abolitionist movements.[10] The scrapbook's pages are a reminder that, in pursuing justice as writers, we draw courage, hope, and strength from one another. We need not "go it alone."[11]

As you try to write in ways that allow more people (perhaps including *you*) to join the feast, you may find yourself working in some decidedly unglamorous genres, such as the grant proposal. (Grant writing typically doesn't earn any accolades, but it does have incredible potential to transform the lives of individuals and communities.) You might also discover that you need to spend more time learning from the people for whom you are writing. In our college's Writing for Social Change class, for example, students who partner with local nonprofits on writing projects often discover that interviewing community stakeholders is the most important research task of the semester. Listening is, once again, paramount in such endeavors as you strive to represent others and their interests well. At some point, you may even realize that you need to get out of the way, allowing community stakeholders to participate in (or take over) the writing process. Writing *with* the members of a community is almost always preferable to writing *for* them, and finding

[9]Josephine St. Pierre Ruffin and Florida R. Ridley, eds., "Editorial: The Convention of the N.F.A.-A.W.," *The Woman's Era* 3, no. 2 (1896), http://womenwriters.digitalscholarship.emory. edu/abolition/content.php?level=div&id=era3_21.09.02&document=era3; also quoted in Holden, "A Presence and a Voice," 72.

[10]Cara Liasson (Collection Manager, Museum of African American History, Boston & Nantucket), email to James Beitler, November 25, 2019.

[11]Paula Mathieu and Diana George, "Not Going It Alone: Public Writing, Independent Media, and the Circulation of Homeless Advocacy," *College Composition and Communication* 61, no. 1 (2009): 130-49.

ways to support them as they represent themselves may be the best thing you have to offer as a writer.[12] That is, after all, how one makes space at the table.

Changing the Dynamics

Our third and final lesson is a general observation about Jesus' conduct here and, indeed, throughout Scripture. On numerous occasions, Jesus is unceremoniously accosted by someone who means to trip him up, embarrass him, and throw his authority into doubt. Jesus is, we might say, regularly called to the field of argumentative battle. As readers over the ages have observed, Jesus has a remarkable ability to change the dynamics of these exchanges. It is perhaps tempting to credit Jesus with being so skilled at parrying that he can wage remarkably effective counter-attacks. But such an account would, in our view, miss the radical nature of what Jesus often does. Time and again, his responses flatly reject the argumentative terms with which his would-be opponents make their assaults. He asks rhetorical questions. He tells intricate short stories. He quotes Scripture. He keeps his mouth shut.

Let us be clear: we are not saying that Jesus never provokes his interlocutors or that he avoids all verbal disputes. He issues firm rebukes in response to sins of hypocrisy, and he meets the moneychangers in the temple with righteous anger. Sometimes loving others well demands such confrontation. But even in these instances, Jesus' exchanges invite us to explore alternatives to argument as war.[13] His words create openings for others to experience the grace and peace of God and leave absolutely no place for fighting for the sake of it. Christians have often felt burdened to defend the truth against what we perceive to be virulent naysayers. They come at us, so we strike back. How can we do otherwise when *the Truth* is at stake? But the Gospels demand that we ask: What did Jesus do?

---

[12]Paula Mathieu, *Tactics of Hope: The Public Turn in English Composition* (Portsmouth, NH: Boynton/Cook, 2005), 66-67, 124-25; see also George, "Changing the Face of American Poverty," 249-51. For those interested in engaging in community-based writing, Mathieu's book is an invaluable resource.

[13]In their writing textbook *In the World: Reading and Writing as a Christian* (Grand Rapids, MI: Baker Academic, 2004), John H. Timmerman and Donald R. Hettinga rightly note that "we may need to speak prophetically to the world or to our communities, but even then we should write under the rubric of the Great Commandment, to love our neighbors as ourselves. The fruits of the Spirit should be evident in our writing, just as they should be evident in other aspects of our lives" (26).

Writing in the Dust

A scene from the Gospel of John offers rich food for thought on this last matter. Much like Socrates's teachings, the words of Jesus only come to us through the writings of his followers. However, while we don't possess a text written by our Lord himself, John does give us an image of him adopting the posture of a writer:

> Early in the morning he came again to the temple. All the people came to him and he sat down and began to teach them. The scribes and the Pharisees brought a woman who had been caught in adultery; and making her stand before all of them, they said to him, "Teacher, this woman was caught in the very act of committing adultery. Now in the law Moses commanded us to stone such women. Now what do you say?" They said this to test him, so that they might have some charge to bring against him. Jesus bent down and wrote with his finger on the ground. When they kept on questioning him, he straightened up and said to them, "Let anyone among you who is without sin be the first to throw a stone at her." And once again he bent down and wrote on the ground. When they heard it, they went away, one by one, beginning with the elders; and Jesus was left alone with the woman standing before him. Jesus straightened up and said to her, "Woman, where are they? Has no one condemned you?" She said, "No one, sir." And Jesus said, "Neither do I condemn you. Go your way, and from now on do not sin again." (Jn 8:2-11)[14]

Three different figures are on trial in this scene. The first is the woman caught in adultery, who stands throughout the episode, awaiting sentencing. The scribes and Pharisees who have brought the woman before Jesus don't really care about her case, however. She's just a pawn in an attempt to trap Jesus and put *him* on trial. But Jesus upends things. From his lowly place on the ground, he reveals that he's actually sitting in the judgment seat, and his would-be accusers are actually the ones on trial. Twice Jesus straightens up to render a ruling. His first ruling is that the scribes and Pharisees ought to judge themselves by their own

---

[14]Though this passage isn't found in the earliest manuscripts, we think it is still instructive for us as writers and disciples.

rule book. After they find themselves wanting and leave, Jesus turns to the woman, who is still standing, and he issues his second ruling. Jesus pardons the woman, allowing her to depart.

Whether Jesus was writing actual words, drawing a picture, or just scribbling, his act helps to turn the tables on the scribes and Pharisees. Composition expert Thomas Deans explains, "Jesus's act of stooping to write functions first to introduce a pause, a quiet but disquieting interruption of expected rebuttals and rejoinders. It disrupts the adversarial back-and-forth, the escalation that typically follows on a direct oral challenge."[15] Jesus refuses to engage in argument-as-war—a response that probably would have provoked the woman's accusers to double down on their position. Instead, he acts in a way that disarms the woman's accusers, simultaneously stopping their violence and unstopping their ears. Deans continues:

> Bending to write the first time primes a reflective turn, quiets the stage for the coming utterance, readies the audience for rhetorical listening. And that makes Jesus's pithy, devastating line register all the more persuasively. Bending to write a second time punctuates that line, bookending Jesus's memorable utterance by presenting a second nudge to individual and collective reflection. The second pause for writing helps the spoken words sink in. The cumulative effect of shuttling between physical acts of silent writing and an eloquently voiced utterance nudges witnesses toward pensive self-examination, stays them from throwing stones, and turns them away.[16]

Jesus' silent act of writing first prepares the woman's accusers to hear his teaching and then invites them to consider the precariousness of their own position. In his book *Writing in the Dust: After September 11*, Rowan Williams describes the significance of Jesus' action in this way: "He does not draw a line, fix an interpretation, tell the woman who she is and what her fate should be. He allows a moment, a longish moment, in which people are given time to see themselves differently precisely because he refuses to make the sense they want. When he lifts his head,

---

[15]Thomas Deans, "The Rhetoric of Jesus Writing in the Story of the Woman Accused of Adultery (John 7.53-8.11)," *College Composition and Communication* 65, no. 3 (2014): 414.

[16]Deans, "The Rhetoric of Jesus Writing," 417.

there is both judgement and release."[17] These are the beginnings of new life for the woman and, perhaps, for her accusers as well (figure 16).

We should not make the mistake of thinking that in pardoning the woman and rebuking her accusers Jesus has ignored the law's demands. His actions have upheld Scripture's injunction to care for the vulnerable and thwart the proud. Biblical justice has been served.[18] Moreover, Jesus hasn't condoned wrongdoing: he instructs the woman to stop sinning

Figure 16. Attributed to Rembrandt, *Christ and the Adulteress?* Many think that this drawing depicts Jesus writing in the dust. But look again. The description of the piece at Sweden's National Museum, where the drawing is held, states, "The subject described [Jesus writing on the ground] is rarely depicted in art, and its identification is not absolutely clear. Although the figures and their actions fit well with the story, it looks as if there is the opening of a grave in front of Christ, and as if he is not writing, but pointing. The woman could be a mourner, and the resurrection of Lazarus comes to mind." Regardless of which interpretation you hold, we contend that the image depicts Christ ushering in "newness of life" (Rom 6:4).

---

[17]Rowan Williams, *Writing in the Dust: After September 11* (Grand Rapids, MI: Eerdmans, 2002), 78.

[18]Etymologically speaking, Jesus models what it means to be a *humble* writer: he is literally writing in the dirt. But like Jesus' other acts of humility in the Gospels, this one brings about a reversal. The high are brought low; the low are lifted up. He is, therefore, also a *just* writer. For a concise summary of biblical justice, see chapter one of Timothy Keller, *Generous Justice: How God's Grace Makes Us Just* (New York: Penguin, 2012).

when he sends her on her way. But the good news of the scene is that even sin does not disqualify the woman (or us) from Jesus' protection. Ultimately, the punishment for the woman's offenses will need to be carried out, but it won't be the woman who is put to death. The cry for justice will be answered, once and for all, on the cross.

Some have guessed at the words that Jesus wrote in the dust—Saint Jerome, for one, suggested that Jesus was listing the transgressions of the woman's accusers—but the marks remain a mystery.[19] He may have simply been doodling! However, what Jesus scrawled is less important than what the act itself helped to accomplish. Reflecting on Jesus' silence when he stands trial before Pontius Pilate, Rowan Williams observes that Jesus "takes the powerlessness that has been forced on him and turns it around so that his silence becomes a place in the world where the mystery of God is present."[20] The scene we have been discussing bears witness to a similar truth: Christ's act of silent writing helped to usher in God's mystery and justice, granting power to the powerless and mercy to the sinner. Thus, while we have no way of knowing what Jesus inscribed, the nature of his act of writing seems perfectly clear. It was, as with all of Jesus' deeds, an act of love. With a finger in the dust, our Lord modeled charitable writing.

---

[19]Deans, "The Rhetoric of Jesus Writing," 413.
[20]Rowan Williams, *Being Human: Bodies, Minds, Persons* (Grand Rapids, MI: Eerdmans, 2018), 95-96.

Part Three

Keeping Time Hopefully

Eleven

Slow Writing

Slow writing is a way to resist the dehumanization
inherent in a world that values speed.

Louise DeSalvo

Writing takes time.[1] When we ask our students to share their goals with us at the start of the semester, several typically report that they wish to learn to write more quickly and more efficiently. They want writing to come more easily. Given all that our students have on their plates, such goals make sense. We confess, moreover, that we often share these desires. Like our students, our lives are tightly packed with other obligations, limiting the amount of time we can spend on our writing on any given day.

The "need for speed" becomes most acute when things don't seem to be going well. When progress is slow, writing is often especially frustrating and disheartening. As deadlines approach and to-do lists lengthen, writing can even be a source of profound anxiety. Facing such woes, who wouldn't want to churn out prose at a speedier clip?

Over the years, you may develop strategies that can increase productivity and shorten wasted time. There is no shortage of authors claiming to promise exactly this: productivity tips pop up in our newsfeeds regularly. While we don't want to discourage the integration of such tactics

---

[1]Louise DeSalvo, *The Art of Slow Writing: Reflections on Time, Craft, and Creativity* (New York: St. Martin's Griffin, 2014), xix; Stephanie Paulsell, "Writing as a Spiritual Discipline," in *The Scope of Our Art: The Vocation of the Theological Teacher,* ed. L. Gregory Jones and Stephanie Paulsell (Grand Rapids, MI: Eerdmans, 2002), 25.

into your writing life, we also believe that there are reasons to think twice about conducting the writing process according to the contemporary ethic of efficiency, efficiency, efficiency. We believe that the Christian tradition gives us an alternative way of conceiving the time of writing. Writing need not simply *take* time; as we will see in this chapter and the next, writing can be a means of *keeping* time.[2]

Slowing Down

One way to describe what we have in mind appears in this chapter's title: *slow writing*.[3] Now, we recognize that for some readers that phrase may seem unhelpful given that their writing already seems slow, even painfully so. Who needs help getting any *slower*? Let us clarify that we have a particular sense of "slow" in mind here, and it is not "slow" in the sense of plodding along as if time didn't matter, nor is it "slow" in the sense of a perfectionist crawl. We don't, in fact, want you to feel like you have to agonize over every word every time you write (though there may be occasions, often at the editorial phase, when you have good reason to weigh your word choices one by one). We don't want you to make a special virtue of doing this or that at a tortoise's pace. We are *not* urging you to write in defiance of the clock. Work still needs to get done, papers submitted, deadlines honored. Our "slow" is not a disguised invitation to procrastinate, either.

---

[2]Michael G. Cartwright, "Being Sent: Witness," in *The Blackwell Companion to Christian Ethics,* ed. Stanley Hauerwas and Samuel Wells (Malden, MA: Blackwell, 2004), 484-86. Cartwright highlights that "keeping time" and "performing liturgy" are important aspects of Christian witness. See James E. Beitler III, *Seasoned Speech: Rhetoric in the Life of the Church* (Downers Grove, IL: IVP Academic, 2019), 17, 216.

[3]For more on this topic, see DeSalvo, *The Art of Slow Writing*; and Nicole Mazzarella, "Facing the Blank Page" (Wheaton College TowerTalks, January 13, 2017), www.wheaton.edu/academics/faculty/towertalks/facing-the-blank-page. Resisting societal pressures "to make life more efficient, more productive, [and] more effortless," Mazzarella invites writers to embrace the spiritual discipline of "slowing" as described in Adele Ahlberg Calhoun, *Spiritual Disciplines Handbook: Practices That Transform Us* (Downers Grove, IL: InterVarsity Press, 2015), 88-91. For a discussion of slow *reading* that connects the practice with humility, hospitality, listening, and charity, see Bethany Williamson, "Reading to Listen and Writing to Speak: A Pedagogical Challenge for the Selfie Age," *Christian Scholar's Review* 49, no. 2 (2020): 149, 155-56, 158. And for reflections on Christian worship and mission that value slowness, see C. Christopher Smith and John Pattison, *Slow Church: Cultivating Community in the Patient Way of Jesus* (Downers Grove, IL: InterVarsity Press, 2014); and Kent Annan, *Slow Kingdom Coming: Practices for Doing Justice, Loving Mercy and Walking Humbly in the World* (Downers Grove, IL: InterVarsity Press, 2016).

What, then, do we mean? The "slow" in "slow writing" is the "slow" of the so-called Slow Movement, which while it now touches many activities found its original, and still its fullest, expression in the Slow Food movement. That movement began in 1986 when Italians protested the installation of a McDonald's near Rome's landmark Spanish Steps.[4] Protesters offered homemade penne pasta to passersby to remind them of traditional culinary culture in Italy. Three years later, the leaders of this protest, along with peers in other countries, signed the "Slow Food Manifesto."[5] The document portrays fast food as the symptom of a much greater problem: "Fast Life," the life "enslaved by speed." Slow Food is thus presented as part of a larger program, one designed to preserve opportunities for "quiet material pleasure"—the pleasures one might have, say, sitting around a home-cooked meal with friends and family.

As a symbol for their movement, the Slow Food folks chose the snail, reminding us that the "slow" of the Slow Movement isn't the slow of the do-nothing, the sluggard, the layabout. The snail may be slow, but it is hard at work. Similarly, doing the "slow" work that members of the Slow Movement cherish actually requires a lot of labor—*skilled* labor.

Consider the example of our friend David Hooker, a sculptor and ceramicist. David is an expert, and yet his route to a finished piece is littered with warped forms and broken pots. "No potter makes *a* cup," David likes to say. "To make one cup, a potter must make ten, twenty, fifty cups."[6] He explains that ceramics requires one to switch from a "mindset of product" to one of *process*. Clay is flexible, but it's also fickle. Each day in the studio presents unique conditions, which take even David's practiced hands a few turns of the wheel to gauge. He may make six attempts at a design before he "gets it right," as in figure 17. David's "slow" art is thus anything but inactive. He produces a lot of material, burning quite a few calories, in order to realize the idea that he sat down with. David's creative process, though, isn't limited to

[4]DeSalvo, *The Art of Slow Writing*, xix; "Frequently Asked Questions," *Slow Food USA*, accessed July 24, 2019, www.slowfoodusa.org/about.
[5]Folco Portinari, "The Slow Food Manifesto," *Slow Food USA*, accessed May 9, 2020, www.slowfoodusa.org/manifesto.
[6]David Hooker (professor of art), conversation with James Beitler and Richard Hughes Gibson, Wheaton, IL, July 31, 2019.

throwing pots. He also spends time looking at the forms that he has created, considering, in particular, how their shapes will affect their use. This looking guides his decisions about where changes might be needed and, if he's satisfied with the form, which glazes to apply. Finally, David must fire his pots, which he often elects to do using the traditional method of wood-firing. This is a time- and labor-intensive process, and it creates an uneven heating environment in the kiln that risks spoiling a sizable portion of the work placed within. David observes, though, that that risk is worth it because of the unique and often unpredictable results. Indeed, he has made a practice of repeatedly wood-firing pieces, which can transform seemingly lost pieces from a previous round of firing into "gems." David's medium, ceramics, thus won't allow him to be a perfectionist about each and every lump of clay he touches. He has sought to master, instead, a set of techniques, a creative process, a craft.

Figure 17. Pottery by David J. P. Hooker

There are many resemblances between this sort of slow making and slow writing. For now, though, we want to highlight what we see as the most significant connection: *both slow making and slow writing are multi-step procedures that play out according to rhythms of activity, contemplation, and rest.* Maya Angelou, who we mentioned in the introduction, was exemplary in her ability to make time (and space!) for all three in the ordering of her writing life. She described her own writing process as follows:

I have kept a hotel room in every town I've ever lived in. I rent a hotel room for a few months, leave my home at six, and try to be at work by six-thirty. To write, I lie across the bed, so that this elbow is absolutely encrusted at the end, just so rough with callouses. I never allow the hotel people to change the bed, because I never sleep there. I stay until twelve-thirty or one-thirty in the afternoon, and then I go home and try to breathe; I look at the work around five; I have an orderly dinner—proper, quiet, lovely dinner; and then I go back to work the next morning.[7]

Despite the fact that Angelou wrote lying down, the hotel rooms she rented were sites for active work, not rest. They were places where callouses formed and slumbering was off-limits. In figure 18, a page from an *Ebony* article by Angelou, we see her at work at her craft, surrounded by the books that were "indispensable" to her as she wrote: a dictionary, a thesaurus, and the Bible. After clocking a day's work in her temporary office, she headed home, where she could engage in the more contemplative practices of breathing and looking. Finally, she allowed herself time to rest: a "proper, quiet, lovely dinner."

In the academic environment in which we swim, the third of these practices, rest, is often seen as most incongruous with writing. "Pulling an all-nighter" is often portrayed as a rite of passage; some students even brag about how many they've done. What's troublesome about the all-nighter is that it messes with one's precious sleep. Worse still, it necessarily diminishes the *communal* dynamics of writing that the previous chapters of this book have championed. In other words, "restless," eleventh-hour writing isn't simply problematic because it's likely to be slapdash; it's also antisocial. It cuts out the opportunities for others to join us on the way. It narrows the window of time that we have to understand what our writing is doing, and for whom. Instead of a feast, we end up dishing out fast food.

So what do we do? What does slow writing entail? Our suggested recipe is no family secret. Like the Slow Food movement, our goal is not to introduce novelty; rather, with the term *slow writing* we would call students back to the traditional practices that have marked strong

---

[7]Maya Angelou, "The Art of Fiction No. 119," interview by George Plimpton, *The Paris Review*, no. 116 (Fall 1990): www.theparisreview.org/interviews/2279/maya-angelou-the-art-of-fiction-no-119-maya-angelou.

Freshman class in expository writing at Wake Forest University get professional advice and instruction from Ms. Angelou. Course is taught by Prof. Dolly McPherson (r.), a close friend of the author.

Spurning typewriter, author prefers to work sprawled across her bed and writing in longhand on a yellow legal pad. Her indispensable working tool, in addition to a thesaurus and dictionary, is The Holy Bible.

132

MAYA ANGELOU Continued

Why, when an American Black can live among the sophisticated concrete mountains of New York City or Chicago, why would one choose to return to the land of painful reminders? When the palm trees of California beckon the Black person to come and live in a sunshine splendor, why would the person reject the invitation and turn her face Southward?

I grew up in the South. In the real South. From three years old until I was 13, I lived in Arkansas in a little village aptly named Stamps —only a little larger than the then three cents postage stamp. My town was mean. Mean and poor. All its inhabitants, save for the few Whites who owned the dying cotton gin and the faded stores along the one block downtown area, were farmers. On our side of town, called quarters (a lingering term used wistfully by Whites), all the men were dirt farmers, and those women who did not work with their husbands in the bottom land, and many who did, took in washing, ironing or actually left their homes to go to care for the houses of women only a little better off than they, economically, but who believed that their white skin gave them the right to have Negro servants.

When I was taken to California by my grandmother, who had raised me, I vowed never to return to the grim, humiliating South. Except for a tentative trip to visit when I was 18, I didn't break my promise until I was 40 years old.

San Francisco became my home. I knew its hills and bridges and bay, and felt at ease with the Whites, who mostly ignored me and whom I ignored in turn.

The love of dance took me to New York City to study with the great dancer and teacher, Pearl Primus. I went to teach at Cleveland's Karamu House, but my inexperience and my radical Afro-hairstyle in 1952, caused me to last there only two weeks. Then back to San Francisco where I became a nightclub singer. Engagements carried me from New York's Village Vanguard to Chicago's Mr. Kelly's.

I pretended the South was far behind me—a shadowy once-was-landscape—when I joined Porgy and Bess as premiere dancer in Montreal, Canada. The painful mysteries and memories were nearly invisible when I looked behind at the Coliseum in Rome and thought of the gladiators enslaved, fighting to their deaths. The mists which rose over the Danube and floated down Moskva Square in Belgrade, Yugoslavia, and over the canals of Venice, may have included hints of Southern Bayous, but I hurriedly rejected them. After all, I was a world citizen who spoke French, Spanish and Italian. What did the South have to do with me?

I taught dance classes in Paris with Bernard Hassel, and gave lessons in Tel Aviv's Habima Theatre. I was a San Franciscan, an elegant cosmopolite whose Southern background was much less important than the pathway to the Parthenon in Athens or the pristine slopes of the Swiss Alps.

Back in New York, I married a South African Freedom Fighter from Johannesburg, whose efforts to solicit support for the freedom of Africans under apartheid, book him to India, Algeria, London, Ceylon and Moscow. I didn't accompany him. I stayed in New York and packed for his departure and unpacked his bags upon his return and fantasized over the foreign capitals, still trying to ignore that distressful land, a day's train ride away, just below the Mason-Dixon Line.

Working as Coordinator of the Southern Christian Leadership Conference in Harlem, I met the heroic men who came North. Martin Luther King, Ralph Abernathy, Wyatt Tee Walker and Andrew Young. The matter they brought to New York was decidedly national and even international in its concern, but it was particularly Southern. That region had formed their speech; they spoke in sugary slow accents and talked of Southern atrocities and Southern protest to those same atrocities. While I listened to speeches, I was moved often to tears and fired to action, but despite the sincere invitation to visit the SCLC headquarters in Atlanta, I declined, knowing that I had had my fill of the South, its hate and horror.

Later, I lived near the pyramids in Cairo and was thrilled by those esoteric erections whose design I had first seen in my grandmother's secret society's handbook which she kept locked in her trunk in Stamps, Ark. After a

Figure 18. Images of Maya Angelou on a page from *Ebony*, February 1982. The image to the left shows Angelou at work. In the image at the top of the page, Angelou shares writing advice with a first-year writing class. The pairing of these images is another reminder that writing is not simply a solitary activity but a social one.

writing for generations. You've probably heard—and maybe attempted to practice—the "stages" of the writing process. These get presented in different ways, using different terms, but the basic skeleton has three overlapping parts: prewriting, drafting, and revising.[8] With the remainder of this chapter, we will describe what these stages might look like if the goal is not to crank writing out but to serve up something substantial.

Prewriting

As our friend and colleague Nicole Mazzarella has suggested, the "blank page" that marks the beginning of the writing process can elicit different reactions from writers, and many of our own students have confessed that they find it *terrifying*.[9] For some students, this terror stems from the belief that they have nothing to say. These writers fear that they are as empty as the page in front of them, and—in a self-fulfilling prophecy— the worry that they won't be able to produce anything makes them clam up. For other students, the page's possibilities are paralyzing. Here is unlimited potential—far too many options!—and these writers worry that any choices they make will take them down false trails, leading to dead ends. Staring into that vast and vacant whiteness with such worries in mind, is it any wonder that many of our students claim to have experienced writer's block?

Feelings of loneliness often accompany such experiences, exacerbated by the fact that many students do their writing alone. (To recall an earlier discussion, writing spaces tend to look more like Dürer's rendition of Jerome's study than Francés's—more like private sanctuaries than communal workshops.) But the simple truth is, *you need not be alone.* And in most cases, we are *not* as isolated as we might sometimes feel. We encourage our students to look around in these moments in order to recognize how many people are primed to offer help—classmates, tutors at your college's writing center, library faculty, and, of course,

---

[8]Other stages of the writing process include research and editing. We encourage you to reflect, preferably with others, on the connections between these other stages and the theological virtues.

[9]Mazzarella, "Facing the Blank Page." Noting that the blank page can hold "possibility" and "promise" or prompt "procrastination," Mazzarella invites writers to cultivate habits of musing, staring, curiosity, and playfulness. We encourage you to watch and discuss her entire talk with your writing group. For additional reflections on the blank page, see Paulsell's essay in appendix C.

instructors (us!). Similarly, professionals who are past their student years often forget how many people surround them (coworkers, professional peers, even interns) who can lend an ear. When you find yourself staring blankly at the blank page, take a minute to remember, and express a prayer of gratitude for, those around you; then email them to ask for a "sounding board" session. (You'll buy the coffee.) Your powerlessness to get going can be an opportunity to acknowledge how much your life depends on others.[10]

There is an even more astonishing reality to be acknowledged here as well. As we brood over the empty page, we can recognize our connection to another, much more immense beginning—and presence.[11] The book of Genesis opens, "In the beginning, God created the heavens and the earth. The earth was without form and void, and darkness was over the face of the deep. And the Spirit of God was hovering over the face of the waters" (Gen 1:1-2 ESV). In the moments before we bring form to the formless page, we recreate this scene of creation. And when we do begin to put words on the page, we reflect the creativity of our Creator and extend the first act of creation into the present moment. This pause before writing reminds us that God has created us to be cocreators. This is, in part, what it means to be created in the image of God (Gen 1:26-27).[12]

When *we* create, though, we do not do so out of nothing (*creatio ex nihilo* is the Latin term for this) as God can. We create out of existing matter (*creatio ex materia*). This distinction is an important one, reminding us of our proper place in the order of things. It also provides a clue about how to move beyond the blank page: we must gather materials with which to work. In his book *Where Good Ideas Come From*, Steven Johnson wisely observes, "The trick to having good ideas is not to sit around in glorious isolation and try to think big thoughts. The

---

[10]Another useful activity of this sort is the group writing session, in which you work on your own writing in the presence of other writers, providing assistance to one another as necessary. Such sessions have been very helpful and encouraging in our experience. Indeed, much of this book was drafted in this manner.

[11]This section of our chapter was inspired by Tish Harrison Warren, *Liturgy of the Ordinary: Sacred Practices in Everyday Life* (Downers Grove, IL: InterVarsity Press, 2016), 27-28. We return to Warren's book in the next chapter.

[12]For more on this interpretation of the *imago Dei*, see chapter two of Dorothy L. Sayers, *The Mind of the Maker* (San Francisco: HarperCollins, 1987).

trick is to get more parts on the table."[13] That's what prewriting is all about. We draw from the plenty of creation, gathering ideas and questions and materials and sources.

From there, we can engage in another creative activity present in the Genesis account. After making humans, God tells them to care for what he has made (Gen 1:28-31). Likewise, once we have at least some material "on the table," prewriting's next act is one of stewardship. We take stock of the research we have done (which isn't ours as much as it has been given to us to care for) and then we tend it: ordering, selecting, developing, synthesizing, and more in order to create new arguments. These first moments of the writing process are often described using the dead metaphor of *brainstorming*, but a "brain storm"—a chaotic and even violent disturbance of the mind—seems to us a less accurate and less useful comparison than those suggested by the creative activities of Genesis 1–3: brooding over the waters, tending a garden, naming the animals, even enjoying a walk in the cool of the day. Let us observe, too, that Genesis suggests that these activities are *enriched* by companionship. The same lesson applies to prewriting. We need not garden our ideas in solitude.

Drafting

We have observed that drafting is the most difficult stage for our students. We see two chief causes. The first is that the writer leaves no time for drafting to take place. The first "draft" ends up being the document that gets submitted. The second cause is more subtle but no less problematic. In this case, students resist the preliminary nature of the draft. They get nettled by minor issues ("Should I put a comma there?"), thereby preventing the draft from being just that: a draft.

Before we proceed any further with these diagnoses, we should address the question that that last statement raises: What is a "draft," anyway? We all know that a draft is a preliminary version of a document, of course, akin to a painter's first sketch. What's left out in some definitions, however, is that drafting is the stage where we can feel the freedom to make mistakes. Most obviously, those mistakes can occur at the

---

[13]Steven Johnson, *Where Good Ideas Come From: The Natural History of Innovation* (New York: Riverhead Books, 2010), 42.

grammatical level. More fundamentally, though, the drafting stage is where ideas can be tried on for size. Sometimes they'll fit the project; sometimes they'll later be abandoned. In her well-known book on the writing life, *Bird by Bird*, Anne Lamott points out that first drafts are typically terrible, containing lots of unusable material.[14] However, such first drafts create possibilities that we simply can't see otherwise:

> The first draft is the child's draft, where you let it all pour out and then let it romp all over the place, knowing that no one is going to see it and that you can shape it later. . . . Just get it all down on paper, because there may be something great in those six crazy pages that you would never have gotten to by more rational grown-up means. There may be something in the very last line of the very last paragraph on page six that you just love, that is so beautiful or wild that you now know what you're supposed to be writing about, more or less, or in what direction you might go— but there was no way to get to this without first getting through the first five and a half pages.[15]

Lamott's description of the first draft as "the child's draft" is especially helpful because it challenges the mentality that we often bring to our drafting: that it has to follow all of the "rules"—whether grammatical, structural, or disciplinary—that are expected of the final product. As Lamott wisely observes, a first draft doesn't have to follow those rules! It need not be shown to anyone, so there is no need for embarrassment. It falls to subsequent iterations of the document to transform these glimmers into sophisticated and effective arguments—to use Lamott's metaphor, to turn this child's play into formal, "grown-up" writing. Exactly by writing crummy first drafts, Lamott continues, good writers "end up with good second drafts and terrific third drafts."[16]

Lamott's advice is also helpful because it challenges a common misconception about writing. Many people believe that writing simply transcribes thought. According to this view of the writing process, thinking *precedes* writing. Therefore, we need to get our ideas in order

---

[14]Anne Lamott, *Bird by Bird: Some Instructions on Writing and Life* (New York: Anchor, 1994), 21-22.

[15]Lamott, *Bird by Bird*, 22-23.

[16]Lamott, *Bird by Bird*, 21.

before we put pen to paper, and writing, in turn, simply involves copying down those (fully formed) ideas onto the page. But that's seldom, if ever, how the process works. Rather, writing *is* thinking: our ideas change and develop as we go. Put another way, writing a first draft always involves setting out into the unknown (recall *The Craft of Research*'s metaphor of writing as exploration). "Very few writers really know what they are doing until they've done it," Lamott rightly notes.[17] Drafting is an occasion, therefore, to cultivate and practice the virtue of hope. We write terrible drafts in the hopes that these drafts are not the end, that our ideas will develop beyond these initial moments of composition, and that the pieces we are working on may ultimately have some small part to play in reflecting the truth, beauty, and goodness of God.

With these suggestions before us, we can now return to the issues with which this section started: our tendencies (1) to put writing off until the last minute, thereby missing the chance to draft (procrastination); and (2) to resist the freedom to fail, to change our minds later, to engage in child's play while drafting (perfectionism).

Let's begin with procrastination. It's no secret that it negatively affects the quality of our writing. Good writing requires rhythms of action and contemplation, work and rest. We have often heard students and colleagues remark on the benefits of "stepping back" or "stepping away" from a project or "giving it a little time." What they are describing is the chance to *return* to a piece of writing with fresh eyes, and often fresh insights, that reveal its strengths and weaknesses. When we procrastinate, we don't leave ourselves the time to enter into these rhythms. First drafts become final drafts—and, frequently, they stink.[18] But more than the quality of our writing may be at stake. Procrastination doesn't just hamper our ability to write well; it can also hamper our spiritual growth.

Procrastination is often the offspring of sloth. That claim has more than once surprised our students (and friends), given that so many of them are anything but couch potatoes. They lead three ministries, take five classes, play on two teams, and sing in the choir! But as philosopher Rebecca Konyndyk DeYoung has observed, sloth is often misconstrued in the popular imagination as merely "being physically lazy or lazy

---

[17]Lamott, *Bird by Bird*, 22.
[18]For another helpful take on first drafts and final drafts, see Paulsell's discussion in appendix C.

about our work."[19] While laziness is indeed one manifestation of sloth, the problem actually runs deeper. According to DeYoung, sloth "is resistance to the discipline and transformation demanded by our new identity as God's beloved children."[20] Sloth, she counterintuitively argues, is *as much a problem for the world's busy people as it is its loafers.* The reason is that sloth is actually opposed not to diligence per se but to fervently seeking to fulfill our *duties.* On DeYoung's telling, the "restless busyness" of our lives is often a form of escapism from the tasks that really require our attention, above all loving God and our neighbors.[21] That's the key point for our purposes: procrastination is often the enemy of charitable writing. When we slap something together late at night as a result of our "restless busyness," we are missing the opportunity to pursue the virtues that we have been describing throughout this book.

Now to the second issue: perfectionism.[22] Agonizing over every sentence—and often every word—perfectionists do far too much editing as they draft. And since they typically don't allow themselves the freedom to make mistakes or generate extra material, they miss out on the new discoveries that result from drafting. The goal of perfectionists is to produce writing that is unassailable—and, thus, to present themselves as faultless—so they tend to dismiss peer feedback and suggestions for revision. Whereas experts in the field of writing studies maintain that "failure is an opportunity for growth," the motto of perfectionists is that failure is not an option.[23] To admit faults in one's writing is to recognize that one is fallen and finite, and the perfectionist wants none of that. Like Gollum's obsession with the ring of power in J. R. R. Tolkien's *The Lord of the Rings*, they view what they've written as "precious," trying to hold on to it at all costs.

Like procrastination, then, perfectionism can get in the way of spiritual growth. Lamott writes,

---

[19]Rebecca Konyndyk DeYoung, *Glittering Vices: A New Look at the Seven Deadly Sins and Their Remedies* (Grand Rapids, MI: Brazos Press, 2009), 92.

[20]DeYoung, *Glittering Vices*, 92.

[21]DeYoung, *Glittering Vices*, 19, 85, 96-97.

[22]For more on perfectionism, see Lamott, *Bird by Bird*, 28-32.

[23]Collin Brooke and Allison Carr, "Failure Can Be an Important Part of Writing Development," in *Naming What We Know: Threshold Concepts of Writing Studies*, ed. Linda Adler-Kassner and Elizabeth Wardle (Logan: Utah State University Press, 2016), 63.

I think perfectionism is based on the obsessive belief that if you run carefully enough, hitting each stepping-stone just right, you won't have to die. The truth is that you will die anyway and that a lot of people who aren't even looking at their feet are going to do a whole lot better than you, and have a lot more fun while they're doing it.[24]

To cast this in more explicit theological terms, perfectionism stems from pride, the root cause of all the vices. Pride tells us that we can go it alone, avoiding sin and its deathly consequences without help from anyone, including God. Here again, cultivating the discipline of writing first drafts can help. They're a low-stakes place to make and learn from mistakes, and they may just teach you to rely on people and processes who are (thank God) outside of your control.

Revising

We must now recognize that the stages of writing are not, in fact, a straightforward linear process whereby one graduates from prewriting to drafting, and from drafting to revising. That description wouldn't be true to experience. Drafting often takes us back to outlining (or word bubbles or zigzag maps or what have you), where we initially laid out our plans, to make physical or mental revisions to that schematic. So, too, the move from the first to the second (and the third, etc.) draft entails revising. The stages are cyclical. To use an important term in writing studies, they are *recursive*: they reoccur throughout the writing process, from the first glimmer of an idea to the final copy that is submitted to some audience's attention.

Our own process of writing this book certainly bears out the idea of recursiveness. During our initial prewriting phrase, we had planned to organize the book into three parts: Creed, Commandment, and Creation. But as we started drafting the first section, we found that our reflections on the creeds were taking us too far afield from the purpose of the book. We started to revise the opening chapters and eventually went back to the prewriting stage. Over several months, as we planned and drafted and revised, we realized that the book actually needed to focus on virtue, and that realization led to another: humility was our

---

[24]Lamott, *Bird by Bird,* 28; see also Mazzarella, "Facing the Blank Page."

proper starting point. This discovery presented us with new challenges. What was the best way to help our readers practice humility as writers? What should humility *look* like? The answers to these questions led us, respectively, to the act of listening and to Benedetto di Bindo's diptych (figure 8). At that point, *Charitable Writing* became a picture book, and many more changes and additions would follow—including the words you are now reading! After reviewing a draft of the book, our editor encouraged us to discuss how we revised this section on revision. The result was this paragraph.

Revision requires work, and it can sometimes seem like *drudgery*—a "slow, grinding business," as writer Gore Vidal once described it.[25] Again, Maya Angelou's writing process is worth highlighting:

> I write in the morning and then go home about midday and take a shower, because writing, as you know, is very hard work, so you have to do a double ablution. Then I go out and shop—I'm a serious cook—and pretend to be normal. I play sane—Good morning! Fine, thank you. And you? And I go home. I prepare dinner for myself and if I have houseguests, I do the candles and the pretty music and all that. Then after all the dishes are moved away I read what I wrote that morning. And more often than not if I've done nine pages I may be able to save two and a half or three. That's the cruelest time you know, to really admit that it doesn't work.[26]

Having already put in a great deal of effort in prewriting and drafting, we now have to muster up the energy to toil at it again and, perhaps, again. Revision also often wounds our pride, which, though ultimately a good thing, still *hurts*. "When we revise our writing," Stephanie Paulsell notes, "we listen for the false notes, we watch for signs of an incomplete train of thought, we read *with an eye for our own failures*."[27] Given the difficulties of revision, it is little wonder that many writers lose heart and stop short of this stage in the writing process.

Part of the problem here, to return to a point we made in an earlier chapter, has to do with the metaphors we use to describe revision, and

---

[25]Quoted in Barbara Tomlinson, "Tuning, Tying, and Training Texts: Metaphors for Revision," *Written Communication* 5, no. 1 (1988): 58.

[26]Angelou, "The Art of Fiction No. 119."

[27]Paulsell, "Writing as a Spiritual Discipline," 25, emphasis added.

you may be able to infuse new life into your revision process by thinking and talking about it differently. It, too, may be an occasion for spiritual formation.

Barbara Tomlinson, whose article on revision we mentioned earlier in the book, presents us with some different options to try out. Beginning with the Vidal quotation we've just cited, Tomlinson examines expert writers' words about the writing process and unpacks eight metaphors that these writers use to describe the work of revision: "refining ore, casting and recasting [a mold], sculpting, painting, sewing and tailoring, tying things off, fixing things (particularly mechanical things), or cutting."[28] Note that these are the activities of artists and artisans—those who have learned how to attend carefully to the world around them and to create objects that help others pay attention, too. Laboring under Tomlinson's list of metaphors as we revise, we can learn how to "focus attention on aspects of revising that we may have overlooked, challenging our current ways of classifying revision."[29] In the same manner that craftspeople frequently find joy in their work, such metaphors may help us take greater delight in the revision process and perhaps even learn to love what we have written. Consider, for example, how Angelou's own metaphors for revision are bound up with her love for her work:

> On an evening like this, looking out at the auditorium, if I had to write this evening from my point of view, I'd see the rust-red used worn velvet seats and the lightness where people's backs have rubbed against the back of the seat so that it's a light orange, then the beautiful colors of the people's faces, the white, pink-white, beige-white, light beige and brown and tan—I would have to look at all that, at all those faces and the way they sit on top of their necks. When I would end up writing after four hours or five hours in my room, it might sound like, It was a rat that sat on a mat. That's that. Not a cat. *But I would continue to play with it and pull at it and say, I love you. Come to me. I love you.* It might take me two or three weeks just to describe what I'm seeing now.[30]

---

[28]Tomlinson, "Tuning, Tying, and Training Texts," 58, 61.
[29]Tomlinson, "Tuning, Tying, and Training Texts," 59.
[30]Angelou, "The Art of Fiction No. 119," emphasis added.

A second, related way to revitalize revision is by recognizing it as an opportunity to love our readers. Revision can be an act of charity. To recall several features of J. I. Packer's definition, charity involves giving of oneself and what one has, freely and without consideration of merit, to meet the actual needs of specific people and promote their greatness.[31] Few of us understand revision in such terms. Instead of viewing it as a gift that promotes others' well-being, we see it as obligatory work we must do to strengthen our writing, earn the "A," get published, or win awards. We may have been taught to revise with the rhetorical needs of our readers in mind, but we typically strive to meet the needs of those who are in a position to promote us—professors, bosses, and other "higher-ups." The social position of our readers should matter to us because, if we're being honest, our desire is usually to make ourselves, not others, great.

Desiring success as a writer is not necessarily a bad thing. We ourselves want to be successful, and it would be extremely strange—and deeply problematic!—if we didn't want our students to strengthen their writing, earn high marks, get published, and win awards. However, we want *more* (not less) for ourselves, our students, and you. While success can be a good worth pursuing, it is of no real value if it doesn't build up love.

The revision stage is thus where some of the most important work of preparing the feast gets done. Revising well means that we seek to know our readers. It is impossible, of course, to know all of our readers in the relational and reciprocal ways that we know our closest friends; nevertheless, we ought to take the time to learn as much as we can about our audience and, when we are able, to develop meaningful relationships with a few of our potential readers. By giving of your time and energy, you may be able to learn what your readers' views about effective writing are, what they know and don't know about your topic, and what types of arguments and genres will best meet their needs. (A writing community or classroom can be an ideal place to practice this work, since several of your readers occupy the seats or offices next to yours.) And when you are unable to get to know your readers personally, you ought to strive to *imagine* what they might need as best as you can.[32] Stephanie

---

[31]J. I. Packer, *Revelations of the Cross*, repr. ed. (Peabody, MA: Hendrickson Publishers, 2013), 126.

[32]For an excellent reflection on the potential and limitations of the imagination, see Elaine Scarry, "The Difficulty of Imagining Other Persons," in *Human Rights in Political Transitions: Gettysburg to Bosnia*, ed. Carla Hesse and Robert Post (New York: Zone Books, 1999), 277-309.

Paulsell speaks to this point: "We don't always know who will read our writing; sometimes we don't know if it will be read at all. Practicing writing as a spiritual discipline requires acts of faith and imagination: we must care about our readers, no matter how anonymous they are."[33] All of this is love's work. It offers of ourselves in the hopes that we might better understand our readers' needs and how to meet them.

Seeking a sense of our readers' needs allows us to do a better job of loving them through the revision process. We are now able to tailor our claims to them and their viewpoints; to recast the contours of the argument so that it's easier for them to navigate; to drop in the definitions and background information they need to follow our trail; to cut out the material they would find outmoded or unnecessary; to meet them on their terms; to fix appeals and evidence to function more effectively given their situation and context; to apply the examples and figures of speech that make our writing more vivid and enjoyable. Revising in these ways doesn't mean we will resort to flattery. Our efforts to meet readers' "observed real needs" as opposed to "their professed wants" (in Packer's language) will sometimes require us to challenge them through our revisions—linguistically, rhetorically, stylistically, intellectually. We may even need to bring our disagreements with potential readers into sharper relief. As we have stressed throughout this book, love does not mean tucking difficult truths under the rug.

Making Time for Others

Reading the previous paragraph, you may have noticed that we consciously drew on Tomlinson's stock of metaphors in our elaboration of the work of revision. But to bring this chapter to a close, we'd like to consider a metaphor related to the feast: hosting guests. Revision, we argue, is a *hospitable practice*. To revise is to strive to welcome the stranger into our thinking. Earlier in this book, we mentioned the importance of hospitality, but now let us underscore that hospitality holds a prized place in Scripture. It is modeled by Abraham's behavior toward his three angelic visitors, inscribed in laws pertaining to the Israelites' treatment of foreigners and sojourners, encouraged among

---

[33]Paulsell, "Writing as Spiritual Discipline," 29. Paulsell continues, "We must . . . discover in our writing how to reunite what has been severed, to connect what seems disparate, to create out of a diversity of material and perspective some new thing."

disciples of Christ in the epistles, and—above all—commended by our Lord (Gen 18; Lev 19:33-34; Deut 10:18-19; Rom 15:7; Heb 13:2; Mt 25:34-40). Remarkably, our acts of hospitality fulfill *both* of the law of love's commands simultaneously. When we welcome the stranger, Jesus tells us, we welcome him (Mt 25:34-40).

When we revise, we're getting our written house in order to host our readerly guests. As with a house, a strong foundation and good structural integrity are of utmost importance. Just as we wouldn't want to invite people to visit our home during a big remodeling project, we don't want them to spend time with our half-formed and disorganized ideas. Once we have the foundation and structure in place, we can turn our attention to the paragraphs and sentences. Like the décor and furniture in the rooms of our house, we want our argument's parts to work well together and to make our readers feel that they belong. If things are too spartan, we may need to add a familiar example or two, like repainting a wall to make it pop or buying a few new decorative pillows. If we're prone to hoarding, we must get rid of extraneous material—the empty boxes and stacks of magazines that will get in our guests' way as they move about the house. Then we ought to concern ourselves with the preferences of our guests. Have we stocked the fridge with their favorite drinks? Are we planning meals that they like and aren't allergic to? As the hosting draws closer, we should turn our attention to beautifying the entryway and our housekeeping tasks. Does our title have enough "curb appeal"? Did we fix the light bulbs in the introduction? Then it's time to straighten things up and clean. Editing grammar and spelling is a bit like dusting and vacuuming: the reader won't notice when you've done it, but it'll be conspicuous if you don't.

All of this housekeeping might sound rather daunting, especially for writers unaccustomed to the practice of revision. Let us offer, therefore, a final reminder and word of encouragement. As we observed when discussing prewriting, the work of revision does not need to be a solo act. Indeed, of the three stages we've discussed, revision is often the easiest one for friends and colleagues to step in and offer immediate aid. The questions that we have just listed about structure, paragraph organization, and sentence-level mechanics are not ones that you must take up alone. These are questions that you can pose *to* a trusted reader. One's local writing community may in fact have established rituals of revision in place, as when members of writing groups workshop each other's pieces. We've noticed that students sometimes worry about being a burden on their peers at such moments. Should that fear creep up on you, we urge you to remember that we are not called to play the part of host exclusively. We, too, are called to be guests, which is to say that we are called both to give love and to receive it. When we ask a peer for help, *we* become the neighbor.

That last observation is a good note on which to return to where this chapter started: what "slow" really means in the context of writing. As this review of the stages of writing has suggested, slow does not mean sluggish. There's much work to be done! "Slow," instead, describes a commitment to conducting our writing according to a properly human rhythm of activity and rest. More importantly still, "slow" writing is like "Slow Food" insofar as the practice is designed to foster *conviviality*. The Slow Food movement has sought to restore not just the old ways of cooking but the communal gatherings that happen around that food. Slow Food is, at base, about the unrushed pleasures of the table where family and friends gather. Slow Food is a *social* vision. Similarly, slow writing treats the composition of polished prose only as a secondary motive. Its goal, ultimately, is to promote charity. In her book *The Art of Slow Writing*, Louise DeSalvo describes slow writing as "a meditative act," which involves "*slowing down* to understand our relationship to our writing, *slowing down* to determine our authentic subjects, *slowing down* to write complex works, *slowing down* to study our literary antecedents."[34] We agree with all of these claims but we also want to add another: *we slow down to let others join in.*

---

[34]DeSalvo, *The Art of Slow Writing*, xix. It is important to acknowledge that DeSalvo's program for slow writing does include "writing partners" (251-53).

Twelve

Liturgies of Writing

Pray without ceasing.

1 THESSALONIANS 5:17

S low writing lets others join in. But it includes more than just our friends, peers, colleagues, and mentors—more than the neighbors of our writing communities. Slow writing also includes God. That may sound more than a little pretentious on our part, we recognize. But the Christian tradition has long taught that God is present in all of our undertakings, however mundane or sublime. As we have argued throughout this book, our writing lives should not be sealed off from the divine presence. What we are proposing now is that we ought to be deliberate about inviting the Lord into the writing process. Writing may be, to recall Stephanie Paulsell's words from the introduction, "a discipline within which we might meet God."

To describe what we have in mind, we need to enlist one last term: *liturgy*. That word is generally taken to describe the formal rituals of worship, often those that are conspicuous in tradition-saturated religious communities. Liturgy, in this standard sense, describes the array of actions that take place within a worship service, such as prayer, Scripture reading, singing, and the celebration of Communion. However, James K. A. Smith has offered an expanded sense of "liturgy" that arises from his observation that humans are fundamentally liturgical creatures—which is to say, we are prone to engage in cultural rituals that express and shape our desires.[1] As an example of what he

---

[1]James K. A. Smith, *Desiring the Kingdom: Worship, Worldview, and Cultural Formation* (Grand Rapids, MI: Baker Academic, 2009), 40.

calls a "cultural liturgy," Smith names the practice of singing the national anthem at a sporting event. Here is an organized ritual that involves certain specific practices (like standing and taking off your cap) and that expresses our allegiance to some higher good (in this case, the well-being of the nation).[2] We *teach* children to join in this activity in order to shape them as citizens. More strikingly still, Smith argues that shopping at the mall is for many moderns a cultural liturgy, an activity that plays out according to what are often carefully orchestrated rituals and that reveals (and provokes!) our desires.[3]

The Power of Liturgy to Shape Us

As the examples above suggest, Smith is concerned to reveal the *unexamined* liturgies that we participate in regularly, perhaps daily, and that may at points challenge—if not subtly undermine—our formation as Christians. Yet his argument has also catalyzed some rich reflections on the overlooked opportunities for spiritual formation that surround us as we go about our days. Among the best of these meditations is a book by the Anglican priest Tish Harrison Warren titled *Liturgy of the Ordinary*.[4] As that title suggests, Warren examines "ordinary" activities of modern life like brushing our teeth, eating leftovers, checking email, and making the bed. Her analysis of that last practice is illuminating for present purposes.

Warren describes an early morning routine that will sound familiar to many readers: looking at her smartphone. "Before getting out of bed," she writes, "I'd check my email, scroll through the news, glance at Facebook or Twitter."[5] She likens this "morning smartphone ritual" to the process by which a rescued animal is "imprinted" by human culture: "From that point on, it will believe that all good things come from people. It is no longer wild and cannot live on its own."[6] She then describes how, as a Lenten exercise, she chose to adopt a new morning

---

[2]Smith, *Desiring the Kingdom*, 105-7.
[3]Smith, *Desiring the Kingdom*, 19-27.
[4]Tish Harrison Warren, *Liturgy of the Ordinary: Sacred Practices in Everyday Life* (Downers Grove, IL: InterVarsity Press, 2016). We also recommend Douglas McKelvey's prayer "A Liturgy Before Beginning a Book," *Englewood Review of Books*, August 26, 2019, https://englewoodreview.org/douglas-mckelvey-a-liturgy-before-beginning-a-book/#more-26409.
[5]Warren, *Liturgy of the Ordinary*, 26.
[6]Warren, *Liturgy of the Ordinary*, 26.

ritual: "I'd stop waking up with my phone, and instead I'd make the bed, first thing. I also decided to spend the first few minutes after I made the bed sitting (on my freshly made bed) in silence."[7] She explains the results as follows:

> My new Lenten routine didn't make me wildly successful or cheerfully buoyant as some had promised, but I began to notice, very subtly, that my day was imprinted differently. The first activity of my day, the first move I made, was not that of a consumer, but that of a colaborer with God. Instead of going to a device for a morning fix of instant infotainment, I touched the tangible softness of our well-worn covers, tugged against wrinkled cotton, felt the hard wood beneath my bare feet. In the creation story, God entered chaos and made order and beauty. In making my bed I reflect that creative act in the tiniest, most ordinary way. In my small chaos, I made small order.
>
> And then there was a little space, an ordered rectangle in my messy home. And that rectangle somehow carved out a small ordered space in my messy, distracted mind.[8]

Notice that Warren does not register the benefits of her Lenten exercise according to the standard worldly indices: making the bed does not suddenly and radically alter her fortune or mood. The tangible benefits are of a far humbler order. She notices a change in her relationship to the world around her. She appreciates the goodness of her bedding, the wooden floor, the small patch of tidiness amidst the household chaos. The practice helps, in a small way, to put her mind in order, and the clearing out of internet distraction breeds a new awareness of her relationship to God.

Warren frames her book as an attempt to "learn how grand, sweeping truths—doctrine, theology, ecclesiology, Christology—rub against the texture of an average day."[9] "How I spend this ordinary day in Christ," she continues, "is how I will spend my Christian life." With little translation, we can use Warren's description of her project as a summary of what we have attempted here. *Charitable Writing* represents our attempt

---

[7]Warren, *Liturgy of the Ordinary*, 27.
[8]Warren, *Liturgy of the Ordinary*, 27-28.
[9]Warren, *Liturgy of the Ordinary*, 24.

to reconcile "grand, sweeping truths" with the perfectly ordinary goings-on of the writing life. Like making the bed, the craft of writing gives us an opportunity to carve a little space of order amidst the chaos of the world around us.[10] As we acknowledged in the last chapter, writing is in this way a sign that we are the bearers of the divine image. And, to borrow Warren's point, our work as writers can make us "cola-borers" with God, and not only in bringing order to things. More important still, if we strive to write charitably, we participate in God's greatest and most astonishing enterprise: loving us.

As Warren observes of bed-making, practicing charitable writing won't suddenly bring you riches and fame. It won't suddenly make you chipper every time you sit down to write. But it may, or so we desperately hope, bring you closer to God. That may happen at moments when everything seems to be clicking, when the words seem to flow from your fingers as if authoring themselves. (Rejoice indeed if this happens!) Yet our experience offers a different lesson. Practicing writing as a discipline of love is difficult. Sometimes, it seems a burden we'd rather throw off so that we can just get the thing done. Sometimes, we'd like to tell our audience how we *really feel*. It is at these moments, if we pause as Alan Jacobs did when he realized his hands were shaking uncontrollably, that we perhaps grasp just how generous, just how unfathomable, just how strange is the love of God. And then, of course, we must strive in our stumbling way to imitate it.

The Virtue of Hope

We have sought across the chapters of this book to imagine how we might go about "writing into virtue." While several virtues have been named, humility and charity have taken center stage. And rightfully so: as we have seen, these virtues were especially demonstrated and advocated by our Lord, and have been, in turn, cherished by Christian teachers down through the ages. But let us now recognize another virtue that is essential to the project of writing under love's dominion: hope.

---

[10]John H. Timmerman and Donald R. Hettinga, *In the World: Reading and Writing as a Christian* (Grand Rapids, MI: Baker Academic, 2004), 12. "All writing is also at once ordering," Timmerman and Hettinga note. "The writer is always making choices—what position to argue, which word to use, or how to arrange sentences and paragraphs. The writer exercises a certain control over language in order to communicate his or her belief of what is true."

Hope has quietly asserted itself from time to time in the preceding pages, but a fuller definition is now in order. In her book *Tactics of Hope: The Public Turn in English Composition,* writing scholar Paula Mathieu explains, "Hope is what mediates between the insufficient present and an imagined but better future." Drawing on the work of philosopher Ernst Bloch, she continues:

> To acknowledge the present as radically insufficient is a hopeful action, when acting as a prerequisite for future actions and imaginings. To see the present as insufficient does not imply that one passively accepts it as such. Nor does it mean that one closes one's eyes, fantasizes, and merely wishes for a better world. Bloch (1988) writes that hope is "the opposite of security. It is the opposite of naïve optimism. The category of danger is always within it. . . . Hope is not confidence. If it could not be disappointed, it would not be hope. . . . Thus, hope is critical and can be disappointed" (16-17).
>
> *To hope then, is to look critically at one's present condition, assess what is missing, and then long for and work for a not-yet reality, a future anticipated. It is grounded in imaginative acts and projects, including art and writing, as vehicles for invoking a better future.*[11]

We think Mathieu's definition is an excellent one, and we encourage you to consider what it might mean for you as a writer.[12] But we also want to thicken it. Hope in a distinctively Christian sense is ultimately grounded in the life, death, and resurrection of Jesus Christ—and the reality it seeks after is resurrection life in the kingdom of God. What is more, as theologian N. T. Wright reminds us, what characterizes people who hope in the resurrection is their love:

> The point of 1 Corinthians 13 is that love is not our duty; it is our *destiny.* It is the language Jesus spoke, and we are called to speak it so that we can converse with him. It is the food they eat in God's new world, and we must acquire the taste for it here and now. It is the music God has written for all his creatures to sing, and we

---

[11]Paula Mathieu, *The Tactics of Hope: The Public Turn in English Composition* (Portsmouth, NH: Boynton/Cook, 2005), 19, emphasis added.

[12]Writing with hope, Mathieu's definition suggests, involves five practices: observing, evaluating, desiring, imagining, and working. We invite you to reflect, perhaps with the members of your local writing community, on ways you might incorporate these practices into your own writing process.

are called to learn it and practice it now so as to be ready when the conductor brings down his baton. It is the resurrection life, and the resurrected Jesus calls us to begin living it with him and for him right now. Love is at the very heart of the surprise of hope: people who truly hope as the resurrection encourages us to hope will be people enabled to love in a new way. Conversely, people who are living by this rule of love will be people who are learning more deeply how to hope.[13]

Now we can acknowledge fully that hope is the virtue that enables us to live through the process of growing into charity and the other virtues. Without hope, every misstep that we make as writers might seem like the failure of the whole scheme. Without hope, the project of charitable writing in fact might seem impossible for us fallen creatures. Hope is the virtue that sees past immediate peril. Hope is the virtue that trusts that there's more to our writing, more possibilities, than we can now see. To adapt wise words about hopeful reading from our friend and colleague Tiffany Eberle Kriner, "Hopeful [writers write] texts in light of their futures as bringers of glory to God. They acknowledge that texts exist in the space and time of the not-yet, that they are incomplete and still developing."[14] And why do we hope? Because we trust in the Lord. Regarding the seemingly unattainable divine commands, such as the law of love, we do well to recall the wise observation of the theologian John Wesley that the Lord's commandments are tantamount to *promises*. As philosopher Jerry Walls explains, "So when God commands us to do something, implicit in the command is his promise that he will enable us to do it."[15] God can, and *will*, love us into charity.

In a number of his writings, Augustine characterizes the Christian life as a "pilgrimage" (*peregrinatio* in Latin).[16] As theologian Sarah Stewart-Kroeker explains, "For Augustine, all human beings are, in the

---

[13]N. T. Wright, *Surprised by Hope: Rethinking Heaven, the Resurrection, and the Mission of the Church* (New York: HarperOne, 2008), 288.

[14]Tiffany Eberle Kriner, "Hopeful Reading," *Christianity and Literature* 61, no. 1 (2011): 110. For more on hopeful reading, see Tiffany Eberle Kriner, *The Future of the Word: An Eschatology of Reading* (Minneapolis: Fortress Press, 2014).

[15]Jerry L. Walls, *Heaven, Hell, and Purgatory: Rethinking the Things That Matter Most* (Grand Rapids, MI: Brazos, 2015), 72.

[16]Sarah Stewart-Kroeker, *Pilgrimage in Moral and Aesthetic Formation in Augustine's Thought* (Oxford: Oxford University Press, 2017), 1.

earthly life, exiles from their true homeland—heaven. Only some become pilgrims who seek a way back to that heavenly homeland, a return mediated by the incarnate Christ. The return journey involves formation, both moral and aesthetic, in *loving rightly*."[17] To recognize our pilgrim condition in life is to see plainly that crossing the threshold into charitable writing won't be achieved in a semester or a four-year degree program or even a decade. It is nothing less than the work of a writing lifetime. We are a people of the threshold; we are pilgrim writers. To name the writing practices that we cultivate to love rightly as *liturgies* is, in this light, absolutely fitting—for they, to recall Smith's formulation, indeed express and shape our ultimate desire and our hope. And that is nothing less than God himself.

Praying Without Ceasing Writing

We began chapter one with a prayer before study, acknowledging with Thomas Aquinas that God should come first in our writing lives. We have now observed that God is also the ultimate direction toward which our lives, writing lives included, ought to move. The beginning and the end of charitable writing are the same. What is more, God should not be thought of as a casual bystander to the rest of the writing process, as if he merely sends us off to school in the morning and cheerfully greets us when we return home in the afternoon. We may ask for God's companionship throughout the writing process, and if you do this you are likely to find—as we have while composing this book!—that writing provides many occasions for prayer.[18]

When confronted by writer's block—the dreaded blinking cursor on an otherwise blank screen—we may, rather than pouting, humbly ask God for patience and guidance. (Aquinas's prayer bears repeating at such moments.) When prewriting, freewriting, or engaging in other practices of invention, we can delight that God has made us colaborers with him. When conducting research, we can beseech God to make us good stewards of others' ideas and ask to be shown the mind of Christ more fully through our endeavors. When participating in workshops,

---

[17]Stewart-Kroeker, *Pilgrimage in Moral and Aesthetic Formation*, 1, emphasis added.

[18]Some examples of prayer in the next paragraph were adapted from Alison Gibson, "Welcoming the Student Writer: Hospitable Christian Pedagogy for First-Year Writing" (faculty paper, Faith and Learning Program, Wheaton College, January 4, 2018).

we can pray that God would teach us how to better love our neighbors through the feedback we give and through the ways we receive feedback on our own work. When plans fall through and writing projects fail, we can offer prayers of lament. When submitting work for official review, a grade, or publication, we can acknowledge our work as a gift from God and give it back to him as an offering, letting it go in the hope that it might be used for his glory. And when a project is completed, we can rejoice, celebrating God's faithfulness in sustaining our work and, ultimately, our lives.

What we want to suggest through the above list of prayers is that, as a slow writer, you can compose two works as you write: a work of learning and a work of prayer. And though these works take very different (and sometimes seemingly independent) forms, they enhance each other like the two melodies of contrapuntal music.[19] By writing slowly in our special sense, we may sing God's praise in two voices.

The sorts of prayers that we've been describing require that you *stop* writing for a few moments and turn your attention to God. But what about the rest of the time? Might we pray *without ceasing writing*? An intriguing argument on this score comes to us from French philosopher Simone Weil in her remarkable essay "Reflections on the Right Use of School Studies with a View to the Love of God." Weil begins the piece by straightaway announcing her claim: "The key to a Christian conception of studies is the realisation that prayer consists of attention."[20] Pause for a moment to reflect on the official and unstated premises of your own education. Were you told, explicitly or implicitly, that the point of the whole exercise was *to improve your prayer life*—and, what's more, to do so in order *to love God* more fully? That is what Weil is arguing here, and lurking behind that argument is the ancient Christian contemplative tradition that we heard Bernard invoke in his

---

[19]We've adapted this metaphor from Dietrich Bonhoeffer, "Letter to Eberhard Bethge, May 20, 1944," in *Dietrich Bonhoeffer Works, Volume 8: Letters and Papers from Prison*, ed. John W. de Gruchy, trans. Barbara and Martin Rumscheidt (Minneapolis: Fortress, 2009), 394. For a brief description of the way that Bonhoeffer uses this metaphor, see James E. Beitler III, *Seasoned Speech: Rhetoric in the Life of the Church* (Downers Grove, IL: IVP Academic, 2019), 208-9.

[20]Simone Weil, "Reflections on the Right Use of School Studies with a View to the Love of God," in *Waiting on God*, trans. Emma Craufurd (Glasgow: Fountain Books, 1977), 66. In "Writing as a Spiritual Discipline," Stephanie Paulsell draws on Weil's essay as well, and her excellent summary points to the two parties that Jesus commands us to love: God and others (23). Paulsell's reflections on Weil can be found in appendix C.

feast metaphor. Recall the end of that passage: "To this food Truth invites the mature, saying: *Eat, my friends, and drink and take your delight, my best-beloved.*" The key word for our present purposes is "mature." Bernard is describing how a monk might, through dedication to prayer, and by God's grace, grow into a richer apprehension of God, which, notably, brings ever-greater delight. Weil would have us understand education as a related process of maturation, whereby the honing of our powers of attention in our studies enhances our prayerful attention to God. Her subtle claim is that we all have the capacity to enjoy something of Bernard's last course, and the development of our palates begins at school.

As an example, Weil describes the result of *not* solving a geometry problem despite considerable effort:

> If we concentrate our attention on trying to solve a problem of geometry, and if at the end of an hour we are no nearer to doing so than at the beginning, we have nevertheless been making progress each minute of that hour in another more mysterious dimension. Without our knowing or feeling it, this apparently barren effort has brought more light into the soul. The result will one day be discovered in prayer.[21]

Notice how Weil turns the tables on our expectations here. We are prone to pity ourselves in moments when the right answer (honestly, *any* defensible answer) simply won't come. What a waste of time! From Weil's perspective, though, there's no need for sulking because the time was not misspent. The goal of education, once again, is the honing of our powers of attention. *That* was accomplished in this scenario. And though we may not have the right answer in the immediate sense, this seemingly fruitless exercise is anything but. It *will* bear fruit in the dimension that really matters: the spiritual life. There is a counterintuitive argument embedded in this example that is worth noting for our purposes. The school exercises that we find difficult now appear among the most beneficial exactly because they tax, and thereby tone, our powers of attention.

What Weil contributes to our reflections is an appreciation for the labor of writing irrespective of its immediate outcome (for example, a

---

[21]Weil, "Reflections," 67.

reader's report or a grade). She urges us to take the long view, and to resist the temptation discussed throughout this book to compartmentalize our writing and spiritual lives. In short, Weil offers a radically different value system by which to judge our daily toil at writing. On this view, the practice of slow writing that we've advocated is to be valued above all because it makes a spiritual discipline of the *whole* of the writing process. No step need be barren. No draft fruitless. No workshop a waste of time.

Draw near to God, charitable writer, and he will draw near to you.

At the Gallery

Across the pages of *Charitable Writing*, we have been steadily assembling a polyptych of writers who saw their craft as a means of practicing their faith. Our aim in this effort of creative remembrance has been to offer you models to imitate, in the hopes that your own acts of writing might become occasions to grow in virtue. Our collection of writers has illustrated that charitable writers listen humbly, argue lovingly, and keep time hopefully. And to help you put these threshold concepts into practice, we have offered you several metaphors and strategies that draw on our rich Christian heritage as well as the insights of writing teachers and scholars. We have sought to bring our religious and rhetorical traditions together—or, at least, to point out some already existing crossroads. We are not the first to attempt this synthesis. We won't be the last. Traditions must be translated, generation by generation.

We began this book in a gallery, and we now conclude in another. This time our destination is the Musée d'Unterlinden ("the museum under the linden trees"), which is located in Colmar, a city in northeastern France not far from the German border. Again there is much to tempt our gaze as we stroll through the galleries: gorgeous images of saints, striking renditions of scenes from the life of Jesus, works by modern masters such as Monet and Picasso. We speed our way past all of these images, though, to reach the Isenheim Altarpiece, a polyptych consisting of painted panels and wooden sculptures, whose various parts were crafted by two German artists, Nikolaus Hagenauer and Matthias Grünewald, from 1512 to 1516. Across its several surfaces, the artists depicted the annunciation, the resurrection, Saint Sebastian,

Saint Anthony, Saint Augustine, and Saint Jerome. The largest image—covering two panels—is the most famous: Grünewald's depiction of the crucifixion, in which our Lord's body is covered with sores, resembling those of plague victims (figure 19). It is a bleak picture to modern eyes, but this depiction of Christ suggested something else to medieval onlookers, particularly the ill: that he shared our afflictions.

Figure 19. Matthias Grünewald, *The Crucifixion*

The Isenheim Altarpiece may seem to be a surprising choice as a concluding image, given that none of the work's many panels features anyone writing. There is no Saint Luke here—or any biblical writer—stationed at a marble desk busily demonstrating the Christian reverence for the written word. (There is a figure reading, though, and we'll get to him shortly.) Our selection springs, instead, from Grünewald's unforgettable depiction of *hands*. As one art historian has well put it, the Isenheim Altarpiece is a "symphony of hands."[1]

---

[1]Randall K. Van Schepen (associate professor of art and architectural history), conversation with James Beitler at Trinity Presbyterian Church, Providence, RI, 2011.

Why is that pertinent now? The reason is so obvious that we often take it for granted: writing is not simply *mental* labor; it is also *manual* (from the Latin *manus,* meaning "hand"). We write with our hands as well as our heads and hearts. Grünewald's study of hands gives us, as we will see in a moment, a chance to reflect on the gestures we make as we compose our works.

Images of hands have long been important to the rhetorical tradition's way of imagining itself. Borrowing an image from the writings of the ancient Roman writer Cicero (himself quoting a still more ancient philosopher, Zeno), rhetoricians have described the difference between rhetoric and dialectic (i.e., philosophical reasoning) using the images of the open palm and the closed fist (figure 20). These images have been glossed many ways over the centuries, but commentators generally treat the palm as a sign of rhetoric's "openness" and expansiveness in contrast to the confident "compression" of philosophical argument seen in the fist.[2] It is important to recognize that the palm and the fist were never seen as mutually exclusive options. One didn't have to make a lifelong commitment to the fist or the palm. Rather, the well-educated person could call on the two postures as the topic or occasion demanded. Sometimes, one's writing or speaking needed to be more fist-like. At other times, the palm needed to be flat.

Figure 20. *Rhetoric and Dialectic*

Those images have lasted for ages because they have more than a little truth about them. You may already foresee projects where your job is to be more openhanded, rhetorically speaking, and

[2]Marcus Tullius Cicero, *De finibus bonorum et malorum*, trans. Harris Rackham (Cambridge, MA: Harvard University Press, 1931), 99. According to Cicero, Zeno maintained "that Rhetoric was like the palm of the hand, Dialectic like the closed fist; because rhetoricians employ an expansive style, and dialecticians one that is more compressed." For other contextualized readings of these images, see Edward P. J. Corbett, "The Rhetoric of the Open Hand and the Rhetoric of the Closed Fist," *College Composition and Communication* 20, no. 5 (1969): 288; and Richard C. Marback, *Managing Vulnerability: South Africa's Struggle for a Democratic Rhetoric* (Columbia: University of South Carolina Press, 2012), 83.

others where the task may require you to tighten your grip a bit. But this simple dichotomy is also a little too tidy. In fact, on this model, the writing life sounds a bit like working a stress ball—at one moment squeezing our ideas as tightly as possible, and at the next relaxing our grasp. Yet our hands must assume many other forms—physical and metaphorical—in our acts of charitable writing. Recognizing that, we can make a productive return to the Isenheim Altarpiece.

Perhaps the most obvious hand gestures that we need as charitable writers are those of the two Marys: Mary Magdalene, who kneels at the foot of the cross, and Mary the mother of Jesus, who has fallen in the arms of John the disciple. Their hands are raised in prayer—quite desperate prayer, in Mary Magdalene's case. Notice that her hands don't align with the two models noted above: they are not closed in confident fists, nor are they open with flat palms. We have made repeated reference in this book to the need for the writing life to become an aspect of our prayer lives, and we even offered a model prayer, that of Thomas Aquinas, back in chapter one. In contrast to the two Marys' apparent pleading, Aquinas's prayer now seems strikingly polished, like a poem that's matured through several rewritings.

The Marys' prayers offer us something else—they are raw, more like scattershot first drafts than Aquinas-the-philosopher's meticulous invocation. An honest account of the writing life will include the Marys' style of prayer alongside that of Aquinas. Their hands are true to the moments when words won't come, ideas won't hang together, when the argument seems to have no legs. A desperate prayer has within it, whether stated directly or not, an acknowledgment of our deep and abiding *dependence* on God. Yet a desperate prayer cannot be the end of the story in our lives any more than it was in the case of the two Marys. We must trust that help will come, likely in a form that we do not expect. And this book has pointed to the first quarter in which to look for that help: the community of writers—friends, peers, coworkers, mentors—that surrounds us.

Let us submit two further sets of hands for consideration: the two Johns in the picture. On the right, we see John the Baptist. Following a medieval convention, Grünewald depicts John as a reader of the Old Testament. He looks up from that book here in order to gesture to the man on the cross. Here again, we have a hand that is neither folded into a fist nor flattened into a palm. John is pointing, his action emphasized by what theologian Karl Barth aptly called a "prodigious index finger."[3] That finger bridges the words in the book and the dramatic scene playing out in the world; his hand is telling us what his reading is all about. But as Barth recognized, Grünewald assigns John's gesture further meaning by including a Latin phrase beside the Baptist's mouth: *Illum oportet crescere me autem minui*, meaning, "He must increase, while I must decrease," cribbed from the Latin translation of John 3:30. Barth asks rhetorically, "Could anyone point away from himself more impressively and completely?"[4]

By enlisting John's index finger among the gestures of charitable writing, we are, of course, confronted by the question of where exactly— or, better said, *to whom* exactly—our writing lives point. If we are being honest, the answer to this question (for most of us at least) will be that the finger points rather "impressively" back to ourselves. And we are not simply being proud in that; our broader cultural way of imagining writing still has no small infatuation with the romantic picture of the solitary writer who summons profundities from the inexhaustible resources of her individual mind.

Throughout this book, we have tried to show how deeply social the writing process should be for Christians. We have tried to imagine, moreover, a set of writing practices that involve rejoicing in the splendor, complexity, and mystery of the world outside our heads. Our efforts to describe that world, we have argued, may comprise testimonies of different orders, whether we explicitly discuss our Lord or not. In so many ways, charitable writing is an art of pointing outward—at others, at the world, at its maker, sustainer, and redeemer. In saying that, we do not mean to suggest that you should take no credit whatsoever for your writings or shy away from writing personally. We are not proposing that you submit your work anonymously or forego occasions to engage in writing as a mode of self-understanding. Putting your name on a piece of writing is a way of taking responsibility for it, and writing can be a profound mode of self-discovery. Our point is simply that charitable writing isn't an exercise in self-enclosure. It is an art "prodigious" in outward gestures.

---

[3]Karl Barth, *Church Dogmatics I: The Doctrine of the Word of God, Part 1*, 2nd ed., ed. G. W. Bromiley and T. F. Torrance, trans. G. W. Bromiley (London: T&T Clark, 2003), 112.
[4]Barth, *Church Dogmatics I Part 1*, 112.

We come, lastly, to the other John, the disciple who stands on the left, cradling Mary the mother of Jesus in his arms. Here Grünewald builds on the examples of past artists who depicted John as Mary's principal comforter at the crucifixion. They were following the text of John's Gospel: "When Jesus saw his mother and the disciple whom he loved standing beside her, he said to his mother, 'Woman, here is your son.' Then he said to the disciple, 'Here is your mother.' And from that hour the disciple took her into his own home" (Jn 19:26-27). Consider the placement of John's hands. His left clutches Mary's left arm as she prays. His right curls around her side. His hold is at once firm and gentle, recalling the closed hand of dialectic and the open hand of rhetoric. Both are required to provide loving support to another. There are lessons to be had in all of the hands that we have reviewed, and surely others to be gleaned in other panels of this picture and other pictures on view in other galleries. But perhaps no symbol is more pregnant with meaning for our effort to write charitably. For if the picture's other John testifies to charitable writing's opening out, this John catches its deeper urge to welcome in. We have offered up many images over the course of this text to capture that generous reception. To write under love's jurisdiction, we have said, is to hold a patient conversation. It is to brave the wild terrains of thought. It is to move in time with other dancers. It is to stage a glorious feast. But in John's pose we find a still more succinct summary of our hopes: *charitable writing as an embrace.*

Afterword

Alan Jacobs

I haven't had many moments of sudden illumination in my life, but around twenty years ago I was granted such a moment, and it changed the direction of my professional life. In retrospect, the truth that I realized that day seems simple and even obvious, but nothing like it had ever occurred to my mind before.

As I was reading, in preparation for teaching, Augustine's great little manual *On Christian Teaching*, I came across this famous passage:

> So anyone who thinks that he has understood the divine scriptures or any part of them, but cannot by his understanding build up this double love of God and neighbor, has not yet succeeded in understanding them. Anyone who derives from them an idea which is useful for supporting this love but fails to say what the writer demonstrably meant in the passage has not made a fatal error, and is certainly not a liar.[1]

Now, this passage was not new to me and I had, I think, for some time grasped the essential idea. But the illumination came when I realized that the deeper point that Augustine was making, beyond the point about biblical interpretation, is that there is *no human endeavor* in which I, as a Christian, am free to neglect the Great Commandment to love the Lord my God with all my heart, all my soul, all my mind, and all my strength, and love my neighbor as myself. Which meant that I

---

[1] Augustine, *On Christian Teaching*, trans. R. P. H. Green (Oxford: Oxford University Press, 1997), 27.

needed to seek to "build up this double love" not just when reading the Bible, but also when reading Augustine. And when reading Toni Morrison. And when reading the morning news.

Again, this was a revelatory insight for me, and I immediately set to work to grasp what it might mean for my work as a teacher and scholar. But there were some closely related corollary points that did not occur to me, or at least not with the same force. One was that any such endeavor could not be pursued in solitude, but only in the midst of Christian fellowship: that is, *charitable* reading is necessarily to some considerable degree *ecclesial* reading. And another was that the same charitable imperative applies, in precisely the same way, to writing as well as reading.

In this book, Richard Gibson and James Beitler have remembered what I forgot, and pursued what I neglected. It is a delight to see how joyfully, as well as shrewdly, they situated the life of writing within what the Book of Common Prayer calls "this fellowship of love and prayer"— the fellowship of the saints, of all faithful believers. In one of his greatest poems, W. H. Auden imagines the redeemed life as one lived "in solitude, for company," and this is the model of writing that Gibson and Beitler have offered to us: a craft in which we may work in rooms alone while remaining nevertheless part of a great company. Again, the Prayer Book speaks of a God "who, in the multitude of thy saints, hast compassed us about with so great a cloud of witnesses, that we, rejoicing in their fellowship, may run with patience the race that is set before us; and, together with them, may receive the crown of glory that fadeth not away."[2] There is in this book much cause for rejoicing.

When Dorothy L. Sayers was writing plays for churches and for the Religious Service of the BBC, she often found herself challenged by well-meaning fellow Christians who wanted to turn her most vigorously imaginative writing into sentimental or inoffensive mush. This experience later led her to reflect, in a letter, on what she saw as a massive "failure to envisage Christian Truth as the great co-ordinate of all truth (whether in science, art, workmanship or anything else)," but a failure which was, paradoxically and yet inevitably, accompanied by a "lack of

---

[2] *The Book of Common Prayer and Administration of the Sacraments and Other Rites and Ceremonies of the Church* (New York: Church Publishing Incorporated, 2007), 347.

respect for what is called 'the autonomy of technique' in all departments of human activity"—that is, a lack of respect for *craft*, for excellent skill. She went on to say that

> the common workman is rather more likely to be exhorted by the Church to use honesty in his work as a Christian duty than the more intellectual kind of worker. The latter, indeed, frequently has to assert his technical integrity in the face of Church opposition or indifference—which is the reason why the Church has to a great extent lost the support and inspiration of the intellectuals and the artists—the two most powerful movers of public opinion.[3]

Her point is that real Christian charity must encompass with equal enthusiasm a commitment to "Christian Truth as the great co-ordinate of all truth" *and* a commitment to serious, honest, rigorous craft—for only the rigorous artist or writer is honest, is faithful to his or her calling from God.

Those two commitments lie at the heart of *Charitable Writing*. I am grateful to these two friends and colleagues, who have shown us what it means to seek truth, to pursue excellence, and, ultimately, to love both God and neighbor through our words.

ALAN JACOBS
Distinguished Professor of Humanities, Baylor University

---

[3]Dorothy L. Sayers, letter to the Rev. Canon S. M. Winter, February 12, 1943, in *The Letters of Dorothy L. Sayers, Volume Two, 1937–1943: From Novelist to Playwright*, ed. Barbara Reynolds (New York: St. Martin's Press, 1997), 388.

Acknowledgments

In this book, we have argued that several virtues are vital to the Christian writing life, focusing on three in particular: humility, charity, and hope. In this space, we want to commend one more: gratitude. As with the other virtues discussed here, we should recognize that gratitude has a particular flavor when practiced by Christians. In his book *The Theological Roots of Christian Gratitude*, Kenneth Wilson argues that gratitude for Christians is far from a passive emotion.[1] It is, rather, a virtue, one that begins with the recognition that Creation itself is a gift. The cosmos in which we live and move and have our being is an ancient and ongoing expression of God's unfathomable love. To pursue the virtue of gratitude, Wilson suggests, is to strive to be ever more mindful to the given-ness of things, and, in turn, to the numerous parties, beginning with God, who contribute to our flourishing. "[G]ive thanks in all circumstances," Paul admonishes us at the end of 1 Thessalonians (5:18). Wilson reminds us that indeed opportunities are never in short supply; we just have to look carefully.

We have found this to be true throughout the composition of this book. There are so many gift-givers to thank!

Thank you, first of all, to our families—especially Alison, Charlotte, and Andrew Gibson, and Brita, James, and Arne Beitler. We love you.

At Wheaton College, we're grateful to our English Department colleagues and fellow first-year writing instructors: Christina Bieber-Lake, Drew Bratcher, Christine Colón, Susan Dunn-Hensley, Jeffrey Galbraith, Alison Gibson, Tiffany Eberle Kriner, Chris Lapeyre, Tom and Dyanne Martin, Nicole Mazzarella, Miho Nonaka, Leland Ryken, Wayne Martindale, Kim Sasser, and Ben Weber.

---

[1]Kenneth Wilson, *The Theological Roots of Christian Gratitude* (New York: Palgrave Macmillan, 2015).

Other Wheaton friends and colleagues who have supported our work on this project include Jeffry Davis, Margaret Diddams, Theon Hill, David Hooker, Sarah Miglio, Matthew Milliner, Timothy Larsen, Alex Loney, Daniel Treier, and Jay Wood. We received valuable feedback from our Wheaton colleagues when we presented portions of the book at a Humanities Colloquium event, a Core Studies faculty workshop, and a session for first-year writing instructors. And Wheaton's sabbatical and travel grants offered the support we needed to jump-start and sustain this project.

We also received generous gifts from Wheaton's English Department (the Dow Fund), Core Studies Program, and Writing Center in order to cover permission and copyright fees. We are especially appreciative of the support of Tom Martin, Sarah Miglio, Alison Gibson, Sherry Austriaco, and Erin McCord Savidge in this regard.

We benefited greatly from the encouragement and guidance that we received during the Conference on Rhetoric and Religion in the Twenty-First Century and the annual conference of the Council of Writing Program Administrators. Thank you to John Duffy and the other members of the Ethics and Religious Tradition Seminar as well as the participants of the roundtable on WPA work at religiously affiliated institutions: Kristine Johnson, Heather Thomson-Bunn, Jeffrey Ringer, Megan Von Bergen, Laurie A. Britt-Smith, Joseph Janangelo, and Marcia Bost. Other helpful conversation partners at these gatherings included Elizabeth Vander Lei, Curry Kennedy, Martin Medhurst, and T.J. Geiger.

Thank you, too, to our editor, David McNutt, and the wonderful staff at IVP for all of the work you have done on our behalf.

We're especially grateful to the artists, gallery and museum staff, and copyright specialists for their contributions and support. Thank you to Sheldon and Lucy Rose Till-Campbell, David Hooker, Leah Samuelson, Jeremy Botts, Greg Halvorsen Schreck, John Collier, John Bergstrom, John August Swanson, Chris Romano, Joseph Brown, Cara Liasson, Tom DeVries, Elizabeth Burnett, Tucker Smith, Mallory Gibson, Amy Hood, Epco Runia, Mohara Gill, Sean Mooney, Sara Palmer, Subaas Gurung, and Lisa Renninger.

We also want to offer special thanks to this book's other contributors, who have served as our teachers, mentors, and friends. To Anne Ruggles

Gere, for helping to make space for matters of faith in writing studies. To Alan Jacobs, for modeling the virtue of charity in our reading and writing lives. To Jeffry Davis, for encouraging our development as teacher-scholars. And to Stephanie Paulsell, for inspiring us to think more about writing as a spiritual practice.

Finally, thank you to our students. Your voices have helped to shape *Charitable Writing*, and our hope is that your engagement with this book and your future writing would serve as occasions to grow in charity. The next chapters are yours to write. We dedicate the book to you.

Appendix A

Practicing Charitable Writing

Discussion Questions and Writing Prompts

Introduction: At the Threshold

1. According to Meyer and Land, a threshold concept is "a portal, opening up a new and previously inaccessible way of thinking about something."[1] Compose a paragraph in which you reflect on your own growth as a student or writer thus far. What experiences have you had that sound like what Meyer and Land are describing? What about experiences that felt less like a portal than a *closed* door? How did you respond to the latter?

2. We have proposed that the writing life needs to be fully integrated into the spiritual life. Before turning to our own suggestions about how to do that, we encourage you to consider your current writing habits. What spiritual practices do you already have in place? What practices have been suggested to you? What can you imagine adding to your writing routine? Make a list of each. Don't worry if you have empty columns. Once you've put some ideas down, ask your peers about what made it into their lists. This exercise can be repeated as you proceed through this book.

Chapter 1: Entering the Study

1. We have offered Thomas Aquinas's "Prayer Before Study" as a model for your practice of entering your writing space. While you can use

---

[1] Jan H. F. Meyer and Ray Land, "Threshold Concepts and Troublesome Knowledge: An Introduction," in *Overcoming Barriers to Student Understanding: Threshold Concepts and Troublesome Knowledge*, ed. Jan H. F. Meyer and Ray Land (New York: Routledge, 2006), 3.

Aquinas's prayer as often as you like, we have also seen the benefit of composing our own "writing prayers." Try it out yourself. It does not need to be long. If you feel comfortable, share it with peers.

2. This chapter has encouraged you to reflect on the members of your writing community. Plotting your writing process from prewriting to the final submission of your work, make a chart of all the people who are available to help you along the way. With a small group of your peers, compare your charts.

Chapter 2: On Humility

1. This chapter has offered two pictures of humility, Mary and Jerome. What important images of humility do you have around you? Are there any people in your life that exemplify the virtue? Are there any favorite passages from books or works of art that help you grasp humility? What do these various models reveal to you about humility? Pick one or two of these questions and compose a short reflection.

2. What does humility look like in action within the writing process? With your peers, discuss key moments in the work of writing where humility might come into play. Don't worry now whether or not you are already a "humble writer" in this regard. Rather, focus on what stands out to you about humility as a virtue.

Chapter 3: Humble Listening in
Local Writing Communities

1. Working with your peers, make a list of all of the moves one can make in a discussion setting (such as posing a question or restating an earlier remark in different terms). Once the list is complete (which may take some time), run down the list, asking how each of these moves might be done with humility. Then discuss which items seem easiest and most difficult to conduct humbly. If you believe that some moves *can't* be made humbly, examine together where the problem arises.

2. After testing out this chapter's recommended exercises for meeting your peers, participating in discussion, and workshopping writing, debrief with the members of your local writing community about

how these practices went. How did your thinking about humility and about listening affect the ways that you went about these activities? What did you learn about "humble listening" by trying to do it? When the next occasion to undertake these practices appears, what might you change about the process of one or more steps?

Chapter 4: Humble Listening in Discourse Communities

1. We have named two ways that writing in Christian communities can go awry, the "misdirected sermon" and the "dis-integrating paper." Where have you seen these missteps in your reading and/or writing life? Are there others of which we ought to beware? In a short reflection, describe your experience with such a piece of writing, whether as reader or writer. What went wrong? How could the piece be salvaged? Discuss your response with your peers.

2. Make a list of several of the discourse communities of which you are a part. Now jot down some notes on the special kinds of speech or writing you use in each of these settings. How do members address one another? What special terminology do members employ? What genres do they use? Compare your list with your peers' lists. Discuss the potential for your writing and speaking in these contexts to become "testimony in another key."

Chapter 5: The Law of Charitable Writing

1. Following Alan Jacobs, we have proposed in this chapter that there is no aspect of our academic or professional lives that gets a pass on the law of love. That is a tall order, even for the most sanctified of writers. This a good opportunity for a short self-reflection exercise. Where have you found the law of love easy to practice? Where has it been a struggle? Or, perhaps more honestly, where have you not even tried? If the law of love is a new concept to you, you might use this exercise as a chance to describe areas of your academic or professional life that you now recognize as falling under this charge.

2. The second half of the double commandment calls you to "love your neighbor as yourself" (Mk 12:31). We have argued that that commandment applies to our writing, and we will have suggestions

in subsequent chapters about how to apply it. But it is worth pausing now to consider the distinct terms of being a neighbor through the medium of writing. How can one be a neighbor through the written word? Working as a group, make a list of ideas, however tentative.

Chapter 6: On Argument

1. We started this chapter by discussing the prevailing assumption that argument is war. Consider your own past experience. Have you tended to think (and behave) along these lines? What have been the consequences of conceiving of argument in this way? Write down some observations about your experience as a writer and conversation partner. Ask other members of your local writing community to describe their experiences.

2. With the help of Don McCormick and Michael Kahn, Deborah Tannen, and others, we have begun to offer alternative metaphorical frameworks in which to conduct academic and professional arguments. What might it be like to argue with one of these suggestions rather than war as the governing metaphor? Consider how your exchanges with others might change. Consider what you might do differently in your writing practices. Share your initial impressions with your colleagues. Discuss the strengths and weaknesses of various alternatives.

Chapter 7: On Charity

1. Discuss the markers of a charitable learning community with your classmates. What are the practices and values of such a community? Based on your discussions, create a charter for your learning community together.

2. Find an example of a text that has several qualities that J. I. Packer describes in his definition of love. Write a response that considers how these qualities of love are exemplified through particular passages.

Chapter 8: Charitable Writing as Love's Banquet

1. We have introduced the feast as a metaphor for argumentative writing. What else might this metaphor illuminate about the

nature of the writing process? Discuss your answers in small groups or as a class.

2. Working with a peer, look back over something you've already written. Examine it in terms of our description of the feast and hospitality. Then revise the piece with these considerations in mind.

Chapter 9: Beastly Feasting

1. Have you ever been a part of a learning community characterized by "beastly feasting"? With your peers, discuss what it was like to learn in this environment. How would the experience have been different if your community had been governed by the law of love?

2. Write a short personal reflection about a time when you were a "beastly feaster." In light of our discussions, how might you have responded differently? What might have been a better way?

Chapter 10: Making Space at the Table

1. This is a good moment for us to look around and consider who *is* and *is not* at the table with us, both in our local writing communities and in our discourse communities. Who is present? Who is excluded? Discuss with the members of your writing community what it might mean to make space at the table.

2. Analyze a biblical passage in which Jesus responds to an antagonistic interlocutor. What rhetorical moves does Jesus make? How might the nature of his responses inform your own writing and speaking practices?

Chapter 11: Slow Writing

1. The ceramicist David Hooker asks his students to make ten pots, select the best one (with the help of their classmates), and then make ten more pots based on the selection. Write three different versions of the same paragraph. With the help of your peers, select the best one. Then put the paragraph aside for at least two days. Finally, review your chosen paragraph and revise it again.

2. Keep a writer's logbook as you work on one of your paper assignments. Track the stages of your writing process in as much detail as

possible, noting the activities you did, when you did them, and with whom. Include remarks about how the ideas and form of the piece developed (or not) at each stage of the process, highlighting moments of recursivity. Submit your log with the final draft of your paper, along with a brief paragraph that notes specific ways you could apply some of the material we discuss in this chapter to enhance your writing process and/or practice writing as a spiritual discipline.

Chapter 12: Liturgies of Writing

1. This chapter has reflected on the importance of the metaphor of the pilgrimage in the Christian tradition. To enrich that metaphor, we invite you to plan and embark on a pilgrimage of your own. It need not be far. You could walk to church or to an important religious site. Upon your return, freewrite about your experience, noting particular details you saw, conversations you took part in, and reflections you had along the way. Then answer the following questions: (1) How is the Christian life similar to and different from your pilgrimage? (2) How might the metaphor of the pilgrimage shape your writing life?

2. In chapter one, we invited you to compose a "prayer before study." Now compose prayers for other stages of the writing process. What ought a prayer in the midst of research look like? What should a prayer upon submitting a paper consist of? Once again, share your prayers with your peers if you are comfortable doing so.

Appendix B

Teaching Charitable Writing

Choosing a *Via Nova*

Jeffry C. Davis

Jeffry C. Davis serves as professor of English, Director of Interdisciplinary Studies, and Dean of Humanities at Wheaton College. Dr. Davis's scholarship and teaching explore themes in higher education, particularly the literacy skills that are central to the liberal arts. The author of Interdisciplinary Inclinations: Introductory Reflections for Students Integrating Liberal Arts and Christian Faith, *Davis has worked extensively with other faculty, future teachers, and writing center consultants on issues related to pedagogy and interdisciplinarity, and he is also the recipient of Wheaton's Senior Teaching Achievement Award and the Leland Ryken Award for Teaching Excellence in the Humanities. In the following piece, Davis provides guidance for instructors on how to incorporate* Charitable Writing *into their classes.*

At the outset of this book, the authors confess that the impetus for *Charitable Writing* emerged from a troubling realization about their own pedagogy: "We had been teaching the craft of writing *in almost the same way* that we had previously done at state universities" (see the Introduction). They were forced, in turn, to ask themselves whether they should continue teaching in the manner they were familiar with or attempt to change their classroom practices, integrating biblical convictions with current scholarship to create something more authentic and invigorating. Their choice was between two paths: instruction as *status quo* or instruction as *via nova*. With a concern for their students' needs and a dedication to their profession, Gibson and Beitler have chosen to reconceptualize their writing courses, taking a leap of faith, believing that a new thing is possible. Such a choice represents one of the most difficult pedagogical steps for faithful teachers of college writing. There is a challenge in this book for all instructors: to have the courage to make such a radical self-evaluation and to remain alive to the possibility of a new and better way.

Undoubtedly, maintaining an established classroom methodology is always easier than adopting a novel one, because the latter requires greater intention and effort. Yet our calling as teachers demands exactly that. A good instructor models the very habits of a curious and conscientious student. As Charles Duhigg reveals, "Habits are powerful, but delicate. They can emerge outside our consciousness, or can be deliberately designed. They often occur without our permission, but can be reshaped by fiddling with their parts."[1] Effective teachers cultivate an attitude of receptivity, even eagerness, toward the consideration and adoption of healthy new habits, particularly as they pertain to instructional motives and modes. And as *Christian* educators, we have a faith tradition that encourages us to acquire holy habits of the heart and mind. These habits prove to be life-giving, for ourselves and our students. Writing classrooms are, at their best, spaces where we join our students in cultivating practices of open inquiry, self-scrutiny, and proactive change. *Charitable Writing* promotes such a vision of Christian education.

My goal in this appendix is to offer fellow writing instructors some possibilities for teaching this book. I begin by briefly highlighting the historical roots of certain common assumptions that Christian students bring to conversations about Christ and culture. Exposing students to some of the ancient debates on these matters, I argue, will help them to understand how they have been shaped by their particular tiles of the Christian denominational mosaic. It should also help them to articulate why they resonate more with some aspects of the book than with others. Then I offer three practical activities to try out, corresponding to the

---

[1]Charles Duhigg, *The Power of Habit: Why We Do What We Do in Life and Business* (New York: Random House, 2012), 25.

book's three main sections: humble listening, loving argument, and keeping time hopefully. Echoing the authors' own position, my suggestions are not intended to be the last word on pedagogical practice but an invitation to consider some creative options.

The Great Conversation of Faith and Learning

The authors argue that education in writing needs "to be interwoven with education in Christian Scripture and tradition" (see the Introduction). Of course, this is no small task. For centuries, the church has wrestled with the question of whether, and how, to integrate biblical faith with earthly knowledge. In the early church, two important thought leaders responded to this question, both coming from North Africa within the span of two hundred years—Tertullian (154–240 CE) and Saint Augustine (353–430 CE). The two had more in common than just geography. As curious teenagers, both benefited from a solid liberal arts education in Carthage, one of the great learning centers of late antiquity. As self-acknowledged sinners who initially lived outside of the Christian faith, both experienced a radical conversion from brokenness to redemption, finding peace with God. As young adults, both sensed a quickening of the Lord toward a Christian calling, dedicating their lives to serving the church. And as disciplined wordsmiths, both became prolific writers who used their words to examine humanity according to God's salvific plans, each with remarkable insight and expressive style.

Yet despite these similarities, the two leaders reached distinct conclusions on the question of whether Christians should adopt secular knowledge for God-ordained purposes. For Tertullian, the worldly education of the ancient Greeks and Romans brought more negative baggage than it was worth. "What you reject in deed," he warned, "you are not to bid welcome to in word."[2] Tertullian knew that, setting aside their refined cultural accomplishments, the pagans were responsible for all sorts of destructive social vices; they also persecuted countless devout followers of Christ, martyring many of them. Consequently, he admonished Christians to stay away from the formative ideas and practices of classical culture. Notwithstanding these concerns, Saint Augustine

---

[2]Tertullian, *The Writings of Quintus Sept. Flor. Tertullianus,* vol. 1 (Edinburgh: T&T Clark, 1869), 25.

disagreed with Tertullian's response, affirming the path of grace that merged secular truths and saintly aims: "Any statements by those who are called philosophers, especially the Platonists, which happen to be true and consistent with our faith should not cause alarm, but be claimed for our own use, as it were from owners who have no right to them."[3] In other words, if truth is indeed truth, it ultimately comes from the Creator of all things, regardless of who communicated it. Just as the Israelites "plundered the Egyptians" for things that could be used on their trek into the wilderness, so too Christians could appropriate knowledge and skill from those who did not claim God's name (Ex 3:21-22; 12:35-36).

Never fully resolved, the Tertullian-versus-Augustine debate continues in various permutations among modern Christians. Proponents of separatist movements affirm Tertullian's cautionary concerns, attempting to avoid the deleterious influences of secular culture. Meanwhile, advocates of cultural engagement adopt Augustine's mindset, upholding the need for reasonable appropriation.

Charitable Writing's approach is without a doubt Augustinian. The saint is, in fact, one of the leading lights of the whole project. In the introduction, the authors cite his "recovery" of rhetoric in *On Christian Teaching* as one of the primary inspirations for the book, and he appears in multiple subsequent chapters, as well as several of the images. Instructors, however, cannot assume that students will automatically agree with the Augustinian stance. Even within the limited terrain of Christian higher education, students come from diverse denominational backgrounds and faith commitments. Therefore, every teacher of this text should be prepared to encounter students with convictions consistent with Augustine or Tertullian, even if they may not be able to articulate them fully (especially at the outset of their college studies).

Writing instructors may thus find it useful to discuss the debate between Tertullian and Augustine (or some subsequent iteration of it) early in the course, helping students to contextualize their own church

---

[3] Augustine, *On Christian Teaching*, trans. R. P. H. Green (Oxford: Oxford University Press, 1997), 64.

tradition and hermeneutical inclinations.[4] This instructional step is consistent with what Crystal VanKooten describes as "meta-awareness," a chief interest in writing studies, which she defines as "an ability to move consistently between enacting compositional choices and articulating how and why those choices are or might be effective or ineffective within a rhetorical context."[5]

Writing instructors, I am suggesting, do not need to sweep this ancient and ongoing disagreement under the rug. Giving careful consideration to these divergent viewpoints can spark productive disagreement and serious reflection among faithful thinkers. There is space to model hospitality here to students holding differing perspectives. Certainly, Christians have benefited from periodic retreats from the world—for example, in order to concentrate on loving God and building his church. Yet clearly there are times, too, when Christians have felt a special urgency in their interactions with culture. Moreover, the command to love one's neighbor is a powerful corrective to the temptation to wall ourselves in. Ideally, undergraduate institutions that take the Bible and liberal arts seriously should give measured credence to multiple positions, holding them in constructive conversation and tension.[6] Although "All truth *is* God's truth, wherever it may be found," as Arthur F. Holmes reminds us, it is not always easy to discern verity from falsity.[7] This is one reason why Christian liberal arts education really matters: it continues to affirm that truth is real, that it should be pursued, and that it can change lives for the good. If students in Christian college writing courses are to experience God's truth in its fullness, then the artful instruction of disciplinary knowledge and skill must be directed by wise teachers who possess an abiding knowledge of Scripture and theology, motivated by God's love.

---

[4]Helpful resources on this topic, which could become the basis for an entire course, include Andy Crouch's *Culture Making*; James Davison Hunter's *To Change the World*; Rod Dreher's *The Benedict Option*; Lesslie Newbigin's *The Gospel in a Pluralist Society*; and H. Richard Niebuhr's *Christ and Culture*.

[5]Crystal VanKooten, "Identifying Components of Meta-Awareness About Composition: Toward a Theory and Methodology for Writing Studies," *Composition Forum* 33 (Spring 2016): http://compositionforum.com/issue/33/meta-awareness.php.

[6]See Jeffry C. Davis, "The Countercultural Quest of Christian Liberal Arts," in *Liberal Arts for the Christian Life*, ed. Jeffry C. Davis and Philip Graham Ryken (Wheaton, IL: Crossway, 2012), 35-36.

[7]Arthur F. Holmes, *The Making of a Christian Mind* (Downers Grove, IL: InterVarsity Press, 1985), 14.

From Conversation to Banquet

Locating writing instruction within this larger context of honest dialectic is especially important if students are going to develop mature intellectual, moral, and spiritual virtues. After all, college writing should be about something of serious consequence, not just learning punctuation rules and avoiding spelling errors (which the authors shrewdly sidestep). Properly taught, writing courses captivate students imaginatively, intellectually, and ethically. Too often, college writers are asked to consider inane topics and to complete irrelevant assignments that lack the gravity to prompt their passions toward the work of earnest composing. Those who teach writing in Christian higher education, especially, should be eager to continue the great conversation of faith and learning, welcoming students to take a seat and enter into the longstanding dialogue on ultimate values for life, as the authors of this book encourage.

Within writing studies, the well-known touchstone for reflecting on the nature of "unending conversation" that involves interactive reasoning is Kenneth Burke's famous metaphor of entering a parlor. He relates it as follows:

> Imagine that you enter a parlor. You come late. When you arrive, others have long preceded you, and they are engaged in a heated discussion, a discussion too heated for them to pause and tell you exactly what it is about. In fact, the discussion had already begun long before any of them got there so that no one present is qualified to retrace for you all the steps that had gone before. You listen for a while until you decide that you have caught the tenor of the argument; then you put in your oar. Someone answers; you answer him; another comes to your defense; another aligns himself against you, to either the embarrassment or gratification of your opponent, depending upon the quality of your ally's assistance. However, the discussion is interminable. The hour grows late, you must depart. And you do depart, with the discussion still vigorously in progress.[8]

---

[8]Kenneth Burke, *The Philosophy of Literary Form* (Berkeley: University of California Press, 1973), 110-11.

As Gibson and Beitler rightly observe, Burke's illustration shows how our ideas connect to those of others: "They build on past arguments, some quite ancient" (see chap. 6). From a liberal arts orientation, most notably emanating from the trivium, the structures of arguments are analyzed in various forms of written and verbal expression (the art of grammar), they are investigated and debated through rigorous logical discussion with other stakeholders (the art of dialectic), and they are interpreted and formally re-presented to members of specific discourse communities (the art of rhetoric). This is *all* the work of the writing teacher.

Charitable Writing's approach is consistent with Burke's conversational metaphor, but it also subsumes it under a larger image—the banquet. Burke draws us into a parlor; Gibson and Beitler suggest that such threshold crossings should to be accompanied by prayer. Burke calls us to listen; Gibson and Beitler urge us to understand listening as an occasion to develop the virtue of humility. Burke depicts a scene of passionate argument between rivals; Gibson and Beitler demonstrate that charity ought to govern these exchanges. And while Burke rightly highlights that these exchanges are "interminable" and will outlive us, Gibson and Beitler remind us that we should strive to order our days faithfully and hopefully. Burke leads us into a fireside debate; Gibson and Beitler invite us to feast with one another.

What should students do once they get to this banquet? Gibson and Beitler offer numerous suggestions over the course of the book. To that list of possibilities, allow me now to add three: meditative journals, sequenced assignments, and slow feedback. These three practices track with *Charitable Writing's* three "spiritual threshold concepts," modeling the task that lies before each of us: to translate these concepts into practices. The activities that follow are attempts at that translation and may prove useful even to instructors who are disinclined to use one or all of them. The authors encourage readers to develop robust "liturgies of writing" (see chap. 12). Instructors enjoy a corresponding charge: to imagine invigorating "liturgies of learning" that help students to grow as charitable writers.

Humble Listening Through Meditative Journals

Learning how to write charitably in response to the writing of others demands that we listen well—and listening well, as Gibson and Beitler observe, is intertwined with the virtue of humility. The first section of the book, therefore, invites students to reflect on the spiritual threshold concept of humble listening. As the authors define it, humble listening requires "paying careful attention to our neighbors and their ideas"— but, notably, it doesn't stop there (see chap. 3). "Humble listening declares itself," Gibson and Beitler wisely observe. Though there are many ways to help students learn both of these aspects of humble listening, I recommend inviting students to keep what I refer to as "meditative journals."

Here is how they work. At the start of each class session, students enter the classroom, look for a prompt on the board, and quietly sit down to begin expressing their thoughts. Always related to the theme of the current assignment, the daily prompt asks a question, features a select quote from a reading, or presents a composing exercise. My college writers understand that they are expected to adopt a monk-like habitus when they cross the threshold of the classroom door: devout, intentional, and meditative. Instead of bringing the chaos of the hallway with them into the classroom, they resist the temptation to chitchat or distract others. They willingly still themselves, gradually become silent, focus their thoughts, and then write.

Considering the prompt at hand, they concentrate their energies on being attentive writers who push themselves to "freewrite" steadily for the next several minutes.[9] This is a time to be calm, open, and expectant, allowing creative and cognitive inclinations to have their way, even if they are not fully understood during the moment of expression. I cajole my novitiates to lean into this time with zeal and effort. "Push yourselves to the next level of your best writing," I tell them, "and take yourself seriously as you compose your *selves*." Opposing the ever-present anti-intellectual inducements of amusement and distraction, I charge my students to actively participate in the long-standing Christian practice of active contemplation.

As Martin Laird reminds us, the Christian faith has a unique history of contemplation, including Scripture and prayer. He explains, "There are two contemplative practices of fundamental importance in the

---

[9]Peter Elbow, "How to Improve Your Writing Through Freewriting Exercises," accessed May 13, 2020, http://peterelbow.com/pdfs/How_to_Write_Better_through_Freewriting_by_Peter_Elbow.pdf.

Christian tradition: the practice of stillness (also called meditation, still prayer, contemplative prayer, etc.) and the practice of watchfulness or awareness. These contemplative skills are not imports from other religious traditions."[10] Recognizing the busyness of the typical college day, with students moving from class to class, thinking about one discipline and then another, talking to one person and then another, I always make time and space at the beginning of class for contemplation.[11] Although most students are at first uneasy with the practice, eventually they come to realize that they cannot afford to live without it. The regular act of silent, contemplative writing affords students the courage to face the blank page in a manner that makes it less "terrifying," allowing for the flow of ideas.[12] As Laird assures Christians, we have a fundamental need for making time for this spiritual practice: "Contemplation is the way out of the great self-centered psychodrama. When interior silence is discovered, compassion flows. If we deepen our inner silence, our compassion for others is deepened."[13] With this premise in mind, I challenge my students to cultivate love for God, for themselves, and for others through silent writing.

After a sufficient number of minutes, once they have gotten into the rhythm of writing for a sustained period, I sense when it is time to bring the contemplative writing to a close and gently but firmly say, "Stop!" This often frustrates them, and to my delight, several keep on writing in order to complete a thought or capture a sentiment, exhibiting irreverent disobedience. Then, usually on a volunteer basis, two students will read what they wrote, without preliminary apology or explanation. (False humility can be a destructive thing, tempting writers to diminish their own creative efforts before others—so I don't allow it.) Writers must read with volume and gusto, as if what they wrote mattered to them and should matter to others, too. I encourage personal investment at every level of the meditative journaling process, asking students to be vulnerable with each other, at the same time extending basic human decency as each person shares.

---

[10]Martin Laird, *Into the Silent Land: A Guide to the Christian Practice of Contemplation* (Oxford: Oxford University Press, 2006), 4.

[11]For more on students' need to move from one discipline to the next, see the discussion of David Bartholomae in chap. 4.

[12]See the "Prewriting" section on "the blank page" in chap. 11.

[13]Laird, *Into the Silent Land*, 115.

Immediately after each writer reads, a peer is asked to take on the role of a caring respondent, making comments about specific writing virtues exhibited in the prompt piece. (None of the vices are addressed at this time; they are reserved for the peer evaluation time.) The goal of meditation exercises is fortification for the journey, not flattery for the ego. Respondents work hard to provide authentic comments, detailed and granular, without vague phrases such as "I like what you wrote!" or "It's really good!" More accurately, they are channeled into phrases like "Your use of sensory language was effective because . . ." or "The argument you make is original for the following reasons. . . ." And because everyone knows that they could be called on, any day of the week, to give a response, everyone participates in the declarative facet of humble listening. This movement from contemplative writing to communal commenting invites students to live into two of the images of Saint Jerome that we see in *Charitable Writing*: students begin, as in Albrecht Dürer's representation of Jerome (figure 4), by writing in solitude, but as the exercise unfolds they are invited to see themselves, as in Nicolás Francés's version (figure 5), as a community of writers.

Loving Argument Through Ever-Widening Circles

Charitable Writing would challenge our often-unstated assumption that love and argument are "an odd couple"—concepts that just don't fit together. Several chapters of the book are dedicated to showing that Christians can indeed argue lovingly. The authors imply, moreover, that if conducted under the rule of what they variously term charity, *agapē*, and *caritas*, a Christian writer may even *love arguing*, since argumentation is a means of arriving at truth. Through their emphasis on the cultivation of virtues, Gibson and Beitler offer a grand vision of how to create a learning environment in which "loving argument" may take place. Yet the book leaves significant room for individual instructors to work out how this grand vision is to be translated into assignments relevant to their particular milieu. In this section, I offer one such practical translation.

Over three decades of teaching writing at all levels, I have repeatedly observed the benefits of assignments that require a clarification of the writer's moral background, spiritual commitments, and ethical imagination. The basic structure that I have often used is a series of concentric circles, moving from the center outward, with increasing emphasis on exercising empathic moral agency in relation to others. The setups for paper topics and related genre conventions are as follows: My Self—examining a moment of struggle and/or embarrassment, and crafting a personal narrative; My Peer—considering the meaning of a specific aspect of human interaction with a friend or acquaintance, and composing a standard analysis; My Boss—responding to a person who is in authority, and drafting a persuasive letter; My Stuff—reflecting on the spiritual nature of our material habits (especially acquisitive consumption), and developing a formal argument; and My Icon—investigating a famous person or thing that has taken on symbolic significance, and completing a multisource research project. For each assignment—rendered with a full page that includes background controversy regarding the issue, ways to approach it, and specific writing priorities—my goal is to be purposefully clear and ethically challenging.

Gibson and Beitler speak in the introduction of the profound moment in which they realized that Augustine's repurposing of rhetoric demonstrated that "we need not throw out our old textbooks, handouts, and assignments. . . . Yet our engagement with Augustine revealed that we could no longer go about this business in the same way" (see the introduction). The same realization applies to the tried-and-true exercises that I have just outlined. The missing piece is "My Lord." As I reimagine the assignment now, I see the benefits of beginning with Packer's multipart definition of *agapē*, and then inviting the students to reflect on which elements of that definition apply to each of the concentric circles. I remain, in other words, committed to a pedagogy that acknowledges tensions and sites of potential division, be it within the self, the classroom, workplace, community, or even the church. But I see now that the students must be guided in these reflections by the lodestar that is Jesus' world-changing notion of love.

The writing classroom is uniquely positioned to model for students productive, and not merely gratuitous, modes of disagreement, since this is a space that doesn't just ask, "What is the right answer?" but "How did you reach that conclusion?" The writing classroom, in turn, allows students to probe their personal convictions and test their own limitations through the writing process. And by reading key samples of powerful —and charitable—writing related to the theme of the assignment, college writers can gauge the depth of each issue and their options for a real response. Through the concentric-circles approach, students will see that loving argument can apply from the most immanent—the writer's very self—to the global. Charity extends near and far. From addressing the need to deal with failure, to considering whether it is okay to lie for a friend, to considering the spiritual illness of affluenza, to exploring the cultural impact of an iconic leader, writing instructors can create compelling assignments that nudge their students toward the horns of a dilemma, moving them from apparent certainty, to humble dissonance, to charitable conviction.

Following in the steps of Quintilian, an early theorizer of writing instruction who was a contemporary of the apostle Paul, writing instructors discover that they can shape the character of their students by encouraging them to use words well in the face of controversy, especially as a prelude to consequential action.[14] "Controversial" assignments, crafted to elicit salubrious student struggles, have the purpose of arousing the self-aware writer as an agent of moral and spiritual influence in the world.

Keeping Time Through Slow Feedback

Charitable Writing resists our age's common view of college as a game, if not a blood sport. Operating under the sway of this metaphor, students adopt strategies to "win the game" with as little emotional attachment or personal investment as possible. Of course, what suffers under this model is the transformative power of the educational experience that the authors promote.

Saint Augustine offers some wisdom here. Our desires, he argues, can be misdirected toward things unworthy of our affections. *Cupiditas* represents the motion of the soul toward the enjoyment of one's self or any other thing for the sake of oneself, rather than for God. To adopt *cupiditas* is to engage in a form of idolatry, damaging the soul. Like virtue, vice results from repeated attention and practice. But whereas virtue draws us up to God, vice sends us spiraling down into our selves. Arguably, the most common form of *cupiditas* among Christian college

---

[14]See Jeffry C. Davis, "Connected Writing Instruction: Adopting Quintilian's Pedagogy for the College Classroom," *Journal of Teaching Writing* 18, no. 1 (2002): 14-30.

students is the acquisition of "good grades" to appease the academic deity of GPA.

Many students will—if given a moment to make a humble assessment of themselves—confess that grades represent a nagging form of idolatry. Functioning as an extrinsic measure of learning (not to be confused with the substance of actual knowledge and skill, and the capability to apply both with wisdom), the pursuit of high grades can be tantamount to treating money and material goods as the definition for success. Yet experience and theology alike teach us that paper currency—whether monetary or academic—always promises more than it delivers.

I will never forget a conversation that I had with a student in my first-year writing course. One day, after I had returned the first batch of graded papers to my class of twenty-two students, I heard a knock at my office door. The student nervously came in, and I asked him to sit down near my desk. "How can I help you?" I asked. With a grimace of frustration and a deep sigh, he unlatched his backpack and pulled out the paper that I had returned to him earlier in class. "Well," he confided with a tone of slight irritation, "I was really disappointed when I got my paper back, and I just want to know one thing: How can I turn this B paper into an A paper?" As sincere as he was, it was very apparent to me that his question revealed more about his motivation than he realized. He did not ask, "You know, I read your comments about my weak persuasive reasoning and my lack of substantiation through examples, and I was wondering if you could show me how to make a better overall argument." Frankly, he wasn't interested in that—he wanted to pass over specifics. In talking with him, he showed little patience or perseverance (both intellectual virtues) as I set out to analyze and explain the particular defects of his paper. By the end of our fifteen-minute session, one thing was clear: he had not humbly listened to me. He wanted a quick fix, a painless solution. The grade was all that mattered, not a noble struggle to the next level of proximal development as a writer.[15]

In *Counterfeit Gods: The Empty Promises of Money, Sex, and Power, and the Only Hope That Matters*, Tim Keller assumes that all people,

---

[15]Lev S. Vygotsky described the Zone of Proximal Development (ZPD) as "the distance between the actual developmental level as determined by independent problem solving and the level of potential development as determined through problem solving under adult guidance, or in collaboration with more capable peers." *Mind in Society: The Development of Higher Psychological Processes* (Cambridge: Harvard University Press, 1978), 86.

even Christians, serve "rival gods" other than the Lord God. The issue is not whether we are idolaters, but whether we are willing to identify which gods we live for and how they operate in our lives. Keller writes, "The question is: What do we do about them? How can we become increasingly clear-sighted rather than remaining in their power? How can we be freed from our idols so we can make sound decisions and wise choices that are best for us and those around us?"[16]

As a teacher who enacts a writing pedagogy that I trust to be consistent with the tenets of God's love, I have an abiding regard for the well-being of my students, including a consideration of those things that prevent them from experiencing abundant life. For this reason, and others, several years ago I decided to stop putting grades on student papers. I became convinced that assigning grades to written work proved to be counterproductive to their actual learning about how to improve as writers. With rare exceptions, grades operated as idols, harmful to their souls.

Nevertheless, although I stopped grading the writing of my students, I continued to assess their work. (When I tell people this, they are often confused.) Whereas grading involves the act of appending a letter or number to a discrete piece of completed student work, assessing comprises a detailed evaluation of the work, apart from any traditional summative notation. To do assessment well, and with a sincere commitment to the advancement of my students, I employ detailed rubrics for every written assignment my students complete. The rubrics unambiguously indicate the elements of the student's work that represent areas of strength and weakness.

Furthermore, I decided that I was not going to waste any more of my time marking student papers without the assurance that they had read my comments and marks. Research on student responses to instructor feedback suggests that students do not in fact benefit all that much; the influence from such input does not conduce as much constructive change as teachers would like to think. In light of this, I decided that the best way to ensure writing students understood my input was to require them to respond to my commentary, in some cases to every jot and tittle.

---

[16]Timothy Keller, *Counterfeit Gods: The Empty Promises of Money, Sex, and Power, and the Only Hope That Matters* (New York: Penguin, 2016), 167.

Designing a dialogical assessment system has revolutionized my interaction with students regarding their papers. Once they submit a written assignment to me, I assess it, using a targeted rubric that is tailored to the assignment expectations. (Clear expectations become the truthful standards by which I fairly evaluate.) I also mark the paper, placing corrections and comments directly on each page. Then, I turn the paper back to the students for their detailed written responses. For every comment written to address a weakness, they must suggest a way to redress the weakness. For every correction noted, they must explain the violated grammar rule. And for every compliment noting a strength, they must affirm the legitimacy of the strength in a way that shows reflective awareness and integration. The conversation continues, bringing enlightenment and awareness. They put their oar into the water, and then I do, back and forth.

Charitable Writing has given me a category for these activities: "slow writing." Perhaps we can say that these procedures match the student's labor of writing with an instructor's "slow feedback." The result is a writing "liturgy"—to use another of Gibson and Beitler's terms—that student and instructor perform together. The approach strives to crystallize what works and does not work for students, which, as students have often remarked to me, is invigorating and empowering to them. It gives them a chance to ask me questions, make sense of my observations, and even challenge some of my conclusions. And then I take the opportunity to read their responses and provide further clarification and direction for them.

It has been a thrilling adventure for me, first and foremost because this back-and-forth exchange is always *about the writing*, not about the grade. I learn a great deal about my students through these conversations, and they about me. I stop being a grade machine to them, and they grade junkies to me. The structure allows us each to practice the virtues that we preach. We meet as humane and caring persons who would cultivate intellectual virtues, including not only the charity, humility, and hope at the center of this book but also fair-mindedness (approaching various viewpoints with consistency), empathy (imaginatively putting myself in the place of others to understand them), and integrity (being consistent in applying standards of judgment across the board). This dialogical assessment approach, though it takes a bit more time, significantly reinforces student understanding and growth, moving them to the next level as writers. This is a "right and good" thing to do—a loving way to teach.[17]

Making All Things New

A writing course that places charity at the center of its aims and activities necessitates a bold vision. The authors of *Charitable Writing* find their vision in the living Word, who transcends time and space. In love, he promises to cross the threshold and enter the abode of every humble learner who will open the door; even more, he declares that he will be a friend, and that he will share a sumptuous meal to nourish the whole person—mind, body, heart, and soul (Rev 3:20). Such an encounter seems a strange thing to base a writing course on, especially in an age of social discord and incivility. But that is precisely what is needed: a *via nova*. "Behold, I make all things new!" (Rev 21:5 KJV).

---

[17]A phrase often found in church liturgies, including the 1979 *Book of Common Prayer* (286).

Writing as a Spiritual Discipline

Stephanie Paulsell

Stephanie Paulsell is the Susan Shallcross Swartz Professor of the Practice of Christian Studies at Harvard Divinity School. Her work focuses on religion and literature, Christian spirituality, and the spiritually formative dimensions of the practices of reading and writing, and her most recent book is Religion Around Virginia Woolf *(Pennsylvania State University Press, 2019). Paulsell's essay "Writing as a Spiritual Discipline," which originally appeared in* The Scope of Our Art: The Vocation of the Theological Teacher, *served as a model and an inspiration for* Charitable Writing. *We include it here, with gratitude to Dr. Paulsell and Wm. B. Eerdmans Publishing Company, and recommend it to writing instructors, theological educators, future teachers, and students who want to continue to explore the matters discussed in our book.*

Imagine yourself in a room where a young woman is sitting at a table before a blank page. Or perhaps she's standing at a desk; the year is 1286, and our vision can't be completely clear from such a distance. But imagine that you can see that she holds a goose quill pen in one hand and a knife for sharpening it and scraping away mistakes in the other. These tools rest easily in her hands because she is a member of an order dedicated to the production of manuscripts, and she uses them every day. She is a Carthusian nun, and like her Carthusian brothers and sisters, she believes that the contemplative and active dimensions of the Christian life can be united in the work of the scribe. Copying the works of others protects the solitude of the monastic cell from more intrusive forms of ministry. But it also allows silent monks and nuns to "preach," as the Carthusians liked to put it, "with their hands." It allows them to reach across the boundaries of geography and time to be in intimate communion with people they will never meet, but whom they hope to lead to God. The tools and the work of the scribe are very familiar to this woman, but the work she plans to do on this day is not. Today she does not take up her pen as a copyist.

If you can draw a little closer to this woman, you'll see that her eyes are rimmed with shadows, for she has not slept or eaten well for several days. She is, in fact, reeling in the aftermath of an intense experience of God's presence, an experience for which she is profoundly grateful, but which has left her exhausted and ill. Several days earlier, the words of lamentation in a pre-Lenten liturgy had made her anxious about her salvation, an anxiety she attempted to resolve through further medi-tation on Scripture. Her meditation led her to prayer, in the midst of which God came to her, full of sweetness, and she felt herself changed and renewed. But the God known by this woman is a God who writes, an author whose chosen parchment is the human heart. Her own heart is now congested with God's writing and overburdened with the re-sponse to it that is taking shape within her. She believes she will die if she cannot relieve her wounded heart, but she is afraid of losing what her heart contains. And so, knowing that she is about to depart from her role as a scribe, she puts her pen to the page and begins to write, probably for the first time, without a text from which to copy.

She writes in Latin, the language of the liturgy with which her life is permeated and the literature that nourishes her prayer, although she breaks into the vernacular now and then when she cannot make Latin words say what she wants them to say. And as she writes, not only is her festering heart soothed, but she finds that the act of writing brings her to another experience of God, an experience of God working in her. She acknowledges that it is impossible to find accurate words to describe divinity, but her pen nevertheless gathers up images for God as it moves across the page: mother, father, brother, friend; creator, judge, blessed food; true refreshment, precious stone; mirror into which the angels peer; medicine, physician, health itself; fragrant rose; life of the soul. Now imagine time passing, and one century giving way to another. Imagine meeting the same woman, older now, at her desk again. If you can come close enough to look over her shoulder, you'll see that she is composing a letter this time, not in Latin, but in the vernacular of her correspondent. Latin is no longer the language of her growing body of writings; she now writes most often in her native Francoprovençal. She knows enough French, however, to maintain a correspondence with friends and fellow religious who do not share her dialect.

As she writes, we see that she is still preoccupied with the way a word can wound a heart, can inscribe itself so deeply that it swells and festers there. She tells her correspondent a story about a woman who is deeply vulnerable to the power of words. Hearing the word "vehement" in pious conversation, it becomes lodged in her heart, and she can think of nothing else. She believes that if she could only understand the word, she would find relief from the pressure it is creating inside her. Someone tells her that "vehement" means "strong," but that doesn't help. Finally, she prays to God to teach her the word's meaning and remove it from her heart.

Before she can finish her prayer, God answers her in such a way that she seems to be standing in a desert. She sees before her a dry and dying tree at the foot of a solitary mountain. The leaves on its drooping branches are inscribed with the names of the five senses. "Sight" is written on the leaves of the first branch, "hearing" on the leaves of the second, "taste" on the third, "smell" on the fourth, "touch" on the fifth. A large circle, like the round bottom of a barrel, rests on top of the tree, keeping out everything the tree needs to flourish — the sun, the rain, the dew.

The woman gazes at the tree, and then lifts her eyes to the mountain. She sees a great stream rushing from the mountain toward the tree with such strength that the tree is uprooted and replanted upside down. With its top in the ground, the roots of the tree turn upwards, its branches reach toward the sky, its once dry leaves become green and lush.

Suddenly a door opens, and the woman looks up from her writing. There's a problem in the fields, or in the kitchen, or with one of the sisters. She's the prioress of the community now, so such matters are her

Stephanie Paulsell, "Writing as a Spiritual Discipline," in *The Scope of Our Art: The Vocation of the Theological Teacher*, ed. L. Gregory Jones and Stephanie Paulsell (Grand Rapids, MI: Eerdmans, 2002), 17-31. Used with permission.

responsibility. She puts down her pen and leaves the room. We can't see how the letter ends, whether the vision has brought healing to the woman with "vehement" written on her heart. The vision itself, however, suggests that when the woman makes herself available to God's own vehement presence, the stifling, oppressive weight of the word will be lifted. For the vehement river of God restores not only the five physical senses, but reaches even deeper, to a place where expression and understanding are intertwined. The woman in the letter is wounded by a word because she cannot understand it. The woman writing the letter seems to say that it is in the work of expression, in the struggle to unite human and divine creativity, that understanding begins.

■   ■   ■

This portrait of a medieval woman writing is of a woman named Marguerite d'Oingt, a Carthusian nun in southern France, who died in 1310. I read her collected works[1] for the first time in 1987, in my first years of language study. Writing in three languages, she posed an almost insurmountable obstacle to my fledgling language skills: I would spend hours over a sentence, over a phrase, trying to figure out what she was saying. I felt like I was standing outside an unfamiliar house with dirty windows, and slowly wiping away the grime until I could see what was inside. What I've described above is what I found: the story of a woman who sought God through the practice of writing, who wrote to understand God and language and the world around her, a writer whose every word was a response to what God had written in her heart.

The rest of the way through my graduate studies, Marguerite was my constant companion, not just as the subject of my dissertation, but also as a challenge to me as a writer. Marguerite worked hard to forge an authorial identity in the midst of a culture that often mistrusted women's writing, and she pushed me to embrace the identity of writer as well. Writing matters, she seemed to say. On days when cleaning my apartment seemed preferable to writing my dissertation, she goaded me. Do your work, she said. Writing is your work. Finishing a degree or

---

[1] Marguerite d'Oingt, *Les oeuvres de Marguerite d'Oingt*, ed. Antonin Duraffour, Pierre Gardette, and Paulette Durdilly. Publications de l'institut de linguistique roman de Lyon 21 (Paris: Société d'édition "Les belles lettres," 1965).

getting a grade is the least of it. Write to learn, to understand, to communicate with another, to seek what is real and true.

For Marguerite, writing was a spiritual discipline, one of the ways she sought to deepen her relationship with God. As a theological teacher, I've tried to let Marguerite's voice penetrate the often competing commitments of my vocation to remind me why writing is important. So many things conspire to obscure writing's potential to be for us a spiritual discipline. Because writing is the currency we trade for tenure, for promotion, for a better job, the usual terrors of sitting down to a blank page are multiplied many times over. We must produce to advance. Many departments require that faculty list the number of pages of each book and article listed on their vitae, as if the accumulation of pages were a good in itself.

In recent years, many thoughtful voices in theological education have sought to question the academy's commodification of writing and its embrace of publications as the central criterion for advancement. The critique of these practices, however, has unfortunately sometimes led to the conviction that writing is the opposite of teaching. The teacher who writes is imagined as one forever turning away—turning from students, colleagues, and responsibilities, in order to sit alone in a room and write. New graduates on the job market are imagined as mercenaries who don't care where they teach as long as they have time to do their research and writing.[2] The constant murmur of faculty complaint that there is no time for writing is heard as an inability to shake free of the sticky hegemony of graduate education, a reluctance to embrace wholeheartedly the vocation of teacher.

Of course, having to write in order to stay employed does force us to embrace the discipline of writing when we might otherwise never make time for it. And the critique of those who seem to disappear into their writing, leaving no energy for the classroom or for work with colleagues, does remind us that the vocation of the theological teacher is made up not only of the work we do alone but the work we do together. But neither of these ways of articulating the relationship of writing to our vocation offers any clue as to how writing might be embraced as part of our spiritual formation and the formation of our students. Indeed, the

---

[2]Barbara Wheeler, "The Faculty Members of the Future: How Are They Being Shaped?" *Christian Century* 115 (1998), 109.

twin problems of the commodification of writing and the suspicion of writing in theological education obscure the ways in which writing might be practiced as a creative, meditative, intellectual activity that might gradually change our lives. In this essay, I want to suggest some ways in which writing might be embraced as such an activity, a discipline within which we might meet God.

The Difficulties of Writing

Making writing an integral part of the vocation of the theological teacher is not easy, and not only because there is so little time in our day for it. Writing is frequently unbearable — not only because of the work it must do on behalf of our careers, but because it is so difficult, because we are not always able to find the right words, because language is never quite under our control. Marguerite d'Oingt shifted back and forth between languages, trying to say what she meant. Anyone who has ever tried to express something one is interiorly convinced of in spoken or written words can identify with Augustine's complaint: "I am saddened that my language cannot suffice to my heart."[3]

Writing theologically, writing words about God, presents even more difficulties. When ancient and medieval Christian writers tried to describe the difficulties of writing theologically, they often quoted Psalm 115:11: *omnis homo mendax*. Everyone is a liar. Augustine, one of the most persistent worriers over language, laments the fact that there is no way of speaking and writing of God that is completely true. One can never speak fast enough to say Father, Son, and Holy Spirit at the same time, and no matter how carefully one writes, Father, Son, and Holy Spirit always occupy their places separately on the page.[4] For Augustine, writing is but a poor human remedy for the way spoken syllables strike the air and immediately pass away. We try to catch them with our pen, but even after we fasten them to the page, they refuse to say precisely what we had hoped.

But of course these worries over the inadequacy of language never stopped Augustine from writing. Indeed, in response to the dilemma he seemed to write more and more. He came at the same ideas over and

---

[3]St. Augustine, *De catechezandis rudibus*, in Patrologia Latina 40:310-48.
[4]Augustine, *De trinitate*, ed. W. J. Mountain, Corpus Christianorum Series Latina (Turnhout, Belgium: Brepols, 1968), IV.21.30.

over, recasting them in different forms, putting them in conversation with different texts, burnishing them with his pen until they glowed.

For writers like Marguerite d'Oingt and Augustine, writing required a combination of audacity and humility (more audacity, perhaps, for Marguerite; more humility for Augustine). Audacity, for attempting to write anything of God at all; humility, because all one's attempts will have to be revised and, even then, will never be wholly satisfactory.

It is precisely this need for both audacity and humility in approaching the blank page that opens a space for writing to become for us one of the spiritual disciplines from which our life as theological teachers might take its shape. We need the audacity to believe that our writing matters, to stick with a difficult task, to live a life that makes room for the discipline of writing. We also need the humility to know that our writing must always be under revision, to do slow, painstaking work with no immediate external rewards, to be willing to seek and receive the critical response of others. Allowing writing to focus our attention, we may have our capacity for attention honed and increased.

Writing and Attention

Simone Weil famously wrote that academic work, when pursued with the love of God as its end and practiced as a set of tasks that require us to be rigorously attentive to what is other than ourselves, is nearly sacramental because it increases our capacity for attention. Without attention, she insists, we can neither pray nor be present to those who suffer. Every effort put forth in learning languages, solving mathematical problems, or grappling with ideas in reading and writing could bear fruit, she argues, in prayer and in our relationships with others. For Weil, academic work done not for some external reward but out of a desire for a deeper life with God and others, is a pearl of great price, worthy of the sacrifice of our time and resources to pursue.[5]

Writing is an academic task that can sharpen our capacity for attention, but in a slightly different way from learning a language or solving a mathematical problem. Those activities require us to enter into a logic wholly outside of ourselves, a grammar not our own. Writing

---

[5]Simone Weil, "Reflections on the Right Use of School Studies with a View to the Love of God," *Waiting for God*, trans. Emma Craufurd (New York: G. P. Putnam's Sons, 1951), 105-16.

can also require us to enter into unfamiliar ways of thinking, depending upon what we are writing about, but it also requires us to make choices from within a wider array than if we are struggling to translate from Latin into English, or to untie the knots of a mathematical problem. When we write, we must constantly make choices: this word, instead of that one; this form, this voice, this tone. Weil says that there is "a way of waiting, when we are writing, for the right word to come of itself at the end of our pen, while we merely reject all inadequate words."[6] But how do we know the right word when it comes? On what basis do we make our choice?

We are only able to recognize a word as the right one if we are attending closely to the words with which we are working, to what they mean, to how they sound, to what is evoked when one is placed against another. We only know the right word if we have a feel for what we are writing and for whom we are writing. We only know the right word if we have been living with our ideas in our reading and our teaching, our conversation and our meditation.

Weil's image of the writer waiting for the right word to spill out of her pen makes it sound as if a first draft can be a final draft. But that is hardly ever the case—and in my case, never. I am comforted in this matter by Botticelli's image of Augustine in his cell. In his painting, Botticelli imagined Augustine at his desk, writing. But there are no angels whispering the right word into his ears, no ghostly hand guiding his. Instead there is a floor littered with broken quills and, best of all, crumpled bits of paper, signs of Augustine's having to abandon a draft and start again, of having to try again and again to work out in writing something true about God. And although Augustine most likely dictated his writings to a scribe, Botticelli is right about one thing: there are traces in his writing of his having gone over and over his words, trying to get it right.

Sometimes the most difficult thing about writing is staying with it as the wads of paper accumulate around us. For most of us, writing is slow, daily work. I do have one friend who reads and reads and reads and reads, and then, over a weekend, can produce a chapter that is rigorously argued, brilliantly articulated: a thing of beauty. But this kind of virtuosity is rare,

---

[6]Weil, "Reflections," 113.

I think. So disciplined is her mind and so exhaustive is her reading—she reads absolutely everything—that the constant conversation between books and ideas that shapes her life allows her writing to unscroll inside of her long before her fingers touch the computer keys.

I have often wished I could write this way. But the truth is, I write in order to do what my friend does through reading and thinking: to figure things out. A minister with whom I once worked used to explain church rituals to me like this: we do not do these things because we know exactly what they mean. We do them in order to find out what they mean. That is what writing is for me. Writing can be a kind of reading, a kind of thinking. A way of receiving and considering the work of others, a way of discovering what we think about particular questions. A way of articulating what we think in a way that invites others into the process of reading, thinking, and articulating.

So it matters what words we choose, what voice we speak in, what tone we take. It matters both for the quality of our own thought, and for the quality of our invitation to our readers. The intellectual and aesthetic choices we make when we write are also moral, spiritual choices that can hold open a door for another to enter, or pull that door shut; that can sharpen our thinking or allow it to recline on a comfortable bed of jargon; that can form us in generosity and humility or in condescension and disdain.

With so much at stake, no wonder revision is such an indispensable part of writing. Even my friend, who writes a first draft so quickly and so well, painstakingly revises until she can hardly bear to look at her words one more time. It is revision that leads Kathleen Norris to call writing a way of life that requires "continual conversion."

No matter how much I've written or published, I always return to the blank page; and . . . to the blankness within, the fears, laziness, and cowardice that, without fail, will mess up whatever I'm currently writing and, in turn, require me to revise it. The spiritual dimension of this process is humility, not a quality often associated with writers, but lurking there, in our nagging sense of the need to revise.[7]

---

[7]Kathleen Norris, "Degenerates," *Ploughshares* (Fall 1994), 116-17.

When we revise our writing, we listen for the false notes, we watch for signs of an incomplete train of thought, we read with an eye for our own failures. While it is deeply pleasurable to improve a piece of writing, it is not always easy to contemplate our paragraphs of cluttered thinking and blurry sentences. It is even more difficult to submit our writing to another—a colleague, a spouse, a friend—and ask them to show us our mistakes. But that is where we have the choicest opportunity to sharpen the faculty of attention that Simone Weil describes. For we have to hold our writing lightly in those moments: we have at the same time to be convinced of its importance and willing to change it radically or even to crumple it up and toss it out. We have to care about it enough to make it better while at the same time cultivating a detachment toward it. The combination of loving attention with detachment is a spiritual discipline of long-standing in many religious traditions. We have an opportunity, in a small way, to cultivate it through our writing.

All of this, of course, takes time. And who has an excess of time? Certainly not the theological teacher, who must respond to students and colleagues, church and academy, community and, oftentimes, family. For the theological teacher, writing cannot happen in our spare time, for we have none. Writing must be made a part of the daily practice of our vocation, like grading papers, sitting on committees, teaching classes. If we are going to write, we have to learn to live a life that has room for writing.

Annie Dillard notes that "a work in progress quickly becomes feral. It reverts to a wild state overnight."[8] Part of shaping a life that has room for writing is to learn to write every day—a simple lesson, but one I am constantly having to relearn. Like any spiritual discipline, we must practice it regularly in order for it to do its work on us, to form us in attention, to draw us more deeply into the life of the world. If we do not tend our writing daily, we are always starting over, always gearing up for it. When we write daily, even in small snatches of time, we come each day to a more or less well-tended garden: we know where things are planted, we see where we might prune and trim, we sense where we need to dig more deeply. If we visit our writing only on the weekends or holidays, we have to cut our way through brambles and weeds, trying to recover the seed of our idea.

---

[8]Annie Dillard, *The Writing Life* (New York: Harper and Row, 1989), 52.

Of course, it is so much easier for me to write this than to practice it. I am a beginner at the spiritual discipline of writing; I am always beginning again, always recommitting myself to the task. Marguerite d'Oingt complains in her letters that the work of running the monastery keeps her from writing all she would like to write as well as she would like. But she kept at it, starting over and over, first in one language, then in another, trying to practice writing as a way of learning something about God and her life with God, trying to find a place within God's creativity for her own. Our goals are, perhaps, more modest: to explicate a complicated text, to narrate a historical moment that sheds light on our contemporary situation, to argue for a theological position. But in the ordinary, daily work of explication, of narration and argument, we learn to hold in our attention both what we study and what we think about what we study, what it means for us and what it might mean for others. Choosing our words with care each day, we nourish the soil of our vocation and perhaps, on occasion, catch a glimpse of a creativity that makes our choices possible.

Writing and Community

In the dichotomized conversations we so often have in theological education about teaching and writing, writing is often portrayed as isolated, isolating work. We write only to please our respective guilds, according to some. Our writing diverts our attention from our classroom, from the life of our institution. It is only in our teaching and our work among our colleagues that we live in relationship; in writing, we separate ourselves from the community.

Certainly it is possible to practice writing as a way to distance ourselves from our lives as teachers and colleagues. But if we practice writing as a spiritual discipline, our writing ought to deepen our life in community. This does not mean we will not need to apply for sabbatical grants, to ask our institutions for time off to complete sustained writing projects. This does not mean that we will not need to protect part of every day for writing. It means that, in our writing, our engagement with the world will not stop at the boundaries of our own lives.

Some of the richest descriptions of how writing leads us into the life of the world can be found among the most cloistered of people. Medieval monks often thought of writing, by which they meant not the production of original manuscripts, but the copying of the manuscripts of others, as manual labor, as indeed it was in an age when all writing was done by hand. For the Carthusians, the order of which Marguerite d'Oingt was a part, writing was understood as silent, manual labor that performs great works in hiddenness. Writing gave the Carthusians an active form of ministry; through writing, cloistered monks and nuns moved about in the world, traveling wherever their books and letters traveled, offering nourishment to persons they would never meet.

Practicing writing as a spiritual discipline means holding potential readers, and the other writers with whom we think and write, in our hearts. Writing is work we do alone, certainly: we sit before a blank screen, a blank page, and slowly begin to arrange words on it. But writing is also work we do with others: like medieval copyists, we have before us, in our memories and imaginations if not before us on our desks, the work of others. We respond to that work, argue with it, re-shape it to help us construct our own argument. And we write toward others, reaching out to them from the scaffolding of our words. When we write with attention, we write in and for community.

Before I got swept into medieval studies by the thought of being able to recover neglected women's writing, I had hoped to study Virginia Woolf. What interested me about Woolf was this: that for her, writing seemed to be a spiritual discipline, a practice that helped her explore what she believed was really real. Although not a theist, Woolf does write of something just beyond her grasp, something she senses even in the midst of her profound depressions, something she seeks when she writes in her diary, "it is not oneself, but something in the universe that one's left with . . . one sees a fin passing far out."[9]

Virginia Woolf believed that we are all wadded in by the cotton wool of nonbeing which is occasionally punctured by what she calls moments of being that hit with the force of a sledgehammer. It is her own susceptibility to these moments of being that Woolf believes made her a writer. She has a revelation, often painful, of some real thing behind appearances and, she writes, "I make it real by putting it into words. It is only by putting it into words," she continues, "that it has lost its power to hurt me; it gives me, perhaps because by doing so I take away the pain,

[9] *The Diary of Virginia Woolf*, Volume 3, 1925-1930, ed. Anne Olivier Bell (New York: Harcourt Brace Jovanovich, 1980), 113.

a great delight to put the severed parts together. Perhaps this is the strongest pleasure known to me. It is the rapture I get when in writing I seem to be discovering what belongs to what."[10] Her daily practice of writing gives birth to what she calls her "philosophy," which she articulates in the rhythm of a creed. She believes, she writes, "that behind the cotton wool is hidden a pattern; that we—I mean all human beings— are connected with this; that the whole world is a work of art; that we are parts of the work of art. Hamlet or a Beethoven quartet is the truth about this vast mass that we call the world. But there is no Shakespeare, there is no Beethoven; certainly and emphatically there is no God; we are the words; we are the music; we are the thing itself."[11] This philosophy drives her vocation as a writer. "I prove this now," she writes in her memoir, "by spending the morning writing, when I might be walking, running a shop or learning to do something that will be useful if war comes. I feel that by writing I am doing what is far more necessary than anything else."[12]

Doing what is far more necessary than anything else—isn't that what we want to discover, isn't that what we want to shape our lives and our vocations as theological teachers? Those moments in our classrooms when we seem to reach our students in a way that matters, when they find their voices and engage the material we offer with passion, when they come alive to all the ways what they study could shape their ministries —those are moments when we know we are doing something necessary. It is perhaps more difficult to know how necessary our writing is: no eyes look back into our eyes, no one breaks in with questions, no one interrupts to take our thinking to another level. We don't always know who will read our writing; sometimes we don't know if it will be read at all. Practicing writing as a spiritual discipline requires acts of faith and imagination: we must care about our readers, no matter how anonymous they are. We must, like Woolf, discover in our writing how to reunite what has been severed, to connect what seems disparate, to create out of a diversity of material and perspective some new thing. Writers are lovers, Woolf suggests in *To the Lighthouse*. "There might

---

[10]Virginia Woolf, "A Sketch of the Past," *Moments of Being*, 2nd ed. (San Diego: Harcourt Brace Jovanovich, 1985), 72.

[11]Woolf, "A Sketch of the Past," 72.

[12]Woolf, "A Sketch of the Past," 73.

be lovers whose gift it was to choose out the elements of things and place them together and so, giving them a wholeness not theirs in life, make of some scene, or meeting of people (all now gone and separate), one of those globed compacted things over which thought lingers and love plays."[13]

To write in such a way as to invite both thought and love is to write on behalf of others. It is to practice writing as a spiritual discipline that has the good of others at its heart. It is to write in a way that exposes one's hopes and motivations, that betrays one's love. It is to write in language that invites rather than excludes, in forms that are full of doors through which a reader might walk. To write this way requires time and a certain measure of solitude. But it also requires that each writing project begin and end with others, both those near at hand, and those we may never know, but to whom and for whom we write.

Teaching Writing as a Spiritual Discipline

How might we teach our students to embrace writing as a spiritual discipline? Can only our best students, our best writers, do so? Certainly not. All a student needs is the desire to sharpen his or her attention through attending to words and the desire to write toward others. Some students will write more proficiently than others, but all can write with attention. In order to invite our students into this discipline, we will have to ask them to write more than a final paper at the end of the course. We will have to encourage the kind of daily writing we aspire to ourselves. This can be done in many ways: short papers, journals, in-class writing assignments, reviews of the writing of others can all accustom students to daily writing and, hopefully, introduce them to the pleasure of it. Asking students to explore the same idea in several forms—in an academic paper and a sermon, for example—can show students how different forms give rise to different thoughts, how it is possible to learn through writing. Showing students how to read and critique each other's writing can further sharpen their attention to words and to others and help shape not only generous writers but generous-spirited readers as well.

We should also be willing to talk with students about our own writing, the frustrations and excitements we experience in writing. We should

---

[13]Virginia Woolf, *To the Lighthouse* (New York: Harcourt Brace and World, 1927), 286.

model writing as a way of reading, a way of receiving the world that turns what we read and experience over and over in the crucible of language until we learn something new and say something meaningful.

Writing is too difficult, and too potentially transformative, for us to write out of motives other than love and generosity. This does not mean we should not write critically, or polemically, or prophetically. But it means we should write in a way that betrays what we care most deeply about, a way that betrays our love.

For the contemporary American novelist Carole Maso, the act of fixing words on a page is itself an act of love. Every moment of life, she writes, is a precious, disappearing thing. To which one says when one writes, "Stay a little." To which one says when one writes, "I love you."[14]

Our students' years in school are an irreplaceable chance for them to grow intimate with language, to find a voice that's true, to write in a way that betrays their love. If we speak of this in our classrooms, it will bear fruit in our students' ministries: in their scholarship, in their sermons, in their liturgies and prayers. We should teach them, and teach ourselves, that if we write from any other motive than to find out what belongs to what, or to heal and reunite, or to reach across boundaries, or to seek communion with others, or to respond to what is written on our hearts, or to peel back the cotton wool of nonbeing, or to seek the real behind appearances, or to illuminate invisible connections, or to open a path between solitude and community, or to find God, then writing will not change us. Nor will we know the rapture Virginia Woolf speaks of, or the deep understanding Marguerite d'Oingt describes. The very best writing emerges from generosity, the desire to meet and nourish another. No matter how inadequate our words may seem to us, in our struggle to find the right ones, we make room for others to find words of their own.

---

[14]Carole Maso, "An Essay," *American Poetry Review* 24, no. 2 (March/April 1995): 27.

Bibliography

Adler-Kassner, Linda, and Elizabeth Wardle, eds. *Naming What We Know: Threshold Concepts of Writing Studies.* Logan: Utah State University Press, 2016.

Alighieri, Dante. *Purgatorio.* Translated by Jean Hollander and Robert Hollander. New York: Anchor Books, 2003.

Angelou, Maya. "The Art of Fiction No. 119." Interview by George Plimpton. *The Paris Review*, no. 116 (Fall 1990): www.theparisreview.org/interviews/2279/maya-angelou-the-art-of-fiction-no-119-maya-angelou.

Annan, Kent. *Slow Kingdom Coming: Practices for Doing Justice, Loving Mercy and Walking Humbly in the World.* Downers Grove, IL: InterVarsity Press, 2016.

Augustine. *The Confessions.* Translated by Maria Boulding, OSB. New York: Vintage, 1998.

———. *On Christian Teaching.* Translated by R. P. H. Green. Oxford: Oxford University Press, 1997.

———. *The Letters of St. Augustine.* Translated by J. G. Cunningham. North Charleston, SC: CreateSpace, 2015.

Barth, Karl. *Church Dogmatics 1: The Doctrine of the Word of God, Part 1.* 2nd ed. Edited by G. W. Bromiley and T. F. Torrance. Translated by G. W. Bromiley. London: T&T Clark, 2003.

Bartholomae, David. "Inventing the University." *Journal of Basic Writing* 5, no. 1 (1986): 4-23.

Beitler, James E. *Seasoned Speech: Rhetoric in the Life of the Church.* Downers Grove, IL: IVP Academic, 2019.

Bernard of Clairvaux. *Liber de gradibus humilitatis et superbiae.* In *Sancti Bernardi Opera*, vol. 3, edited by Jean Leclerq, C. H. Talbot, and H. M. Rochais, 13-59. Rome: Editiones Cistercienses, 1957–1977.

Bonhoeffer, Dietrich. "Letter to Eberhard Bethge, May 20, 1944." In *Dietrich Bonhoeffer Works, Volume 8: Letters and Papers from Prison.* Edited by John W. de Gruchy. Translated by Barbara and Martin Rumscheidt. Minneapolis: Fortress, 2009.

Bonowitz, Bernard, OCSO. *Saint Bernard's Three-Course Banquet: Humility, Charity, and Contemplation in the* De Gradibus. Collegeville, MN: Liturgical Press, 2013.

Book of Common Prayer and Administration of the Sacraments and Other Rites and Ceremonies of the Church: Together with the Psalter or Psalms of David According to the Use of the Episcopal Church. New York: Church Publishing Incorporated, 2007.

Booth, Wayne C., Gregory G. Colomb, and Joseph M. Williams. *The Craft of Research.* 3rd ed. Chicago: University of Chicago Press, 2008.

Bourlakas, Martha Johnson. *Love Feast: Together at the Table.* New York: Morehouse Publishing, 2016.

Brooke, Collin, and Allison Carr, "Failure Can Be an Important Part of Writing Development." In *Naming What We Know: Threshold Concepts of Writing Studies,* edited by Linda Adler-Kassner and Elizabeth Wardle, 62-64. Logan: Utah State University Press, 2016.

Bullock, Richard. *The Norton Field Guide to Writing.* 2nd ed. New York: W. W. Norton, 2009.

Burke, Kenneth. *The Philosophy of Literary Form.* Berkeley: University of California Press, 1967.

Butler, Clementina. *Pandita Ramabai Sarasvati: Pioneer in the Movement for the Education of the Child-Widow of India.* New York: Fleming H. Revell, 1922.

Calhoun, Adele Ahlberg. *Spiritual Disciplines Handbook: Practices That Transform Us.* Downers Grove, IL: InterVarsity Press, 2015.

Calvin, John. *Institutes of the Christian Religion.* Edited by John T. McNeill. Translated by Ford Lewis Battles. Philadelphia: Westminster, 1960.

———. *Tracts Containing Treatises on the Sacraments, Catechism of the Church of Geneva, Forms of Prayer, and Confessions of Faith.* Vol. 2. Translated by Henry Beveridge. Eugene, OR: Wipf and Stock, 2002.

Cambridge Dictionary. S.v. "Humility." Accessed July 15, 2019. https://dictionary. cambridge.org/us/dictionary/english/humility.

Capon, Robert Farrar. *Kingdom, Grace, Judgment: Paradox, Outrage, and Vindication in the Parables of Jesus.* Grand Rapids, MI: Eerdmans, 2002.

Carruthers, Mary. *The Book of Memory: A Study of Memory in Medieval Culture.* 2nd ed. Cambridge: Cambridge University Press, 2008.

Cartwright, Michael G. "Being Sent: Witness" in *The Blackwell Companion to Christian Ethics,* ed. Stanley Hauerwas and Samuel Wells. Malden, MA: Blackwell, 2004.

Celarent, Barbara (pseudonym for Andrew Abbott). "Review of *The High Caste Hindu Woman* by Pandita Ramabai Sarasvati; *Pandita Ramabai's America:*

Conditions of Life in the United States (United Stateschi Lokasthiti ani Pravas-vritta) by Pandita Ramabai Sarasvati, Kshitija Gomez, Philip C. Engblom, Robert E. Frykenberg." *American Journal of Sociology* 117, no. 1 (2011): 353-60.

Chesterton, G. K. *Orthodoxy*. San Francisco: Ignatius Press, 1995.

Chrysostom, John. "Homily XV." In *The Homilies of S. John Chrysostom, Archbishop of Constantinople, on the Gospel of St. Matthew,* translated by Frederic Field. London: Walter Smith, 1885.

Church, Ian M., and Peter L. Samuelson. *Intellectual Humility: An Introduction to the Philosophy and Science*. London: Bloomsbury, 2017.

Cicero, Marcus Tullius. *De finibus bonorum et malorum*. Translated by Harris Rackham. Cambridge, MA: Harvard University Press, 1931.

Cipriani, Nello. "Rhetoric." In *Augustine Through the Ages: An Encyclopedia*, edited by Allan D. Fitzgerald et al., 724-26. Grand Rapids, MI: Eerdmans, 1999.

Collins Online English Dictionary. S.v. "Humility." Accessed July 15, 2019. www.collinsdictionary.com/us/dictionary/english/humility.

Conybeare, Catherine. "Augustine's Rhetoric in Theory and Practice." In *The Oxford Handbook of Rhetorical Studies*, edited by Michael J. MacDonald, 301-11. Oxford: Oxford University Press, 2017.

Corbett, Edward P. J. "The Rhetoric of the Open Hand and the Rhetoric of the Closed Fist." *College Composition and Communication* 20, no. 5 (1969): 288-96.

Corder, Jim W. "Argument as Emergence, Rhetoric as Love." *Rhetoric Review* 4, no. 1 (1985): 16-32.

Daly, Kerry J. *Families and Time: Keeping Peace in a Hurried Culture*. Thousand Oaks, CA: SAGE Publications, 1996.

Deans, Thomas. "The Rhetoric of Jesus Writing in the Story of the Woman Accused of Adultery (John 7.53–8.11)." *College Composition and Communication* 65, no. 3 (2014): 406-29.

deClaissé-Walford, Nancy L. "Psalms." In *Women's Bible Commentary*, 3rd ed., edited by Carol A. Newsom, Sharon H. Ringe, and Jacqueline E. Lapsley, 221-31. Louisville, KY: Westminster John Knox, 2012.

DePalma, Michael-John. "Re-envisioning Religious Discourses as Rhetorical Resources in Composition Teaching: A Pragmatic Response to the Challenge of Belief." *College Composition and Communication* 63, no. 2 (2011): 219-43.

DeSalvo, Louise. *The Art of Slow Writing: Reflections on Time, Craft, and Creativity*. New York: St. Martin's Griffin, 2014.

DeYoung, Rebecca Konyndyk. *Glittering Vices: A New Look at the Seven Deadly Sins and Their Remedies*. Grand Rapids, MI: Brazos Press, 2009.

Dow, Philip E. *Virtuous Minds: Intellectual Character Development*. Downers Grove, IL: IVP Academic, 2013.

Duffy, John. "The Good Writer: Virtue Ethics and the Teaching of Writing." *College English* 79, no. 3 (2017): 229-50.

———. *Provocations of Virtue: Rhetoric, Ethics, and the Teaching of Writing.* Logan: Utah State University Press, 2019.

———. "Writing Involves Making Ethical Choices." In *Naming What We Know: Threshold Concepts of Writing Studies*, edited by Linda Adler-Kassner and Elizabeth Wardle, 31-32. Logan: Utah State University Press, 2016.

Duhigg, Charles. *The Power of Habit: Why We Do What We Do in Life and Business.* New York: Random House, 2012.

Evans, Gillian Rosemary. *Bernard of Clairvaux.* Oxford: Oxford University Press, 2000.

Finn, Thomas M. "Agape (Love Feast)," in *The Encyclopedia of Early Christianity*, edited by Everett Ferguson. 2nd edition. New York: Routledge, 1999.

Fitzpatrick, Kathleen. "Listening." *Generous Thinking: The University and the Public Good.* Accessed August 13, 2019. https://generousthinking.hcommons. org/2-on-generosity/listening.

Fox, Robin Lane. *Augustine: Conversions to Confessions.* New York: Basic Books, 2015.

"Frequently Asked Questions." *Slow Food USA.* Accessed July 24, 2019. www.slow foodusa.org/frequently-asked-questions.

George, Diana. "Changing the Face of Poverty: Nonprofits and the Problem of Representation." In *Popular Literacy: Studies in Cultural Practices and Poetics*, edited by John Trimbur, 235-52. Pittsburgh: Pittsburgh University Press, 2001.

Gere, Anne Ruggles. *Intimate Practices: Literacy and Cultural Work in U.S. Women's Clubs, 1880–1920.* Chicago: University of Illinois Press, 1997.

———. "Kitchen Tables and Rented Rooms: The Extracurriculum of Composition." *College Composition and Communication* 45, no. 1 (1994): 75-92.

Gibson, Alison. "Welcoming the Student Writer: Hospitable Christian Pedagogy for First-Year Writing." Faculty paper, Faith and Learning Program, Wheaton College, January 4, 2018.

González, Justo L. *The Mestizo Augustine: A Theologian Between Two Cultures.* Downers Grove, IL: IVP Academic, 2016.

Graff, Gerald, and Cathy Birkenstein. *They Say/I Say: The Moves That Matter in Academic Writing.* 4th ed. New York: W. W. Norton, 2018.

Greene, Stuart. "Argument as Conversation: The Role of Inquiry in Writing a Researched Argument." In *The Subject Is Research*, edited by Wendy Bishop and Pavel Zemliansky, 145-56. Portsmouth, NH: Boynton/Cook, 2001.

Haswell, Richard, and Janis Haswell. *Hospitality and Authoring: An Essay for the English Profession.* Logan: Utah State University Press, 2015.

Hitz, Zina. *Lost in Thought: The Hidden Pleasures of the Intellectual Life*. Princeton, NJ: Princeton University Press, 2020.

Holden, Teresa Blue. "A Presence and a Voice: Josephine St. Pierre Ruffin and the Black Women's Club Movement." In *Bury My Heart in a Free Land: Black Women Intellectuals in Modern U.S. History*, edited by Hettie V. Williams, 59-82. Denver: Praeger, 2018.

Hugh of Saint Victor. *The Didascalicon of Hugh of Saint Victor: A Medieval Guide to the Arts*. Translated by Jerome Taylor. New York: Columbia University Press, 1991.

Hyde, Lewis. *The Gift: Creativity and the Artist in the Modern World*. 25th anniv. ed. New York: Vintage, 2007.

Jacobs, Alan. *How to Think: A Survival Guide for a World at Odds*. New York: Currency, 2017.

———. *A Theology of Reading: The Hermeneutics of Love*. New York: Westview Press, 2001.

Jeffrey, David Lyle. *People of the Book: Christian Identity and Literary Culture*. Grand Rapids, MI: Eerdmans, 1996.

Johnson, Steven. *Where Good Ideas Come From: The Natural History of Innovation*. New York: Riverhead Books, 2010.

Julian of Norwich. *Revelations of Divine Love*. Translated by Elizabeth Spearing. New York: Penguin, 1999.

Keller, Timothy. *Generous Justice: How God's Grace Makes Us Just*. New York: Penguin, 2012.

Kriner, Tiffany Eberle. *The Future of the Word: An Eschatology of Reading*. Minneapolis: Fortress, 2014.

———. "Hopeful Reading." *Christianity and Literature* 61, no. 1 (2011): 101-31.

Laertius, Diogenes. *Lives of Eminent Philosophers, Vol. 2*. Translated by R. D. Hicks. Cambridge, MA: Harvard University Press, 1931.

Lakoff, George, and Mark Johnson. *Metaphors We Live By*. Chicago: University of Chicago Press, 2003.

Lamott, Anne. *Bird by Bird: Some Instructions on Writing and Life*. New York: Anchor, 1994.

Larsen, Timothy. *The Slain God: Anthropologists and the Christian Faith*. Oxford: Oxford University Press, 2014.

Leff, Michael C. "Hermeneutical Rhetoric." In *Rethinking Rhetorical Theory, Criticism, and Pedagogy: The Living Art of Michael C. Leff*, edited by Antonio de Velasco, John Angus Campbell, and David Henry. East Lansing: Michigan State University Press, 2016.

Leiva, Simeon. "Editor's Foreword." In *Saint Bernard's Three-Course Banquet: Humility, Charity, and Contemplation in the* De Gradibus, by Bernard Bonowitz, OCSO, ix-xii. Collegeville, MN: Liturgical Press, 2013.

Lewis, C. S. *The Four Loves.* Repr. ed. New York: Harcourt, 1991.

———. *Mere Christianity.* New York: Macmillan, 1960.

———. "The Weight of Glory." In *The Weight of Glory: And Other Addresses.* Rev. ed. New York: HarperCollins, 2001.

"The Luminous One." Wheaton College website. Accessed April 8, 2020. www .wheaton.edu/academics/programs/art/the-presidents-art-commission/the -luminous-one.

Lunsford, Andrea A., John J. Ruszkiewicz, and Keith Walters. *Everything's an Argument: With Readings.* 7th ed. Boston: Bedford/St. Martin's, 2016.

Lynch, Paul, and Matthew Miller. "Twenty-Five Years of Faith and Writing: Religion and Composition, 1992–2017." *Present Tense: A Journal of Rhetoric in Society* 6, no. 2 (2017). www.presenttensejournal.org/volume-6/twenty-five -years-of-faith-in-writing-religion-and-composition-1992-2017.

Maiorani, Arianna. "Pandita Ramabai (1858–1922)." In *Great Women Travel Writers: From 1750 to the Present,* edited by Alba Amoia and Bettina L. Knapp, 113-25. New York: Continuum, 2005.

Marback, Richard C. *Managing Vulnerability: South Africa's Struggle for a Democratic Rhetoric.* Columbia: University of South Carolina Press, 2012.

Mathieu, Paula. *Tactics of Hope: The Public Turn in English Composition.* Portsmouth, NH: Boynton/Cook, 2005.

Mathieu, Paula, and Diana George. "Not Going It Alone: Public Writing, Independent Media, and the Circulation of Homeless Advocacy." *College Composition and Communication* 61, no. 1 (2009): 130-49.

Mazzarella, Nicole. "Facing the Blank Page." Wheaton College TowerTalks, January 13, 2017. Accessed August 11, 2019. www.wheaton.edu/academics/ faculty/towertalks/facing-the-blank-page.

McCormick, Don, and Michael Kahn. "Barn Raising: Collaborative Group Process in Seminars." *Exchange: The Organizational Behavior Teaching Journal* 7, no. 4 (1982): 16-20.

McInerney, Joseph J. *The Greatness of Humility: St. Augustine on Moral Excellence.* Eugene, OR: Pickwick Publications, 2017.

McKelvey, Douglas. "A Liturgy Before Beginning a Book." *Englewood Review of Books.* Accessed April 1, 2020. https://englewoodreview.org/douglas-mckelvey-a-liturgy-before-beginning-a-book/#more-26409.

Merriam-Webster Dictionary. S.v. "Humility." Accessed July 15, 2019. www.merriam-webster.com/dictionary/humility.

Meyer, Jan H. F., and Ray Land. "Threshold Concepts and Troublesome Knowledge: An Introduction." In *Overcoming Barriers to Student Understanding: Threshold Concepts and Troublesome Knowledge,* edited by Jan H. F. Meyer and Ray Land, 3-18. New York: Routledge, 2006.

Miller, Henry Wise. *All Our Lives: Alice Duer Miller.* New York: Coward-McCann, 1945.

Nationalmuseum. "*Christ and the Adulteress?* Description." Accessed April 1, 2020. http://collection.nationalmuseum.se/eMP/eMuseumPlus?service=ExternalInterface&module=collection&objectId=132133&viewType=detailView.

Noll, Mark A. *Jesus Christ and the Life of the Mind.* Grand Rapids, MI: Eerdmans, 2011.

Noll, Mark A., and Carolyn Nystrom. *Clouds of Witnesses: Christian Voices from Africa and Asia.* Downers Grove, IL: InterVarsity Press, 2011.

Nowacek, Rebecca. *Agents of Integration: Understanding Transfer as a Rhetorical Act.* Carbondale: Southern Illinois University Press, 2011.

O'Connor, Flannery. *The Habit of Being: Letters of Flannery O'Connor.* Edited by Sally Fitzgerald. New York: Farrar, Straus and Giroux, 1988.

Oden, Amy G., ed. *And You Welcomed Me: A Sourcebook on Hospitality in Early Christianity.* Nashville: Abingdon Press, 2001.

Packer, J. I. *Revelations of the Cross.* Repr. ed. Peabody, MA: Hendrickson Publishers, 2013.

Paltridge, Brian. *Discourse Analysis.* New York: Bloomsbury Academic, 2012.

Paulsell, Stephanie. "Writing as a Spiritual Discipline." In *The Scope of Our Art: The Vocation of the Theological Teacher,* edited by L. Gregory Jones and Stephanie Paulsell, 17-31. Grand Rapids, MI: Eerdmans, 2002.

Pieper, Josef. *Faith, Hope, Love.* San Francisco: Ignatius Press, 1997.

Portinari, Folco. "The Slow Food Manifesto." *Slow Food USA.* Accessed May 9, 2020. www.slowfoodusa.org/manifesto.

Radcliffe, Timothy. *What Is the Point of Being Christian?* New York: Burns and Oates, 2006.

Rice, Eugene F., Jr. *Saint Jerome in the Renaissance.* Baltimore: The Johns Hopkins University Press, 1985.

Ringer, Jeffrey M. "The Dogma of Inquiry: Composition and the Primacy of Faith." *Rhetoric Review* 32, no. 3 (2013): 349-65.

———. *Vernacular Christian Rhetoric and Civil Discourse: The Religious Creativity of Evangelical Student Writers.* New York: Routledge, 2016.

Roberts, Robert C. "Forgivingness." *American Philosophical Quarterly* 32, no. 4 (1995): 289-306.

Roberts, Robert C., and W. Jay Wood. *Intellectual Virtues: An Essay in Regulative Epistemology*. Oxford: Oxford University Press, 2007.

Rogers, Carl R. "Communication: Its Blocking and Its Facilitation." In *Rhetoric: Discovery and Change*, edited by Richard E. Young, Alton L. Becker, and Kenneth L. Pike, 284-89. San Diego: Harcourt Brace Jovanovich, 1970.

Roozen, Kevin. "Writing Is a Social and Rhetorical Activity." In *Naming What We Know: Threshold Concepts of Writing Studies*, edited by Linda Adler-Kassner and Elizabeth Wardle, 17-19. Logan: Utah State University Press, 2016.

Ruffin, Josephine St. Pierre, and Florida R. Ridley, eds. "Editorial: The Convention of the N.F.A.-A.W." *The Woman's Era* 3, no. 2 (1896). Accessed August 12, 2019. http://womenwriters.digitalscholarship.emory.edu/abolition/content.php?level=div&id=era3_21.09.02&document=era3.

Sayers, Dorothy L. "Why Work?" In *Letters to a Diminished Church: Passionate Arguments for the Relevance of Christianity*. Nashville: Thomas Nelson, 2004.

Scarry, Elaine. "The Difficulty of Imagining Other Persons." In *Human Rights in Political Transitions: Gettysburg to Bosnia*, edited by Carla Hesse and Robert Post, 277-309. New York: Zone Books, 1999.

Smith, C. Christopher, and John Pattison. *Slow Church: Cultivating Community in the Patient Way of Jesus*. Downers Grove, IL: InterVarsity Press, 2014.

Smith, James K. A. *Desiring the Kingdom: Worship, Worldview, and Cultural Foundations*. Grand Rapids, MI: Baker Academic, 2009.

———. *You Are What You Love: The Spiritual Power of Habit*. Grand Rapids, MI: Brazos Press, 2016.

Stewart-Kroeker, Sarah. *Pilgrimage in Moral and Aesthetic Formation in Augustine's Thought*. Oxford: Oxford University Press, 2017.

Tannen, Deborah. *The Argument Culture: Stopping America's War of Words*. New York: Ballantine Books, 1998.

———. "How to Turn Debate into Dialogue: Why It's So Important to End Americans' War of Words and Start Listening to One Another." *USA Today Weekend*, February 27–March 1, 1998.

———. "Surviving Higher Learning's Argument Culture." *Chronicle of Higher Education*, March 31, 2000. www.chronicle.com/article/Surviving-Higher-Learnings/18745.

Timmerman, John H., and Donald R. Hettinga. *In the World: Reading and Writing as a Christian*. Grand Rapids, MI: Baker Academic, 2004.

Tomlinson, Barbara. "Tuning, Tying, and Training Texts: Metaphors for Revision." *Written Communication* 5, no. 1 (1988): 58-81.

Vander Lei, Elizabeth, Thomas Amorose, Beth Daniell, and Anne Ruggles Gere, eds. *Renovating Rhetoric in Christian Tradition.* Pittsburgh: University of Pittsburgh Press, 2014.

Vidmar, John. *Praying with the Dominicans: To Praise, to Bless, to Preach.* New York: Paulist Press, 2008.

Walls, Jerry L. *Heaven, Hell, and Purgatory: Rethinking the Things That Matter Most.* Grand Rapids, MI: Brazos, 2015.

Wardle, Elizabeth, and Doug Downs. *Writing About Writing: A College Reader.* 3rd edition. Boston: Bedford/St. Martin's, 2017.

Warren, Tish Harrison. *Liturgy of the Ordinary: Sacred Practices in Everyday Life.* Downers Grove, IL: InterVarsity Press, 2016.

Weil, Simone. *Gravity and Grace.* New York: Routledge, 2002.

———. "Reflections on the Right Use of School Studies with a View to the Love of God." In *Waiting on God,* translated by Emma Craufurd. Glasgow: Fountain Books, 1977.

Westerfield Tucker, Karen B. *American Methodist Worship.* Oxford: Oxford University Press, 2001.

Williams, Rowan. *Being Christian: Baptism, Bible, Eucharist, Prayer.* Grand Rapids, MI: Eerdmans, 2014.

———. *Being Human: Bodies, Minds, Persons.* Grand Rapids, MI: Eerdmans, 2018.

———. *Writing in the Dust: After September 11.* Grand Rapids, MI: Eerdmans, 2002.

Williamson, Bethany. "Reading to Listen and Writing to Speak: A Pedagogical Challenge for the Selfie Age." *Christian Scholar's Review* 49, no. 2 (2020): 147-59.

Wilson, Kenneth. *The Theological Roots of Christian Gratitude.* New York: Palgrave Macmillan, 2015.

Wolterstorff, Nicholas. "It's Tied Together by Shalom." *Faith and Leadership,* March 1, 2010. www.faithandleadership.com/qa/nicholas-wolterstorff-its-tied-together-shalom.

———. *Justice: Rights and Wrongs.* Princeton: Princeton University Press, 2008.

Wright, N. T. *Surprised by Hope: Rethinking Heaven, the Resurrection, and the Mission of the Church.* New York: HarperOne, 2008.

General Index

Scripture Index

Finding the Textbook You Need

The IVP Academic Textbook Selector
is an online tool for instantly finding the IVP books
suitable for over 250 courses across 24 disciplines.

ivpacademic.com